CRUSHING IT

CRUSHING IT

IN
APARTMENTS
AND
COMMERCIAL
REAL ESTATE

HOW A SMALL
INVESTOR
CAN MAKE IT
BIG

BRIAN
MURRAY

SACKETS HARBOR PRESS

SACKETS HARBOR PRESS
215 Washington Street, Suite 001
Watertown, New York 13601

Library of Congress Control Number: 2016920040

Developmental editor: Maria Gagliano
Copy editor: Jennifer Eck
Interior designer: Pauline Neuwirth, Neuwirth & Associates, Inc.
Cover designer: Zoe Norvell

NOTE TO READER

THIS PUBLICATION CONTAINS THE opinions and ideas of its author. It is intended to provide helpful and informative material on the subject matter covered. It is sold with the understanding that the author is not engaged in rendering professional services in the book. If the reader requires personal assistance or advice, a competent professional should be consulted.

The author specifically disclaims any responsibility for any liability, loss, or risk, personal or otherwise, which is incurred as a consequence, directly or indirectly, of the use and application of any of the contents of this book.

The book provides general information that is intended, but not guaranteed, to be correct and up-to-date. The information is not presented as a source of tax or legal advice. You should not rely on statements or representations made within the book or by any externally referenced sources. If you need tax or legal advice upon which you intend to rely in the course of your business or legal affairs, consult a competent, independent accountant or attorney.

The contents of this book should not be taken as financial advice. It should not be taken as an endorsement or recommendation of any particular company or individual, and no responsibility can be taken for inaccuracies, omissions, or errors. The information presented is not to be considered investment advice. The reader should consult a registered investment adviser or registered dealer prior to making any investment decision.

The author does not assume any responsibility for actions or non-actions taken by people who have read this book, and no one shall be entitled to a claim for detrimental reliance based upon any information provided or expressed herein. Your use of any information provided here does not constitute any type of contractual relationship between yourself and the provider of this information. The author hereby disclaims all responsibility and liability for all use of any information provided in this book.

Although effort has been expended to ensure that meaningful resources are referenced in these pages, the author does not endorse, guarantee, or warranty the accuracy, reliability, or thoroughness of any referenced information, product, or service. Reference to other sources of information does not constitute a referral, endorsement, or recommendation of any product or service. The existence of any particular reference is simply intended to imply potential interest to the reader.

To the memory of Johnny Einbeck, who possessed a rare

combination of toughness, integrity, work ethic, pride, and compassion.

When they made John, they broke the mold.

∎

CONTENTS

PREFACE

"The best investment on Earth is earth."
—LOUIS GLICKMAN

"The fastest way to succeed is to look as if you're playing by somebody else's rules, while quietly playing by your own."
—MICHAEL KORDA

■

ACK IN 2007, I took a leap of faith and bought my first commercial investment property. Seven years later, I found myself walking up onstage at the American Business Awards in Chicago to accept the Gold Stevie Award for National Real Estate Company of the Year. It seemed surreal.

The acknowledgment was humbling and I was sincerely grateful for the recognition. At the same time, my accomplishments had piqued a lot of peoples' interest. Everybody was asking the same question: "How did you do it?" I remember one reporter shook his head and commented that I was amassing properties like he collects socks in his underwear drawer. "What's your secret?" he asked.

The question was not a new one for me. Yet for a long time I didn't know how to respond to this seemingly simple query, and it bothered me that I struggled with the answer. It's not that I was trying to hide anything. I just didn't know what to say. At times, figuring out how to grow my nascent business seemed like trying to solve a giant Rubik's Cube.

Why? For one thing, I certainly never felt like I had it all figured out. I was just an ordinary investor trying to find my way... somebody who was making plenty of mistakes and trying not to screw things up. And for the most part I still am! Yet my properties were thriving while others around me headed to foreclosure.

So when confronted with the inevitable "what's your secret?" I usually just mumbled something about how important it is to reinvest back into your properties (a boring response, by the way, that is pretty much guaranteed to be met with a blank look of disappointment). People want to hear something a lot more exciting. They figure there has to be some kind of trick.

In the months after receiving the Gold Stevie Award, I gave the question more thought. I found that it proved far more enlightening to stop looking in the mirror and instead take a harder look at what other commercial investors were doing.

Closely examining my investment approach in contrast with other methods allowed me to deconstruct my strategies and pinpoint what led to my success. This helped me realize the extent to which my investment philosophies, while not particularly complicated, were surprisingly unique.

In retrospect, I realized how great of a blessing in disguise it was that I didn't have any commercial real estate experience when I started out. Because I've since discovered that many of the traditional ways of doing things in the industry are ripe for improvement.

My inexperience gave me the freedom to figure out how to do things *the right way*—how to run my real estate investments like an actual business, and not some bloated, passive source of easy money. I had too much at stake to do it any other way.

By ignoring convention and staying laser-focused on making the best possible business decisions, I exploited a variety of weaknesses that are pervasive in the industry. And in doing so, I was able to achieve extraordinary growth over a relatively short period of time.

Ironically, while my methods had been highly effective by any measure, they were also fairly straightforward. I didn't have any "secrets"... or at least they didn't seem like secrets to me. My way of doing things had just evolved over time as my business grew.

I hadn't taken any real estate courses, and I didn't have a mentor. I read lots of books and latched onto ideas that made sense. I relied heavily on intuition, embraced sound business principles, and made the best decisions I could—even when they seemed to go counter to mainstream. I continuously tried different things and learned from my mistakes.

From all of this emerged a set of principles that allowed me to achieve success with my investments. In the chapters that follow, I reveal each of the strategies that were the most important keys to my success.

I should acknowledge that my strategies for investing in commercial real estate are by no means the only ways to do things. And they're certainly not going to be the best approaches for everyone. But they worked for me, and they can be used as a roadmap for you to follow, if you so choose.

I believe that if you're determined to make a better life for yourself and your loved ones through real estate, the opportunity is there for the taking. Whether you're already an investor or just getting started, commercial real estate remains more accessible than most people realize.

So if you want to invest in real estate, you don't need to limit yourself to single-family homes and duplexes. You can think bigger than that. Office buildings. Plazas. Apartment complexes. Commercial real estate offers real potential to create wealth and change your life, as it already has not only for me, but for countless others before me.

But while the strategies in this book offer a real opportunity for wealth creation, I want to be clear up front that they don't promise overnight success or "easy money." This book does not feed into the sense of entitlement, culture of immediacy, and "something for nothing" attitudes that are ubiquitous in today's society.

So just to clarify, here is what this book is *not*:

First, this book is *not* a get-rich-quick scheme. In fact, it's just the opposite. Many of the strategies here require that you effectively position yourself to make the effort and sacrifices necessary to be successful.

The best way to be successful is to EARN IT. Understand that despite what you might hear on a late-night infomercial, real estate is a business like any other, and it takes *hard work*. Nine times out of ten the easy path isn't the right path. If you're going to be a successful real estate investor, you'd be well served to hold yourself to a high standard and do things the right way.

Investing in commercial real estate can yield tremendous rewards, but it still requires perseverance. It's not for everyone, but the sky is the limit if you're willing to put in the effort. The strategies here are most likely to work for investors with grit—a trait that some would argue is the single most important key to success, both in business and in life.

Second, this book is *not* a guarantee of success. It's unique in that it focuses on specific strategies to put you in the best position to control your own destiny. By embracing the recommendations, you can reduce your risk, but by no means eliminate it. All investments carry risk and you should never invest anything you're not prepared to lose. The goal is to manage this risk to the best of your ability, and achieve the greatest possible returns.

One way to mitigate risk is by leveraging your small investor's work ethic and feet-on-the-ground presence to secure an advantage over the competition. But these competitive advantages don't guarantee success, and they require you to roll up your sleeves and make short-term sacrifices.

Lastly, this book is *not* intended to be a comprehensive introduction to the world of commercial real estate. There are innumerable potential paths to riches in real estate . . . and many more to bankruptcy! Some strategies are more risky and complicated than others. The intention here is to focus on the more straightforward and proven methods.

In general, the more complicated the project, the more difficult it is to accurately assess the risks involved. This book's goal is to distill commercial real estate investing to a specific set of basic, down-to-earth strategies designed to leverage the advantages of the small-to-medium-sized (but highly motivated) investor.

My journey in commercial real estate has been rewarding, yet fraught with challenges and mistakes. My motivation for writing this book is simple—so that others can reap the benefits of what I've learned. In the end, if you read this book and walk away with even one thing that can make a difference, or slightly improves your chances of success, then writing this book was a worthwhile endeavor.

Now get out there, roll up your sleeves, and *crush it*.

DISPELLING THE MYTHS

*"Everything around you that you call life was made up by people
that were no smarter than you, and you can change it, you can
influence it, you can build your own things that other people can
use. Once you learn that, you'll never be the same again."*
—STEVE JOBS

"Screw it. Let's do it!"
—RICHARD BRANSON

■

REMEMBER WHEN I FIRST started looking at investment properties. A few years prior I had quit my job at a tech startup to
become a teacher, and I was finding it increasingly difficult to
make ends meet. I was hoping to supplement my teaching salary
with extra income and had decided that real estate might be the
way to go.

I had always been intrigued by real estate, but the idea of buying
that first investment property was intimidating. My real estate experience at that point was very limited. I had once renovated a
townhome I was living in and did well when it sold. On another
occasion I had rented out my house after relocating. But both were
more happenstance than purposeful investments, and at best could
be characterized as "dipping my toe in the water."

So, like most aspiring real estate moguls, I started off cautiously
looking at small residential properties and never gave a thought to
larger investments. It just seemed like the logical way to begin. After all, you should walk before you run, right? I thought I was just
being realistic.

I would do my homework each time I evaluated prospective houses or duplexes. I read a lot of real estate books and learned how to calculate my return on investment. When I found a promising property, I requested income and expense information so I could calculate what the cash flow would be. I talked to lots of brokers and asked a lot of questions.

There was a lot of learning going on, but I couldn't seem to find the "right" property, and I wasn't even certain that I knew what the "right" property even meant. One thing I did know was that the houses and duplexes I was looking at were not offering the kinds of returns I had hoped for.

As the months passed, I started to become frustrated. But I kept at it, until a new problem emerged: my pool of prospective properties was drying up. Being new to the game, I had limited my search to properties listed for sale. And since I wanted to stay local, I eventually worked my way through all the listings.

Running out of options, I gradually began to widen my search parameters and, little by little, the size of the properties I was considering started to increase. I became intrigued by commercial real estate, and before I knew it, I was looking at things that would have seemed absurd to me just months earlier.

WHAT IS COMMERCIAL REAL ESTATE?

These "larger properties" that I tentatively began to investigate were more expensive than duplexes, and ranged from small apartment buildings to offices, and even some retail buildings. I remember when I first did some serious due diligence on a 6-unit apartment building. A little while later I evaluated a 21-unit. And then a small office building, and it progressed from there.

These investments were well beyond my original budget, but through my reading and interactions with brokers, I began to realize that there might be ways to make my money go a lot further than I had originally thought. I remember when the broker for one commercial property explained that the seller was highly motivated. In order to help make the property more attractive to prospective buyers, the seller was offering owner financing that would allow a buyer to close the deal with very little cash.

That particular investment didn't work out, but it really opened my eyes. A lightbulb went on and some of the seemingly abstract financing strategies I had been reading about became a lot more real.

This exposure to the concept of commercial real estate changed my way of thinking,

> *"The common question that gets asked in business is, 'why?' That's a good question, but an equally valid question is, 'why not?'"*
>
> —JEFF BEZOS

and I began to see the world around me through a different lens. It hadn't ever occurred to me that the commercial buildings all around me were investments, and something that a regular person like me could own.

While I was primarily looking at apartments, offices, and retail at this point, I've since learned that "commercial real estate" can be a fairly broad term and encompass a vast array of property types. In fact, ask 10 different people what "commercial real estate" is, and you're likely to get 10 different answers—even from people working in the industry!

At its most expansive, commercial real estate can encompass any property held for the purpose of generating a return on investment. Among many other things, this typically includes such popular asset classes as apartments, offices, retail, and industrial facilities. But it can also include things like self-storage facilities, agriculture, and parking lots.

Other published definitions of commercial real estate are narrower and might exclude major categories of investment property, such as multifamily. "Multifamily" is a fancy way of describing any residential property that includes more than four dwelling units. Most people use the word "multifamily" interchangeably with apartments, but it can also encompass things like mobile park homes or even retirement communities.[1]

THINKING BIG

Most small real estate investors have the same mentality that I did initially—they believe they need to start with single-family homes or duplexes, and slowly grow their real estate portfolio over an extended period of time. They tend to rule out the option of purchasing apartment complexes or commercial properties without giving it a whole lot of deliberation.

In fact, most investors only consider such properties fleetingly, if at all. When commercial properties *are* contemplated, it's usually with wide-eyed wonder and a distant dreaminess. Kind of the way a high school nerd might look at a runway model.

Now there is absolutely no doubt that gaining some experience with smaller properties is valuable, and I highly recommend it. But you don't need to have 20 duplexes before you purchase your first apartment building or strip plaza. Just like you don't need to get experience dating 20 ordinary people before you have the courage to ask out somebody fantastic.

In the immortal words of the Roman poet Virgil, "Fortune sides with him who dares." If you don't buck up and try, you'll never know what could have been. I had the same mental barrier to thinking big that most people have, and tearing that barrier down was the first step.

As I got progressively crazier with my large property shopping, I started to notice that commercial properties tended to offer substantially better returns and more upside potential compared to

---

1 Though many definitions of "commercial real estate" are inclusive of apartments, you will notice that there are some references throughout the book to "apartments and commercial real estate," including in the book's title. This apparent redundancy is intentional—it is done for clarity, since some definitions of commercial real estate omit apartments. It is also done for emphasis, because apartments represent one of the greatest segments of investor interest and opportunity.

smaller residential properties. Mulling over the prospect of superior returns, together with this newfound idea that I might be able to find ways to reduce the amount of cash I needed, my mind was opening to bigger and bigger possibilities.

Eventually, almost on a whim, I decided to request information on a 50,000-square-foot office building in downtown Watertown, a small city near my home in Upstate New York. Even with my higher budget, the property's $1.2M asking price was about three times higher than what I thought I could afford, so I almost didn't bother. But after a lot of wrangling with a motivated seller, I eventually worked out a deal to purchase the building for $950K that involved assuming the seller's mortgage.

> *"There is no passion to be found playing small—in settling for a life that is less than the one you are capable of living."*
> —NELSON MANDELA

As I did my due diligence over the subsequent months, I discovered substantial inaccuracies in the information provided by the seller, and ended up renegotiating the purchase price. I also negotiated some credits to help reduce the amount of cash I would need to come up with at closing. In the end, I purchased the property for $836,500. When I assumed the seller's mortgage it covered about 90% of the purchase price, and the credits I negotiated covered another $50K. After cobbling together the rest in cash, I was off and running.

IT'S NOT COMPLICATED

Do you ever feel misunderstood? If you could talk to an office building, it would likely appreciate the opportunity to commiserate with you! An office building like the one I purchased might bemoan the fact that people think it's too expensive, overly complicated, risky, and only suitable for larger, institutional investors.

It would ask you questions like "Why can't people understand that I'm really no more complicated than a duplex?" or, "I have so much to give, yet I feel completely unappreciated and overlooked—I just want someone to take care of me—someone who can see my potential and love me for who I really am!"

Commercial real estate is a subject of fascination, but it's generally considered to be a sophisticated, lucrative playground reserved for the wealthy or rigged for institutions. It seems impenetrable for the little guy. Acquiring a plaza, office building, or apartment complex seems too far out of reach, requiring specialized knowledge and millions of dollars.

"The odds of me coming into the rocket business, not knowing anything about rockets, not having ever built anything, I mean, I would have to be insane if I thought the odds were in my favor."
—ELON MUSK

Commercial real estate misperceptions are widespread and are often perpetuated by large investors or brokers who feel compelled to speak in jargon and inflate their status. For all their bluster, the truth is that the amount of work and complexity associated with a large property doesn't necessarily increase all that much with its size. And you don't need to work with self-aggrandizing brokers to get a deal done. There are plenty of down-to-earth and friendly brokers out there who would be glad to help you, or if you prefer, you can bypass brokers altogether and find your own investments.

People also assume they can't afford commercial properties. Lenders will typically tell new investors they need to put 25% down in cash to purchase a commercial property, plus closing costs. That may be true in some cases, but the reality is that alternative financing arrangements are a lot more commonplace in commercial deals than in residential investments. So your cash can sometimes go a lot further, yielding much better cash-on-cash returns.

On top of that, there are economies of scale in real estate—both acquisition and operating expenses are often substantially lower on a per-square-foot basis for larger properties, so investment returns can sometimes be significantly better than are typically found on smaller residential investments.

The bottom line is that while people are intimidated by commercial real estate, they don't need to be. Don't assume that apartments or commercial properties are too complex or too expensive. In many cases they are not. In fact, if you've already experienced success with smaller rental properties, you're more qualified to make the leap than I was.

You can read and ask questions, and learn everything you need to know to get started. You should do your homework and make decisions based on the facts. Just like anything in life, you can make it as complicated as you want it to be. But the knowledge is out there for the taking, and you can fill in the gaps as you go.

> *"I am always doing that which I cannot do, in order that I may learn how to do it."*
> —PABLO PICASSO

Commercial real estate can be lucrative for the small investor. It does *not* have to be complicated, and it can be just as accessible as a residential property. You can do it! You can acquire a commercial property. You can compete with the bigger players—*and you can win.*

DAVID AND GOLIATH

As a small investor, it's easy to get intimidated when you're stepping into an industry that is dominated by much larger and more established investors. You're going to be David—competing against the Goliaths of commercial real estate. But that doesn't actually mean you don't have any advantages, or that you can't compete and win. Because you can. Don't underestimate your own strength!

In his book *David and Goliath: Underdogs, Misfits, and the Art of Battling Giants*, author Malcolm Gladwell explores the balance between the small and mighty, examining why underdogs succeed so much more often than we expect. In one of Gladwell's many fascinating stories, he digs a little deeper into an event that took place 3,000 years ago, when the Philistine and Israeli armies agreed to settle their dispute through single combat between each army's mightiest warrior.

In an apparent gross mismatch, a small Israeli shepherd boy

named David confronts Goliath—a terrifying, six-foot-nine armored Philistine giant. Miraculously, David fires a stone from his sling and hits giant Goliath right between the eyes, knocking him out. David then runs up, takes the giant's sword, and cuts off his head.

Gladwell proceeds to turn this epic story upside down, revealing why everything we thought we knew about the story of David and Goliath is in fact completely wrong. As it turns out, there were a variety of reasons why David had a distinct advantage over the giant.

For example, Gladwell points out that an examination of the physics involved proves that twirling a sling can launch a stone with as much stopping power as a .45 caliber handgun. Gladwell also exposes some of Goliath's inherent weaknesses, including his likely affliction with a form of gigantism whose side effects include severe vision problems. To David's credit, he used the giant's weaknesses to his distinct advantage.

As Gladwell concludes in his popular TED Talk on the subject:

> So the Israelites up on the mountain ridge looking down on [Goliath] thought he was this extraordinarily powerful foe. What they didn't understand was that the very thing that was the source of his apparent strength was also the source of his greatest weakness. And there is, I think, in that, a very important lesson for all of us. Giants are not as strong and powerful as they seem. And sometimes the shepherd boy has a sling in his pocket.[2]

Small investors are akin to David because, counter to common belief, they enjoy a wide range of advantages over the commercial real estate giants. And just like Goliath, the commercial real estate industry is actually bloated and vulnerable.

As you'll learn later in this book, the industry is *layered* with inefficiencies and poor business practices. It is ripe for disruption

---

2 Malcolm Gladwell, "The Unheard Story of David and Goliath," filmed September 2013, TEDSalon NY2013, 15:40, https://www.ted.com/talks/malcolm_gladwell_the_unheard_story_of_david_and_goliath?language=en.

and disintermediation—particularly for the small investor at the local level. You may be a small fish in the big pond, but your local knowledge and presence put you in a far better position to compete than you might realize.

If you are careful, diligent, and determined in your approach, you can use the principles in this book to help you keep it simple, find a property that works for you, and stack the deck in your favor.

SECTION

PRE-ACQUISITION   1

CHAPTER 1

MASTERING THE FUNDAMENTALS

*"Give me a lever long enough and a fulcrum on which to place it,
and I shall move the world."*

—ARCHIMEDES

*"The effects of compounding even moderate returns over many
years are compelling, if not downright mind boggling."*

—SETH KLARMAN

■

WIDELY HELD BELIEF ABOUT owning commercial real estate is that it can make you rich. Well, the good news is that this notion is true! Commercial real estate *can* help investors achieve financial freedom. The bad news is that this outcome is far from guaranteed. Not all commercial real estate investments are lucrative, and a bad investment can drag you under, even if you give it your all.

Your first step on the path to successful real estate investing is to understand and appreciate the basic financial concepts. What separates the good investments from the poor ones? How can a property increase in value and provide a good return? How can you invest to minimize your risk and create the most wealth?

The underlying principles are not complicated and are the same regardless of the property size or type, so many investors with smaller residential properties will already have a basic understanding and appreciation for their importance.

Being able to properly evaluate a property from a financial perspective is critical to your success. As you'll see, there are a lot of factors to consider. But at the core of the decision-making process is an accurate assessment of the property's financials.

KEEP IT SIMPLE

Let's start by acknowledging that finance is not an exciting topic for many of us. And it can sometimes be unnecessarily complicated. A financial discussion with somebody deeply ensconced in the commercial real estate industry is definitely at risk of devolving into a painstakingly boring and baffling dialogue.

But the truth is that real estate finance can be as complicated or as easy as one decides to make it—worthy of a PhD dissertation, or kept straightforward and simple.

For most small investors, I would recommend my own tried-and-true approach to real estate finance, which is to fully embrace the KISS (Keep It Simple, Stupid) principle. Investing the time and effort into thoroughly understanding just a few basic principles can reap great dividends and is a prerequisite for success.

If you can add up all of a property's income and expenses, then you're off to a great start! By simply subtracting these total annual expenses from the annual income, you can calculate a property's net operating income, or "NOI," which is the most important number for an investor to understand in commercial real estate. It really is that simple. The basics introduced in this book are enough for most investors. You can leave the scarier equations to the self-professed experts.

Using basic financial analysis can be equated with driving a car. You don't have to understand how to build a car from scratch in order to be an excellent driver. That said, you would be well served to understand the fundamentals of how a vehicle operates. In real estate finance, these fundamentals consist of a few basic concepts that we're going to review.

Yes, there are plenty of people in the world making their for-

NOI = annual income – annual expenses

tunes through complicated real estate instruments, but many of those paths are full of potential pitfalls for those of us who are un- initiated. The more complicated the deal, the more unnecessary risk you're taking on. There is plenty of opportunity available without having to get sexy. So if you want to get a healthy return with less risk, then you're well served by just keeping it simple.

> *"Remind people that profit is the difference between revenue and expense. This makes you look smart."*
> —SCOTT ADAMS

CASH IS KING

 The first and perhaps most valuable step you can take toward success in real estate investing is to fully under- stand and embrace the significance of cash, leverage, and compounding.

A long time ago, I took a finance class, and while I honestly don't remember very much of what I learned, I vividly recall my profes- sor emphatically proclaiming (on multiple occasions) that "CASH IS KING!"

This stuck with me. I admit thinking he was a little extreme at the time, but my experience as a businessperson and real estate investor has convinced me that the old guy knew *exactly* what he was talking about.

Cash is the lifeblood of any business. It's what pays the bills, de- termines valuation, and ultimately is the spigot controlling your growth. But there are a variety of factors in real estate that magnify the importance of cash.

Every investment decision you make should weigh the near- term and long-term cash implications. Even the smallest expendi- tures can add up and have surprisingly significant consequences, for better or for worse. Cash really *is* king, and you should remem- ber this if you want to grow your portfolio.

To fully appreciate the value of cash, it's worth digging a little deeper into the underlying factors that make it so powerful for your business's growth and success. Real estate offers the prospect of astonishing growth potential by combining two basic principles that allow you to create wealth at an astonishing rate: financial leverage and compound returns.

If there is a "secret sauce" to wealth creation through real estate, then financial leverage and compound returns are two of the main ingredients.

LEVERAGE AND COMPOUNDING

What exactly are leverage and compounding in the context of real estate? Let's start with leverage. "Leverage" simply refers to borrowed money. The more you borrow, the more "leveraged" you are. Leverage is debt, whether it's a bank mortgage or funds secured from a private lender. It encompasses any funds extended to you that must be paid back.

Debt is called "leverage" because, similar to how you can move a heavy object by applying less force to a lever, debt enables an investor to buy more property with less cash.

Real estate is somewhat unique in the investment world in that it is so commonplace to make investments using predominantly other people's money. Unlike investments such as stocks and bonds, for example, you finance a high percentage of your real estate acquisitions by borrowing money. In fact, an entire industry has evolved around the lending of money specifically for real estate.

Compound returns, or "compounding," on the other hand, is a phenomenon that occurs when you earn a return on something and then reinvest those proceeds, thereby increasing your earning power. In other words, if you earn income on the money you invest, that income then gets added to the amount

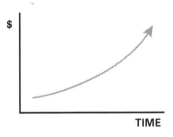

you started with. The combined higher amount then earns even more income. You thus experience a powerful acceleration in growth over time as you "earn income on the income."

Compounding is the same principle that underlies the more widely known concept of "compound interest"; the only difference being that real estate earnings are not technically interest, which is a fee paid in exchange for borrowing money.

Now, when you combine leverage with compounding, you can experience this acceleration in growth on a much greater scale. For example, if you are able to purchase a $100K investment by putting in only $25K in cash, you have managed to acquire an investment that is four times larger than if you had purchased your entire investment in cash. Every $1 you put in has now been invested with the power of $4.

In this scenario, you only put in $25K but you are now in a position to earn compound returns on that larger $100K investment. And if you can do that, something special happens.

 When leverage and compounding are optimized in a real estate business, they create extraordinary growth potential. These two principles can turn your cash into rocket fuel.

The concepts might seem overly simplistic on their surface, but understanding the true implications of properly combining leverage with compounding is essential. Until you fully grasp the enormity of their power, you won't appreciate the importance of cash.

And if you don't appreciate how important it is to prioritize cash, you won't make the right decisions when you're running your real estate business. You'll pay people to do things you can do yourself. You'll underestimate the long-term cost of selling a property. You'll make mistakes that could have been avoided. There are irreversible long-term implications for every short-term cash decision.

CASH-ON-CASH RETURNS

Used wisely, leverage and compounding can yield some pretty incredible "cash-on-cash" returns. Cash-on-cash returns are typically expressed as a percentage. It is a measure of how much cash is generated by your property annually in comparison to how much cash you contribute up front as part of your initial investment.

Cash-on-Cash Return = Annual Cash Flow / Initial Cash Investment

For growing a portfolio, it's important to focus on investments that can produce an immediate cash flow so you can harness the incredible power that leverage and compounding can provide.

Healthy cash-on-cash returns are particularly critical for investors just getting started, since such investments also tend to be less risky relative to the return. Investors with larger portfolios are better positioned to take more risks if they choose to since they will have established a strong enough cash flow to help carry them through if something unexpected happens. This is another reason why cash is so important—it can help you survive the mistakes and hiccups that are part of doing business.

Though not everyone likes math, there's no better way to illustrate the full implications of leverage and compounding in real estate than by walking you through an example. So let's examine a project to demonstrate a cash-on-cash return.

Apartment Complex Example

You decide to acquire a 30-unit apartment complex for $1M. First, you add up all of the income, which, in addition to the rent, might include things like income from on-site laundry machines, rental application fees, or pet fees. Some landlords generate extra income by having tenants reimburse them for utilities, or charging separately for things like parking and storage. In the case of this 30-unit complex, when you add these sources up you find that the property currently generates $200K per year in rent and other associated income. This is called your gross income.

Next, you add up all of the operating expenses, including things like maintenance and repairs, property management, insurance, property taxes, landscaping, advertising, etc. For the 30-unit apartment complex, you find that the total annual expenses are approximately $100K. When adding up the expenses, you exclude mortgage payments. You should always analyze the debt separately, and we'll get to that in a moment.

As mentioned early in the chapter, this difference between the gross income and expenses is called your net operating income, which is commonly referred to as "NOI":

Annual Income – Annual Expenses (Excluding Debt Service) = NOI
$200K – $100K = $100K

Now let's examine the debt. You use bank financing for 75% of the purchase price. As part of the deal, the seller has agreed to lend you another 15% of the purchase price. So you are financing a total of 90% of the purchase price, leaving you to come up with the remaining 10%, or $100K, in cash at closing.

Bank Financing	$750,000
Seller Financing	$150,000
Cash	$100,000
Total	$1,000,000

You are comfortable with financing 90% of the project because you have identified ways that you can add value to the property after closing. In this case, the primary way that you will add value is to boost the property's income well above the current income of $200K per year. There is a high vacancy rate, and you have come up with a solid plan to get the vacant units filled. The property is also charging rents that are well below market, and you plan to gradually raise them. More strategies for adding value to a property will be covered in a later chapter.

So since you are financing 90% of the purchase price, your total debt is $900K. To secure this financing, you're borrowing from both the bank and the seller at a 5% annual interest rate with a 25-year amortization period. Your resulting combined mortgage payment is $5,261 per month, or approximately $63K per year. This total of your payments for the year is called your "annual debt service."

Now you have everything you need to calculate how much money you will make from this investment. You subtract your mortgage payments (annual debt service) from the NOI, and find that the investment generates $37K in cash flow per year.

Net Operating Income	**$100,000**
Annual Debt Service	**−$63,000**
Cash Flow	**$37,000**

Since you put $100K of cash into the project out of pocket, you are in a position to clear a 37% cash-on-cash return in the first year of operation, if you so choose. And this is before you take any steps to boost income.

Cash-on-Cash Return = Annual Cash Flow / Initial Cash Investment
= $37,000 / $100,000
= 37%

You are also on pace to get all of your money back in 2.7 years, a number commonly referred to as your "payback period."

Payback Period   **= Initial Cash Investment / Annual Cash Flow**
= $100,000 / $37,000
= 2.7 Years

Now let's consider that when you make loan payments, you're also decreasing your debt by paying down your principal. In fact, in this scenario your total principal pay-down over the first five years of your loan totals approximately $103K (an average of more than $20K per year).

Principal pay-down can eventually be accessed as cash by refinancing or selling. So if we include the principal pay-down in our returns, then our potential annual cash return increases to approximately $57K per year. *This yields a gaudy 57% annual rate of return.*

If you continue to invest this cash back into both this property (and others) that meet a similar criteria, over the long term you can sustain this return. What does this mean?

If you run the calculations, you will find that, thanks to the power of compounding, a 57% annual return means that your payback period is only 1.75 years. In fact, with a 57% annual return, every $1 you put into your business (or keep in your business) can turn into approximately $9.50 in five years, and a whopping $91 in 10 years. That's some pretty extraordinary value creation!

YEAR	VALUE
0	$1.00
1	$1.57
2	$2.46
3	$3.87
4	$6.08
5	$9.54
6	$14.98
7	$23.51
8	$36.91
9	$57.96
10	$90.99

It's also worth noting that the above scenario doesn't reflect the even better returns you can achieve by following some of the strategies introduced in later chapters. For example, what do you think happens when you boost your cash flow an *additional* 5% by doing your own property management? And *even more* by making investments that boost rental income and curtail expenses?

This is the financial rocket fuel that will take you to the stars. How far you get depends on how closely you preserve and recycle your rocket fuel (that is, your cash)! One of the keys to success in real estate investing is to avoid pulling cash out unnecessarily, and carefully reinvesting as much of it as possible back into your properties. And to strategically put your cash to work for you in places that will boost your long-term NOI as much as possible.

CASH PRESERVATION

Understanding the power of cash, leverage, and compounding helps motivate investors to make the right decisions that create wealth. At the very heart of these decisions is the imperative of preserving cash.

"Beware of little expenses; a small leak will sink a great ship."
—BENJAMIN FRANKLIN

Small investors need to look for ways to improve their cash position across the full lifecycle of an investment, starting with the initial property selection criteria and the deal structure, and ending with the asset's long-term operating expenses.

There are limitless ways to improve your cash position, but certainly some are more accessible and offer more potential than others. For example, when selecting a property, you don't want to pick one with major problems that will necessitate a large cash infusion right after closing. And after closing, you should continuously look for ways to improve efficiency and save money without diminishing the value you deliver to tenants.

Once you own an investment property, the goal is not so much to avoid spending money but to reduce waste and invest money in things that are going to improve the property's long-term value. I'll explore methods for accomplishing this in more depth later in the book, but it boils down to thinking carefully about the implications of money spent. How will each improvement and expense affect the NOI over the longer term? How much value will it create? This analysis will often result in a decision that might go counter to standard industry practices.

Examples might include waiving a few months of rent to attract a new tenant, or paying for the build-out of a prospective office tenant's space in a market where such concessions are not the norm. These types of incentives can backfire if you offer them to unreliable tenants, but they can yield an excellent return when used judiciously, such as to secure a long-term commitment from a great tenant to occupy a space that has been difficult to lease.

Look at tenant build-outs and other property improvements through the same lens as an acquisition—consider your return on investment and how much value you'll be creating to help guide you in your decision-making process.

FEED THE BABY

Perhaps the most important way to conserve cash is to make a commitment to reinvesting as much of the cash flow back into the properties as possible. The property and business is your baby—it should feed off of you, not the other way around! At least not until it grows up... then you can retire and it can take care of you!

On a very basic level, always keep the business finances separate from your personal finances to avoid temptation and to keep your finger on the pulse of how the business is doing.

If your property is cash flow positive, it can be tempting to spend the money on personal luxuries instead of reinvesting it. Will you take some cash out of your business and put it into a new car? Or into a nicer home? Or to pay yourself so you can quit your day job?

Maybe you will, and that's OK. Everybody has different goals and priorities. Just be sure you're making an educated decision with a full understanding of the real cost involved.

It's important to set goals so you know what your endgame is, and how committed you are to getting there. Every dollar you take out of your business or spend unnecessarily will slow your growth and could keep you from hitting your goals.

> *"One half of knowing what you want is knowing what you must give up before you get it."*
> —SIDNEY HOWARD

The real implications of that only become evident if you take the time to run the numbers and figure it out.

CAPITALIZATION RATES

Another financial concept that is important to understand in commercial real estate is capitalization rates, which are used to determine a property's market value. In simple terms, the capitalization rate (or "cap rate") is the percentage return that you would receive on a property if you were to pay for it with all cash.

Cap rates are different than cash-on-cash returns because they are based solely on a property's NOI and purchase price, without adjusting for any debt or mortgage payments. Since there are so many ways to finance an acquisition, cap rates provide a more objective measure of a property's underlying income production relative to the purchase price.

Cash-on-cash returns provide an excellent measure of your return on invested capital, but they can vary widely for a given property depending on how much money you borrow. How a deal is financed and its resulting effect on cash flows is extremely important. But this consideration should be left to individual investors to evaluate based on their personal goals and circumstances, not used to measure a property's market value.

This is where cap rates come in. Recall from our 30-unit apartment example that NOI is the money a property generates without debt payments. The cap rate in this example is the annual return that the NOI represents relative to the price for which the property was acquired.

To calculate the cap rate you take the NOI and divide it by the purchase price of the property. The result is then expressed as a percentage.

Cap Rate = NOI / Purchase Price

To illustrate, let's find the cap rate for the 30-unit apartment complex. You may recall that our NOI was $100K and our purchase price was $1M. So the cap rate would be calculated as follows:

$$\begin{aligned} \text{Cap Rate} \quad &= \text{NOI / Purchase Price} \\ &= \$100{,}000 / \$1{,}000{,}000 \\ &= 10\% \end{aligned}$$

It might seem counterintuitive at first, but the cap rate is inversely proportional to the price. In other words, a high cap rate is indicative of a lower price property (per dollar of income it generates) while a lower cap rate indicates a higher price.

As you might expect, investors pay a premium for the same income when it comes from investments with low risk. Therefore, real estate assets with low risk tend to sell at a lower cap rate (higher price).

For example, a commercial real estate property occupied by a strong national chain with a long-term, corporate-guaranteed lease in place might be considered low risk. Such a property would be desirable to an investor due to its stability and would therefore command a premium price and lower cap rate.

Properties situated in more desirable locations are also perceived to be lower risk due to some inherent underlying value and therefore reduced downside. The logic here is that if you were to lose a tenant, the space is more likely to be quickly and easily re-rented due to the location's desirability. Or, in some cases, it might be redeveloped for another use.

When there is more risk involved, investors demand a higher return on their investment even though they are getting the same NOI. Such properties therefore command a higher cap rate, and are priced lower, relative to the income they generate. Examples of higher risk investments might include a property occupied by a startup (more prone to failure) or a property in a less desirable location. Any factor that might put future NOI in jeopardy will lower the property value and therefore command a higher cap rate.

Higher cap rates mean that the property yields a higher return on your money, meaning you'll also get a higher cash-on-cash return for a given financing structure. But these higher returns need to be weighed against the risks associated with the property and any factors that might threaten those returns over time. This can create opportunities. Sometimes clever investors can identify ways to manage this risk and reap the rewards of superior returns. Examples might include lining up a strong new tenant ahead of time, or getting the current month-to-month tenants to make longer-term commitments, thereby creating more stability in the cash flow.

Capitalization rates are also influenced by the lending environment and cost of borrowing. In order to service their debt (pay their mortgage), investors need to achieve a return on their investment that is higher than their cost of capital (their mortgage interest rate).

How does this work? Well, if you think of the cap rates as boats, the lending rates are like the ocean tides. As the lending rates rise, so must the cap rates for properties in the marketplace. This is because investors need to ensure they can service their debt. And when cap rates rise, it means that property prices fall.

MANAGING LEVERAGE

An introduction to real estate finance wouldn't be complete without a word of caution on the potentially dire consequences of getting too greedy when taking on leverage.

While leverage can extend the reach of your dollar and accelerate investment, you must take on debt with caution. Debt can be a good thing for ratcheting up returns, but when it comes to debt, you can definitely get too much of a good thing. For the most part, banks are likely to keep you in check. But that is not always the case, especially with private lenders and motivated sellers.

If you overextend yourself by borrowing too much, it can be a struggle to make the mortgage payments every month. Don't leave things so close that you can't handle some of the inevitable setbacks you'll face along the way. There are few certainties in any new business venture, but here is one thing you can definitely count on: there will always be some surprises—unexpected things *will* happen. So keep that in mind when borrowing and leave yourself some breathing room.

How much debt is too much? How much risk is too much? The answer is largely a personal one. How much are you prepared to lose if things don't go well? We all have our own levels of comfort when it comes to risk tolerance and each investor has to consider their own unique circumstances.

The ultimate responsibility not to overborrow lies with *you*, the investor. But when a seller agrees to extend owner financing, or you begin looking at hard money loans (risky loans extended to investors at a higher interest rate), I encourage you to be thorough in your analysis and use restraint. The prospective rewards of a project can blind an inexperienced investor to the corresponding risks that are always inherent to such projects. You need to balance the lure of extraordinary cash-on-cash returns versus the risk of overextending yourself. This is easy enough to say but can be difficult in practice, particularly when you're excited about a project with great potential returns.

OTHER FINANCIAL AND BUSINESS CONCEPTS

There are many more ratios and financial concepts used in business and commercial real estate. However, the ones presented in this chapter should be your core principles when acquiring and operating an income-generating commercial property. In Appendix A, you will find a summary of the basic formulas covered in this book for easy reference later on.

As mentioned in the preface, this book is not intended to be comprehensive. It is designed to arm you with a good understanding of the fundamental concepts you need to be successful. Of course as you gain experience and educate yourself your knowledge will naturally broaden. And if you're motivated to learn more, you're strongly encouraged to do so. A commitment to devouring as much educational material as possible will do nothing but make you a better investor.

In Appendix B, you will find a list of supplementary educational resources. A good place to get started would be BiggerPockets.com, a free online networking and information website designed to help educate people in all aspects of real estate investing. What I like about BiggerPockets is that the education is largely accomplished through blog posts and interactions between active investors, which tends to make the information practical. While much of the content is geared toward smaller residential investments, most of the concepts apply to commercial properties as well.

Finally, a word of caution as you explore educational resources: always bring a healthy dose of skepticism and be leery of any approaches or analyses that seem overly complicated or purport to yield easy money. There are a lot of people out there preying on the hopes and dreams of aspiring investors, and their pitches can be compelling and seductive. Others use a lot of fancy terminology and espouse complicated techniques to further their own agendas. *Don't let them dazzle you.* As Warren Buffett cautioned in a letter to investors, "Our advice: Beware of geeks bearing formulas."

Stay grounded with the basics, and remember that there aren't any shortcuts.

THE SOLAR BUILDING PROJECT: PART I

 Once you've mastered the fundamentals and start to invest in more real estate projects, you're likely to face a wide range of challenges and continue to learn as you grow. Every once in a while a project may come along that accelerates this process. One that doesn't just call on everything you've learned thus far, but also pushes you onto a steeper learning curve. These projects can be great opportunities, though they also need to be entered into with caution and careful consideration.

This was the case for me with the Solar Building, a six-story, mixed-use property with commercial storefronts on the ground floor and apartments upstairs. It was located one block over from our main office, and thus I was very familiar with it and its sketchy history. One of our office tenants shared with me that a few years earlier he'd looked out his window one morning to observe somebody committing suicide by leaping from the top floor of the Solar Building.

ALEXA MURRAY

Since that time, things at the Solar Building had really gone downhill. The police were responding to calls there all the time. It had a horrible reputation and its close proximity to our office building had prompted some of our commercial tenants to express concern for their safety.

Even so, given my appetite for turnarounds, the Solar Building was a property that really grabbed my attention when it went into foreclosure. Architecturally it was remarkable, with a wedge shape reminiscent of the Flatiron Building in New York City.

The Solar Building originally got its name from a massive central skylight that on sunny days fills its multistory atrium with sunlight. The interior also features an exposed elevator that runs up and down the atrium. The building was located right on the edge of the business district, an area that was trending in the right direction.

The building had been neglected and mismanaged to the point that people avoided it, but at the same time it practically screamed potential. I went back and forth on what to do, but felt compelled to investigate further.

Was this an opportunity to leverage my local knowledge and familiarity with the property to reap great rewards? Or would this project be my downfall? Only time would tell. To be continued…

KEY POINTS

► New investors should invest the time and effort necessary to master the basic underlying principles of real estate finance. More complicated financial transactions and analysis can require specialized knowledge and are not suitable for most inexperienced investors.

- When leverage and compounding are optimized in a real estate business, they create extraordinary growth potential. Understanding the potential returns can give real estate investors a better appreciation for the importance of cash.
- Capitalization rates are the industry standard for measuring a property's value. The cap rate is associated with the perceived risk and return of a property, and is measured as the ratio of the net operating income to the purchase price, expressed as a percentage. Properties with high cap rates can sometimes present excellent opportunities for small investors.
- While higher levels of debt can drive up cash-on-cash returns, investors should carefully weigh the risks and be cautious about overextending themselves.

CHAPTER 2

BOOTSTRAP IT

*"Opportunity is missed by most people because it is dressed in
overalls and looks like work."*
—THOMAS EDISON

*"People usually know what they should do to get what they want.
They just won't do it. They won't pay the price. Understand there
is a price to be paid for achieving anything of significance. You
must be willing to pay the price."*
—JOHN WOODEN

■

ONE OF THE MORE rewarding aspects of having some success in real estate investing is that it provides me with opportunities to share what I've learned with others. I often serve as a mentor and I'm grateful for the opportunity to help steer aspiring real estate entrepreneurs on the right path. Hopefully I can help them avoid some of the mistakes I've made along the way.

I recently met with a young real estate investor whose unrestrained enthusiasm was a bit jarring. As she sat down in my office, it was immediately clear that she was outgoing and very excited. "Thank you so much for meeting with me!" she exclaimed. "I'm so excited to get started with my investing—I want to do exactly what you've done. I've always thought real estate was interesting, and I can't wait to start buying properties."

She jumped right into her story. "I just moved in with my boyfriend. He has enough savings to get started. I think we have enough for a down payment on an apartment complex of 20 to 30 units, so I thought I'd start with that. I really don't like my job, so I plan to quit this week and jump in with both feet! I've already found a small building for sale that I will buy and use as my business office. It's a little more than I need right now, but I want to make sure I've got plenty of room to grow for when I start hiring people."

My eyes got progressively wider as I listened. I'm fairly certain she believed I was sharing in her excitement as she plowed ahead without taking a breath. "I've already come up with a name for my firm and I've got business cards—here, have one!" She thrust a card at me and continued. "I picked out the furniture for my office and I bought the equipment I'll need—I got a really good deal because it was on sale! The color laser printer was half off!"

By now my eyes were like saucers, and my jaw was starting to drop. From my facial expression, she decided I must be incredibly impressed with her, and she puffed her chest up a little and proceeded to describe how she wanted to decorate her office. She reiterated several times how excited she was to quit her job, and, to my absolute horror, how she was planning to buy a new car since her current vehicle was unreliable and she would be driving around a lot for her new business! She asked me if I recommended a magnet or decal for affixing a logo.

Finally stopping and gulping for air, she was positively *beaming* at me. Holy crap, I thought. This conversation isn't going to go the way either one of us expected. How to rein this young lady in without dampening her excitement? Despite her naiveté and lack of sound judgment, I really liked her enthusiasm. She had that going for her.

We ended up talking for nearly an hour as I gave her the soundest advice I could. Her readiness to take action was impressive and an asset, but it wasn't going to serve her well to leap forward blindly. I encouraged her to first direct all her eagerness toward learning a little more about real estate before she spent any more money. I also strongly urged her to avail herself of some business counseling advice that was available for free through a local business development center.

But perhaps most importantly, I introduced her to the concept of bootstrapping, and emphasized how critical this concept was if she wanted to be successful.

Bootstrapping is essentially being creative at finding ways to leverage your existing resources to accomplish more with less. It's figuring out how to get things done without spending money, or at least minimizing your cash outlay. It's preserving your rocket fuel.

> "He who does not economize will have to agonize."
> —CONFUCIUS

Bootstrapping certainly doesn't involve cutting back on your income or, even worse, taking on unnecessary debt. These are two of the worst things an entrepreneur could possibly do.

This is where the concept of "sweat equity" comes in. You're rolling up your sleeves and doing as many things as you can to build a real business without spending money. All of the work you put in (and the money you save) helps grow the value of the business.

When you start out in real estate investing (or really any business), remember that cash is king and every penny is precious. In practical terms, this means that dollars should be used for deals, and not for office space, cars, furniture, or fancy business cards.

After explaining this to the aspiring investor, she had an undisguised look of disappointment. I challenged her with difficult questions about how hard she was prepared to work and what sacrifices she was prepared to make. I offered encouragement, but I'm not sure she liked my message.

> "It is better to risk starving to death than surrender. If you give up on your dreams, what's left?"
> —JIM CARREY

For most of us, money is a scarce resource. For entrepreneurs, it's everything. Remember that your new business is your baby. You need to nurture it carefully and avoid spending money on anything that isn't necessary.

BEING FRUGAL

After I bought my first office building, you might think I would have picked out a nice suite for myself. There certainly were enough vacant offices to take my pick. But I didn't. My office ended up being what I can best describe as a cramped utility cubby tucked under the basement stairs. Yes, that's right. A cubby under the stairs... just like Harry Potter.

The office was full of old electric panels. If I stood in one spot, I could touch the walls on either side. And my arms aren't very long. One end was just wide enough for a small desk, which was good enough. This was the company office for years, even when my business started to grow and I had three employees. Sure it was a little cozy, but we were mostly out running around anyway, and it got the job done.

Why did I do this? Simple. While I needed to have an office on-site for the sake of the tenants, every single square foot of space I could rent was important to maximizing income, and thereby improving my business's chances of surviving and thriving. So I picked the spot that, in my estimation, would be the least desirable in the building to a prospective tenant. There was just too much at stake to do it any other way.

ASK THE HARD QUESTIONS

When investing in real estate, be prepared to ask yourself the hard questions when making spending decisions—especially when you're just starting out. Carefully think through every expenditure. Is it *really* necessary?

"Be industrious and frugal, and you will be rich."
—BENJAMIN FRANKLIN

Here are the kinds of questions you should consider when first starting your business:

- What are you currently using as a computer? Keep using it until it dies.
- Do you have a place to sleep? If so, it can probably double as an office.
- What are you currently using as transportation? A bicycle? A bus? An old car? Keep using it.
- If you need a website, does it need to be professionally designed? Or can you use a free service like Weebly or WordPress to create a basic one yourself? Or can you forgo a website altogether and instead create a business page on a social media platform such as Facebook or LinkedIn?
- What do you *absolutely need* to buy? If you're convinced it's necessary, can you find a used one? If not, can you rent or lease it instead?

The sacrifices you make early on, and the creativity you employ in getting things done, will reap rewards later on. You should take great pride in the ingenuity necessary to be a successful bootstrapper. It's not something everyone can do, but it's another way to stack the deck in your favor on the road to success.

MY DAILY ROUTINE

I was working as a professor at the time I bought my first property, and I followed the same routine almost every day. After getting up early, I'd head into the office building, where I'd unlock the four building entrances and the elevator, walk the interior hallways on all three floors while turning on the lights and checking the bathrooms. Then I'd walk the grounds, inspecting the exterior and picking up any litter.

If there was snow or ice to clear, I'd come in earlier and start the process well before sunrise. Afterward, I'd tend to a myriad of projects or tasks before heading off to my teaching job at around 8:00 a.m. Most days I'd go back to the office building during my lunch break to address any pressing issues, and then for another hour or two after work, depending on what needed to get done. When school wasn't in session, I could stay there all day.

But I always made it home in time for dinner. I carved out family time religiously and also time to take care of myself and stay healthy. Sometimes you'd find me at the property on weekends with the family in tow, planting flowers or working on projects, but not too often. It's always a challenge to balance work with family, but I was determined to make my first project a success—my life savings was riding on it, and I wasn't about to cut corners. There was a lot on the line.

DON'T QUIT YOUR DAY JOB

Though my revitalized office building could have supported my family and me, quitting my day job was never an option. It was hard, but I continued to teach for seven years after I acquired my first property, all the while performing my teaching duties to a high standard. Why? As I saw it, quitting would have been self-indulgent.

Even though I had originally intended for my real estate investing to help supplement my income, there was no way I was going to siphon off cash in order to pay my personal bills. Taking owner's draws at this stage could put a strain on the business, or worse—jeopardize its ultimate survival. I wanted every penny to go right back into the property, and that's exactly what I did. In fact, it's what I still do for the most part.

I didn't quit my day job until my company's annual revenues surpassed $2M. Personally, I think a lot of entrepreneurs are far too quick to quit their day jobs. In cases where the workload can be balanced, that steady income can be enough to make the difference between the ultimate success and failure in any entrepreneurial venture.

There are certainly times when it's necessary to quit your day job and focus 100% on your venture, but I've seen too many people jump the gun. They speak of their decision to quit their job with pride, when all too often what they actually did was take the easy way out at the expense of burdening their young business with a much heavier load. Now the business doesn't only have to support itself—it has to support you too! And maybe your family to boot! You may have just made the success hurdle a lot higher than it needed to be, or at least slowed your business's growth potential. Be your own biggest investor—bootstrap it and keep your day job for as long as you can manage it! The business will pay you back later.

GRIT

If I had to choose the single attribute that is the greatest key to success as a real estate investor, I would have to say it is grit. The investor has to have an iron will and determination to succeed that can steadily power them over the long term. This will allow them to continue to bootstrap even when they don't have to—to make short-term sacrifices necessary for the longer-term success.

In her famous TED Talk on the subject of grit, researcher Angela Lee Duckworth singles out grit as the key to success. In her talk, Professor Duckworth defines grit as follows:

> Grit is passion and perseverance for very long-term goals. Grit is having stamina. Grit is sticking with your future, day in, day out, not just for the week, not just for the month, but for years, and working really hard to make that future a reality. Grit is living life like it's a marathon, not a sprint.[3]

---

3 Angela Lee Duckworth, "Grit: The Power of Passion and Perseverance," filmed April 2013, TED Talks Education, 6:13, https://www.ted.com/talks/angela_lee_duckworth_grit_the_power_of_passion_and_perseverance?language=en.

Everyone has setbacks every day, some bigger than others. But it's an investor's unbreakable determination and resilience that will eventually lead to success. It's through grit that you will overcome obstacles and create value for both you and your customers. Grit is the foundation on which you can build an empire.

WALKING THE COMMERCIAL REAL ESTATE PLANK

 So what happens when a new real estate investor walks the plank and jumps into the commercial real estate ocean? When they leap into the unknown, ready to swim with the sharks? The answer depends in large part on the extent to which the investor is motivated and prepared. If you understand the basics, keep things simple, and are determined to work hard, you are likely to find it's not only manageable, but can be tremendously rewarding.

I don't mean to imply that a jump into the commercial real estate ocean won't be challenging. The water might be cold, the cur-

> *"There are no secrets to success. It is the result of preparation, hard work, and learning from failure."*
> —COLIN POWELL

rents may be strong, and there are dangers out there. But as an investor with grit you are an absolute force to be reckoned with. You aren't easily discouraged. You are prepared to bootstrap it—to do the hard work and make the difficult decisions necessary. You are willing to put your head down and swim the distance. You will take pleasure in the challenge of the hard swim, and enjoy your life on that tropical island.

On the other hand, if you're the investor who jumps off the proverbial plank intending only to spend the day floating on your back looking for helicopters, then you're probably better off just staying on the boat.

KEY POINTS

► Real estate investors should not expect their path to be easy or glamorous. To successfully start a business in commercial real estate, aspiring investors should be prepared to bootstrap it, being frugal with their cash and using creativity to get the most out of their limited resources.

► Investors can dramatically increase their chances of success if they work hard and preserve supplemental sources of income. It is generally not advisable for a real estate investor to quit their day job until they have assembled a larger portfolio.

► One of the most important attributes in determining whether an investor will succeed is grit. The ability to persevere in the face of setbacks and consistently work hard toward long-term goals can yield great rewards.

CHAPTER 3

EXPLOIT HOMEFIELD ADVANTAGE

"The problem with real estate is that it's local. You have to understand the local market."

—ROBERT KIYOSAKI

"In a fight between a bear and an alligator, it is the terrain which determines who wins."

—JIM BARKSDALE

■

ONCE YOU HAVE A handle on the basic financial concepts of commercial real estate and a heightened appreciation for the power of cash, bootstrapping, and hard work, you're well on your way to start looking for investment properties. But there are a number of other important decisions you'll need to make before you can conduct a productive search. The first step is to determine what geographic area you'd like to invest in.

There is a wide range of factors to consider when choosing a location. In the end, it boils down to identifying a property where you can best compete and achieve your investment goals. Commercial real estate is as intensely competitive as any other industry, so it's wise to fully consider your strengths and weaknesses when choosing your market—any advantage you might have over the competition can help make the difference between failure and success.

One great aspect of owning investment property is that you get to select the playing field in which you're going to compete. Wouldn't it make sense to choose a location that you're familiar with?

It's only natural that investors tend to have the most intimate knowledge of their own communities. Among other things, people tend to know the best and worst neighborhoods, the school districts, who the largest employers are and where they're located, what areas are growing, and what areas are in decline.

Most people even have some micro-level knowledge of their community such as the appeal of particular shop and restaurant locations, the history of individual properties, and sometimes even whether specific businesses or people would be good tenants. And this is just the tip of the iceberg.

Though they often aren't aware of it, through their day-to-day life the average person has already accumulated a wealth of knowledge about their community that can provide a significant competitive advantage over those investing from a distance.

Perhaps this advantage can best be illustrated by contrasting the perspective of a local investor to that of a large institutional investor from outside the community.

Let's imagine a distant large investor dressed in their custom tailored suit, overseeing their investment trust (with hundreds of properties) from their desk in an office on the 42nd floor of a very impressive building. Lots of glass and lots of marble. Their office smells like money. They are a modern-day commercial real estate Goliath.

Perhaps surprisingly, from this imposing position the investor actually has some extraordinary weaknesses. As the small investor sitting at home, you are in position to take on the role of David, prepared to do battle and take advantage of those weaknesses.

One of the large investor's greatest weaknesses is their distance and detachment. They are stretched too thin and they are too removed from the actual brick-and-mortar properties themselves, which are often reduced to nothing more than lines of numbers on a spreadsheet.

This can make them stodgy, overly reliant on distant (and expensive) third parties, and unfamiliar with local market conditions. It also drives them toward the most conservative properties. These large investor weaknesses represent great opportunities for the little guy.

> *"One who does not know the mountains and forests, gorges and defiles, swamps and wetlands cannot advance the army."*
> —SUN TZU

Having your feet on the ground and investing in your own backyard opens up a plethora of potential advantages. In fact, it could be argued that even if you live in an unattractive market by most standards, your backyard is still the best potential location of all when it comes to securing a distinct advantage over competitors removed from the area.

There are multiple potential benefits of investing in your local market. Examples include a far better vantage point to identify opportunities and assess risk, to actively manage and oversee projects, to monitor what is going on, and to react nimbly. Buying local could be the sling in your pocket!

Imagine there are two investors, each of which is going to purchase a small retail plaza.

Investor A is Winston Carter. Winston purchases a plaza that is 2,000 miles away and hires ABC Regional Property Management LLC to manage his property. Winston pays 5% of revenues to the management firm. The property management firm is the best available in that area, but they manage more than 100 properties, some of which they own themselves and will always get priority. Their employees are overextended because margins are thin in property management, so staffing levels have to be held in check. The property management firm uses "preferred vendors," which is a fancy way of saying they award work to the guys they go fishing with.

Investor B is Judy Smith. Judy purchases a plaza just a short drive from her house. She drives by it every day on her way to work and checks on things. Sometimes she stops by during her lunch break or later in the day. She speaks face-to-face with the tenants regularly and builds relationships. Judy is constantly identifying ways to improve the property and operate it more efficiently. She self-manages and takes that 5% of revenue that would have gone toward a property manager and reinvests it back into property improvements. On weekends Judy sometimes piles her spouse, her kids, and the family dog into her minivan for an outing to the property, where they do a family trash pickup or flower planting. The kids are proud and learn the value of hard work. The dog wags his tail because he loves doing anything with the family. Word spreads about the great local ownership, and the property's reputation improves.

Which investor's property is most likely to stay full? Which investor's property is most likely to increase in value? If you had to bet your life savings on which scenario is more likely to yield a higher return, which would you pick?

RELATIONSHIPS AND RESPONSIVENESS

Only a handful of the benefits of local ownership are reflected in the above scenarios. Other examples include knowledge of local trends and culture, and the ability to establish strong relationships with local partners, including lenders, contractors, government officials, etc.

As a local owner, you can also keep a much closer eye on the competition and changing market conditions, and then react accordingly.

I can't tell you how many local properties I've purchased from absentee landlords who were out of touch with market conditions and charging rent that was far too low, or far too high and resulting in high vacancy. In these cases, simply bringing the rents closer to market levels is usually enough to dramatically improve the value of a property.

Direct access to the marketplace and your end customers—the tenants—offers a major competitive advantage, not only for informational purposes, but also for the relationships that you can establish.

From a business standpoint, the bottom line is that being local can significantly lower a project's risk. It can also open an abundance of opportunities to lower operating costs and boost income, dramatically improving your returns.

HOT AND COLD MARKETS

Think you can't find a good deal or achieve an attractive return in your particular market? Think again. This is one of the most common myths in real estate, and one of the greatest excuses for not investing. People think their particular market is too expensive, or that they've already missed the boat. Others think their market is too rural or depressed.

These kinds of negative pronouncements tend to be more of a reflection on the investor than on the market itself. You'd be surprised at what kind of deals investors uncover in the most unlikely places. Challenging markets require diligence, patience, and sometimes even a little creativity. But if you're persistent and look hard enough, most experienced investors agree that deals can be found in any market, or at least within a reasonable driving distance.

Robert Kiyosaki laments this very point in his iconic book *Rich Dad Poor Dad* when he shares with his readers that he hears the same complaint in nearly every city—people claim that they can't find good deals. But his experience and those of countless other investors proves otherwise. "Even in New York or Tokyo, or just on the outskirts of the city, prime bargains are overlooked by most people," notes Kiyosaki. "In Singapore, with their high real estate prices, there are still bargains to be found within a short driving distance."[4]

Likewise there are deals to be had on the opposite end of the population density spectrum—attractive opportunities can often be found even in the smallest cities and towns. Certainly any community large enough to support a grocery store or post office offers prospective commercial investments.

In fact, most of the post office locations themselves are leased from real estate investors, and occasionally they come up for sale.[5] Recognizing post offices to be a good investment opportunity, a small investor named Lawrence Magdovitz began purchasing USPS facilities in rural Mississippi back in 1980, eventually accumulating 850 of them all across the country!

Though the investment pickings can sometimes be slim in more sparsely populated regions, the opportunities are there, and the returns are often healthy. Because smaller communities are less popular among large investors, they are more likely to be buyers' markets where properties sell at higher cap rates than in larger, more competitive metropolitan areas.

BUYING OUTSIDE YOUR BACKYARD

Even though the case for buying local can be compelling, it would be folly to suggest that good opportunities can't be found in more distant and/or unfamiliar locations. Thousands of real estate investors have proven it's possible to be successful by buying outside of their geographical areas.

When considering this option, however, the investor must accept the following:

---

4 *Rich Dad Poor Dad: What the Rich Teach Their Kids About Money—That the Poor and Middle Class Do Not!* by Robert T. Kiyosaki, Plata Publishing, 2011.

5 USPS Leased Facilities Report, https://about.usps.com/who-we-are/foia/leased-facilities/report.htm.

- The less you know about a market, the higher the inherent risk, and thus increased likelihood of failure.
- The more distant a property, the more difficult it will be for you to be actively involved, provide high levels of service, and stay on top of things.
- The more spread out your properties are, the harder it will be to gain efficiencies of scale.

Understanding these risks and considerations, many investors will elect to go ahead and invest outside of their home market anyway, for a variety of reasons. While I do not generally advocate this approach, there are some compelling reasons investors might logically take this path. These reasons may include factors such as:

- Having a trusted partner or family member that will provide the local involvement and presence to mitigate the risk in your absence.
- Lower prices and higher cap rates are too appealing to pass up.
- Lack of nearby opportunities that meet your investment criteria.
- The target location has, or is projected to have, better economic growth and development, providing increased upside potential.
- Intention of relocating to the target location in the future.
- Your portfolio has grown to a level that continued geographic concentration poses a higher level of risk than you are comfortable with.

While nothing can match the value of being present every day, I would encourage investors who are buying in new locations to do everything they can to stay on top of the market and property management. This can mean anything from reading the daily newspaper to hyper-communication with your local representatives, whoever they may be.

It's a powerful natural tendency for people to fall into the trap of "out of sight, out of mind." This is particularly true when dealing with something stressful, such as the myriad of issues that inevitably crop up when you're a landlord. If you can't be there yourself, come up with as many ways as you can to keep your finger on the pulse, and commit to it.

THE SOLAR BUILDING PROJECT: PART II

 Since the Solar Building was only a short walk from our office, I was intimately familiar with its surroundings, but had never been inside. I decided we needed to get a look at the interior before the auction. It was a foreclosure situation so we couldn't schedule a showing, but the building was occupied so my superintendent and I waited near the entrance for an approachable tenant to let us in, and then began exploring the common areas.

Our first reaction was one of fear. The local newspaper called the Solar Building a "haven of criminality" and we could see why. Most of the common area lights were smashed out and drug dealers lurked in the dark hallways. There was trash everywhere and lots of bugs. Cockroaches were visible scurrying out of our path as we walked the common areas, even though it was the middle of the day. They were even crawling around on the hand railings. The air was stale and pungent.

But even though it was scary, I couldn't help notice that underneath the filth were gorgeous mosaic tile hallways and ornate wrought-iron railings. We got a few stare-downs but encountered a tenant who seemed relatively non-threatening and spoke with him about the situation. He invited us into his apartment to sit down and talk. We learned that there were still some good people living there. These scared, rent-paying tenants were hiding behind locked doors. In my mind I imagined they were just waiting for the right investor to help save the day!

After our visit to the property, I did as much due diligence as I could, until I had gathered every possible piece of information I could get my hands on. I leveraged my relationships with local people who had ties to the building, and I was able to speak with a former superintendent and contractors who had completed work there in the past. I had a long conversation with the property manager. I even met with the local police.

> *"True beauty can only be discovered by one who mentally completes the incomplete."*
>
> —OKAKURA KAKUZŌ

I thoroughly researched the history of the property, including all of the court documents associated with the foreclosure. The short version of what I discovered was unexpected. The reason for the foreclosure was rooted in a legal dispute and was unrelated to the financial performance of the property itself. Despite the deplorable conditions, the property was actually generating a healthy cash flow.

I did the best estimating I could and, using highly conservative numbers, I modeled the financials. The results were encouraging. If I could get the property at the right price, it should cash flow even if it were only half occupied. Even with rents that were well below what we knew the local market could support.

After weighing all the information I had gathered, I was determined to bid at the foreclosure auction. When the auction eventually took place, I was amazed to find out that, apart from the bank representative, we were the only ones there! With no other bidders, we were able to purchase it for literally $1 over the bank's minimum bid.

Despite the fact that the building was cash flowing and had tremendous upside potential, nobody wanted to go near it. It just didn't fit the criteria for any large investors, and was too big and too scary to be considered by local investors, many of whom were more focused on duplexes and triplexes.

The fact that nobody else showed up at the auction was exciting, but it was also a bit unnerving. Was I missing something here? Did nobody else know about the auction? Or did everyone know but say "no thank you"? Maybe $1 over the bank's minimum bid was actually too high of a price. Maybe the bank should have been paying me to take it off of their hands!

I shoved my doubts aside and had faith. I had done my homework. I knew the market. And I was ready. At least that's what I told myself. To be continued...

KEY POINTS

▶ Buying local can provide an investor with a wide range of competitive advantages over absentee landlords.

▶ The average person has already accumulated a wealth of knowledge about their community that can be highly beneficial to an investor.

▶ Intimate knowledge of a market and close proximity can sometimes be enough to overcome the disadvantages of investing in an otherwise unattractive marketplace.

▶ There are a variety of reasons why investors may be compelled to invest in a distant market. In these situations the investor should make extraordinary efforts to mitigate the disadvantages of not being local.

CHAPTER 4

PICK THE BEST BATTLEGROUND

"If you try to steal the giant's lunch,
the giant is likely to eat you for lunch."
—SETH GODIN

"An army may be likened to water, for just as flowing water
avoids the heights and hastens to the lowlands, so an army
avoids strength and strikes weakness."
—SUN TZU

■

WHEN I WAS STILL teaching, a local entrepreneur visited my class and shared an all-to-familiar story with the students about how a big-box retailer had driven her out of business. Born and raised in the community, this entrepreneur had realized her lifelong dream of opening a retail shop in her hometown. Her small business thrived until a Walmart opened up, after which sales dropped, and she eventually had to close her doors.

This entrepreneur had all the advantages of knowing her local community inside and out. She knew what was popular and what wasn't. She knew her customers well and worked hard to build relationships. But in the end the advantages of being local just weren't enough to prevail in a head-on war with the largest re-tailer in the world.

One of my students asked the entrepreneur what she could have done differently, and you could tell from the entrepreneur's response that she had already spent time wrestling with this question. "You know, I couldn't see it at the time, but I should have shifted my focus a little and sold things you can't buy at Walmart… maybe offered services they don't provide, or I could have targeted customers who don't shop there."

While on the surface this entrepreneur's experience may not seem relevant to real estate investing, there are definitely some valuable lessons. Yes, you can and should secure significant competitive advantages through your local presence and market knowledge. But sometimes that's not enough by itself. You should also try to prevent unnecessary direct competition with much larger investors by positioning yourself advantageously when selecting your type and class of investment property.

This kind of strategic decision-making involves understanding and watching your competition, and positioning yourself accordingly. As you will see, avoiding toe-to-toe competition doesn't mean you'll have to pass up opportunities with the most potential. Nor is it necessary to make things overly complicated.

SEGMENTS OF COMMERCIAL REAL ESTATE

Some types of commercial real estate, such as industrial, agricultural, hospitality, or specialized properties such as laboratories, marinas, or convalescent homes, are not common choices for new investors for a variety of reasons, including complex regulatory environments or a greater need for industry-specific knowledge.

Even something as seemingly simple as farmland can be a more complicated investment than you might expect. It's not necessarily as simple as just buying a few acres of land and renting them out to a farmer to run his business on your property. Unless they have prior farming experience, investors are unlikely to have the expertise necessary to accurately assess the potential value of this asset, for example, or know how to ensure its long-term sustainability. As a result, tracts of farmland are more likely to be owner-operated, meaning that the same investor owns both the business and the underlying real estate asset.

Another example of an investment requiring expertise that is frequently owner-operated is a hotel. Small investors that acquire hotels are more likely to have worked in the industry and gained the specialized knowledge and experience that will allow them to operate the property more effectively, or at least be capable of hiring the right team and providing some oversight. The learning curve would be exceptionally steep otherwise, dramatically increasing the likelihood of failure.

The categories of commercial real estate most suitable for smaller investors are typically more straightforward, and include existing multifamily (apartments or mobile home parks), multitenant retail, multitenant office, and self-storage properties with strong cash flow. The strategies included in this book are generally applicable to each of these popular investment types.

That's not to say these categories are all the same—they're not. In fact, the nuances of each could fill an entire series of books on their own. That said, the differences are not so vast or complex as to be beyond the ready grasp of most determined, novice investors. The fundamentals of running these property types are also very similar to those underlying a duplex or even a single-family home rental, something that many aspiring commercial investors already have experience with. Overall, they offer the following advantages for small investors:

▶ They require less specialized knowledge than niche property types.
▶ They are less labor intensive than high service-level assets like hotels or convalescent homes.
▶ In most markets they are available in ample quantities for investors to purchase.
▶ They offer significant opportunities to limit exposure to downside risk while retaining the prospect of superior upside returns.

- They are typically easier to finance than specialized properties or development projects.
- They share many of the same basic underlying principles and considerations when it comes to valuation, leasing, and operation.

I want to emphasize that the property you choose should be existing, with an established, strong cash flow. This is primarily because of the higher risk and cash demands typical of new development. Existing, occupied properties can produce attractive cash flows immediately after an investor takes ownership. Such properties also improve an investor's chances of securing a reputable lender. New construction is generally more complicated and has a longer payback period. And while experienced developers can certainly achieve attractive returns, there are many potential pitfalls that can drag a project out and quickly eat up your cash. This tends to be a game better played by those with more experience.

It is also preferable to target properties with a diversified cash flow, meaning the income is derived from as many tenants as possible so as to mitigate the effect of losing a tenant. This is one reason why apartment complexes and self-storage facilities can be attractive—the rental income is typically spread across more tenants. It's also why I recommend that small retail or office investors prioritize multitenanted properties.

On the opposite end of the spectrum would be a commercial property that is fully occupied by a single tenant. These properties should be evaluated with caution because the implications can be severe should this tenant vacate or fail. It becomes easier for an investor to rationalize a single-tenant property if they have a larger portfolio to help offset the potential loss of income. Unless the single tenant is particularly strong with a long-term, corporate-guaranteed lease, it can be harder for a small investor to justify the higher risk.

CLASS A, CLASS B, OR CLASS C

When looking at a prospective investment property, investors will consider its relative age, condition, and overall quality. In commercial real estate, properties are often marketed as Class A, Class B, or Class C, which is a way of communicating their relative grade.

A published definition for Class A, Class B, and Class C can be found in the glossary courtesy of Institutional Real Estate Inc. (IREI), but investors need to be aware that there are no broadly accepted industry standard criteria for these classes. In fact, the exact distinction between these classes is somewhat ambiguous, and depends on both the source and the specific market in question.

The "grading" tends to be done on a curve that factors in local competition. This means a given property might be considered Class B in one market and Class C in another. In an attempt to distinguish that properties fall on the fringe of a class in their market, many people in the industry will also use plusses and minuses. Thus, an apartment complex may be described as a C+ or B– property.

Class A properties are the highest quality in their respective market. They generally tend to be newer and well situated, with higher-end finishes. The expectation is that these properties will offer a level of professionalism and amenities that set them apart from the competition. Class A properties usually attract the best tenants and command higher rents in their market. For retail and office buildings, you will often find national tenants with long-term, corporate-guaranteed leases that include very little or no landlord responsibility.

Class B properties are usually of good quality, though they tend to be a little older and show a little more wear than those in Class A. These properties are "middle of the road" for their respective markets. Class B properties are typically well maintained, but show signs of obsolescence and lack some of the amenities found in the community's finer properties. Commercial tenants are often regional or local.

Class C properties are generally older, outdated buildings that provide a more economical and functional option for their tenants. They sometimes have less stable tenants and lower occupancy rates. These properties are often of particular appeal to small and medium investors who are willing to put in some sweat equity or the time and effort necessary to improve them, particularly if they are well located. This kind of value-add approach can reap rewards in terms of incremental equity.

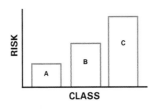

While most commercial real estate references will not mention a Class D, you may hear some investors use Class D to describe properties that are the worst of the worst. These are the properties that you are generally reluctant to enter because you fear for your life, either from lurking criminals, swarms of vermin, or just an overall lack of structural integrity. Though it was structurally sound, the Solar Building could have been considered a Class D asset when we acquired it due to the crime and pest problems.

Selecting which class to target in your search may not be an easy process. Since Class A properties are the best in almost every respect, they tend to command premium prices and thus sell at low cap rates. They are generally well-oiled machines that are ideal for the long-distance investor. They are also the lowest risk properties on the spectrum, which makes them appealing to larger, more conservative investors. Due to this low risk and ease of management, the investors are willing to accept significantly lower returns on their investment.

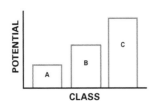

On the other end of the spectrum, Class C properties often leave a lot to be desired. But don't be quick to dismiss them. Sometimes small changes can improve these properties and mitigate the risk. Relatively low-cost improvements such as updated finishes, fresh paint, or sprucing up the landscaping can often make a dramatic difference in how a Class

C property shows, which can in turn boost occupancy and rent. Many Class C properties are also underutilized. When I purchased my first office building, I was able to immediately boost the cash flow just by leasing out excess parking and storage space.

Another thing I like about Class C properties is that the pool of prospective buyers is smaller because many investors are either unwilling or unable to do the work necessary to turn these properties around.

Class B properties are halfway in between and can represent a compromise for investors looking for that happy medium. Some Class B properties that are well located can be improved to Class A, but that can be a challenge. For example, Class B properties may have physical constraints that prevent the addition of certain amenities. In general, raising a Class B property to Class A tends to be a more expensive undertaking than raising a Class C to a Class B.

DON'T STEAL THE GIANT'S LUNCH

In his book *Competitive Strategy*, renowned author and business strategist Michael Porter has the following to say about "picking the battleground":

> Assuming that competitors will retaliate to moves a firm initiates, its strategic agenda is selecting the best battleground for fighting it out with its competitors. This battleground is the market segment or dimensions of strategy in which competitors are ill-prepared, least enthusiastic, or most uncomfortable about competing.[6]

As suggested in the review of classes, most small-to-medium-sized real estate investors are better off focusing on those areas

6 *Competitive Strategy* by Michael Porter, The Free Press, 1980, page 70.

about which larger investors are least enthusiastic and most uncomfortable competing. That might not sound very appealing on its surface, but it is strategic, and it can work.

The good news is, you won't miss out on as much as you might think when you avoid direct competition with larger investors. In fact, you're typically better off. There are plenty of attractive opportunities for smaller investors outside of where institutional investors focus. In fact, the properties that are the best fit for small investors are generally not those of most interest to the large investor.

> *"Do not let what you cannot do interfere with what you can do."*
> —JOHN WOODEN

It would seem logical that most investors are looking to secure properties with superior returns. But despite their size, large investors aren't always in the best position to maximize returns, and it's not even usually their top priority. They typically look for low-risk investments that yield consistent returns, even if those returns are quite low.

The properties of most interest to institutional investors tend to command a price premium relative to their inherent risk and thus tend to yield very pedestrian returns—often equal to or sometimes even less than the cost of capital (i.e., the mortgage's interest rate).

There is no getting around the fact that large investors have access to far more financial resources than most of us. In fact, this is arguably their greatest strength. Access to a large war chest certainly comes in handy if you want to buy a shopping mall or a 2,000-unit Class A apartment complex. But what most people don't realize is that such war chests are often secured with strings attached.

For one thing, it's important to understand that many large investors raise their funds from a private pool of wealthy individuals and/or corporate entities that are trying to diversify their investment portfolios, or otherwise put their money to work in a safe manner. This money is not extended just to be nice. It's delivered with the clear expectation of a steady return.

VIEW FROM THE TOP

Put yourself back in the wingtip shoes of a large investor for a few minutes. Do you feel the uncomfortable itch of that tie cinched around your neck? Imagine that your investment firm has successfully raised money from a pool of powerful, high net worth individuals. In order to secure their buy-in, you've projected dependable 7% annual returns on their money.

Yes, you've given them all the disclaimers and the requisite language saying that such returns cannot be guaranteed, blah, blah, blah. But the bottom line is you're working in a conservative environment, and you know the projected returns are not just hoped for, they are *expected*. In fact, it might be more accurate to say they are *demanded*.

If you can't deliver for some reason, you're going to get your head handed to you. If nothing else, failure to achieve target returns will make it exceptionally difficult to raise money in the future.

So with that as the backdrop, how are you going to deploy the funds? In most cases the answer will be *ultra-conservatively*. You're likely going to seek out commercial properties that are in major metropolitan areas, occupied by the most stable national tenants with long-term, corporate-guaranteed leases.

As a large, conservative investor, you'll also want to find properties with triple net (NNN) leases, which are leases that make all expenses and maintenance the tenant's responsibility. And you'll want to find a lot of them to diversify your risk. If they are multi-family, you'll look for the very largest properties because small or medium-sized properties won't be able to offset the extra administrative and legal costs that burden these kinds of complex deals.

Whether you invest in commercial properties or apartments, you'll look for buildings that are new (or nearly new) construction because after you pay out returns to your investors, there won't be much money left to reinvest back in. Strictly Class A. When all is said and done, you've limited your risk to the greatest extent possible. But at the price of low returns, with very limited upside potential.

You may get an 8% return on your investment, for example, only to forward 7% on to the investors who fronted the capital. This is how a lot of deals get structured. Your rocket fuel has been drained!

Can real estate investors make money this way? Yes, plenty, if you know what you're doing. The firm or individual that pulls it all together might boost their returns by carving out equity for themselves or inserting a variety of fee structures. But it changes the business model entirely and introduces a level of complexity and costs that should give small investors pause.

There are a lot of opportunities to achieve more attractive returns by doing it yourself on a smaller scale with value-add investment that let you keep that rocket fuel in the tank.

WHERE OPPORTUNITIES EXIST

Let's slide back into your own more comfortable shoes. What does all this mean for the small investor? In most cases, it's probably best to stay clear of the institutional "sweet spots," which are primarily larger, Class A assets. As a small investor, you're not going to be in a position to effectively compete for those properties. The good news is, you don't have to, nor should you.

As a small investor, you've got more freedom and you're in a better position to find properties with more upside potential. They might be properties that have strong cash flows in place but don't fit a large investor's rigid criteria. This should be your battleground.

"Know the enemy and know yourself; in a hundred battles you will never be in peril."
—SUN TZU

Keep in mind that there are numerous reasons that a property might be passed over by more conservative investors. For example, a property might carry a risk that's too difficult to accurately document or assess from afar, or it might be full of local tenants, or maybe have shorter-term leases, or even no leases at all! These qualities can make institutional investors very uncomfortable. But that doesn't mean a property isn't a good investment or that it doesn't have strong cash flow.

Large investors will also pass up opportunities that aren't big enough to grab their attention. Small apartment buildings and mobile home parks are a good example of this.

Apartments and Mobile Home Parks

Institutional investors tend to be most enthusiastic about the largest apartment complexes and mobile home parks, primarily due to the economies of scale they can provide, both in terms of absorbing the initial transaction costs, as well as achieving greater efficiencies in their ongoing administrative and operational expenses. They tend to shy away from properties with less than 100 units, while properties of 50 units or less are almost never considered.

As a result, apartment complexes and mobile home parks with 15 to 75 units are often priced attractively relative to larger investment properties because they fall in a kind of no-man's-land. They can't support the overhead of a large deal and can't be managed as efficiently as the 100-plus-unit property. Yet they're also perceived to be out of reach by most small investors.

This is particularly true in secondary and tertiary markets (outside of the major metropolitan areas). Large buyers often eliminate remote properties from consideration altogether. They also lack enthusiasm for the smaller cities, making these locations an attractive battleground for the little guys.

While less populated areas aren't as desirable to large investors, as discussed in Chapter 3, they can still offer plenty of attractive investment opportunities. One recommended type of commercial real estate commonly found in such locations is self-storage.

Self-Storage

Real Estate Investment Trusts (REITs) and the larger self-storage companies focus their attention almost exclusively on the larger metropolitan areas and major arteries. Since drive-by traffic correlates closely with storage demand, they typically look for traffic counts of 15,000 or more per day, even though lesser traveled arteries in secondary markets can still yield a very healthy demand for self-storage.

Outside of the highest demand areas, much of the self-storage market is comprised of small investors, many of whom have erected self-storage as a side business, usually on land they already own and with little to no analysis of the desirability of the location or the market demand.

An investor who does their homework and researches these secondary markets can find lucrative opportunities in self-storage. It's not difficult to estimate market demand based on the population. Most industry data suggests between six and eight square feet per capita, though significantly higher demand can exist among transient populations such as students or military. It's also relatively easy to determine a market's supply and current rental rates by visiting the existing facilities. Meanwhile, traffic counts are usually publicly available through department of transportation websites, which can help identify the most ideal locations.

While the self-storage market is believed by many to be stagnant and saturated, a careful examination of your area may reveal that this is not the case. A methodical and analytical approach can yield sizable returns by focusing on the smaller towns and villages, and avoiding the areas dominated by the bigger players.

Say, for example, that you are contemplating a self-storage investment in a village with a population of 5,000. The total demand for storage space might be estimated as follows:

5,000 people × 7SF per capita = 35,000SF

You then visit the two local self-storage facilities to count the doors and find that there are a total 150 units. To convert this into square footage, you can either take a quick measurement or use an industry average for unit size, which would be approximately 120 to 140 square feet per unit. So the existing supply would be estimated as follows:

$$150 \text{ units} \times 130SF/\text{unit} = 19,500SF$$

The local market self-storage deficit would then be estimated by calculating the difference between supply and demand:

$$35,000SF - 19,500SF = 15,500SF$$
$$15,500SF / 130SF/\text{unit} = 119 \text{ storage units}$$

In this scenario, the deficit is significant and would indicate a shortage of storage space in the community. If the existing facilities are well situated but not full, they are likely poorly managed; meaning new ownership could come with significant upside potential. And there is almost certainly enough demand to support expansion.

The best option for a new investor in an area with unmet demand would be to acquire an existing facility with good location, and then work to fill it and potentially expand. Self-storage construction is much more straightforward (and thus lower risk) than other types of new development, but even so you're better off gaining some experience and establishing positive cash flow before undertaking such a project.

THE PATH FORWARD

Attractive properties with good returns are out there. If you can find and acquire the right one, you'll have more cash flow to work with, which puts you on the path to greater things. Compared to many of the investors that syndicate a deal by raising money from financial institutions or private money, you have a lower risk because you don't have to pay out income to investors.

All that said, remember that even more important than staying out of the crosshairs of the large investor is to make sure you're familiar with the communities and markets in which your properties are located.

Armed with this knowledge and an understanding of the basic financial principles, you're ready for the next step. It's time to take some action. This means finding and evaluating prospective properties.

KEY POINTS

- ▶ The most suitable types of investment property for small investors tend to be existing multifamily (apartments or mobile home parks), multitenant retail, multitenant office, and self-storage properties with strong cash flow.
- ▶ Small investors are better off choosing a market segment that avoids direct competition with larger investors.
- ▶ Larger, more conservative investors tend to gravitate to Class A properties, creating a high demand and lowering returns.
- ▶ Class C properties and secondary markets can sometimes offer overlooked and attractive opportunities for small investors.

CHAPTER 5

FIND THE RIGHT PROPERTY

"The way to find a needle in a haystack is to sit down."
—BERYL MARKHAM

*"There comes a time in every rightly constructed boy's life
when he has a raging desire to go somewhere and dig for
hidden treasure."*
—MARK TWAIN

■

AFTER YOU'VE DETERMINED THE location, type, and class of investment you're interested in, it's time to start looking for the right property. The goal at this stage is to find as many prospective properties as possible that meet your criteria. But filling up your pipeline is not always as simple and straightforward as it might seem—particularly if you're new to commercial real estate.

In an ideal world, you would know the exact profile of your dream investment, and then you would promptly identify a property that's the perfect match—one that also happens to be for sale at a great price. Wouldn't that be nice? The reality is it's rarely that easy.

To start with, it's hard to even know what your exact criteria is when you have limited experience. Your ability to effectively narrow search criteria will evolve as you look at more properties, make acquisitions, and manage them. Absent such experience, just jump in and do the best you can. Also recognize up front that you're unlikely to find the 100% "perfect" property. A more realistic goal is to find an investment opportunity that meets your criteria as closely as possible, while also recognizing that it's probably going to take a lot of work.

Finding the right investment opportunity generally involves casting a wide net and being persistent as hell. You have to be prepared to look at a lot of properties, make a lot of offers, and get a lot of nos before you find the right one. But it's out there. Unless you're incredibly lucky, there is no substitute for patience, tenacity, and a willingness to kiss a lot of toads.

From a practical standpoint, you can begin the search process by looking online, which will allow you to get the lay of the land without wasting anybody's time. The more properties you look at, the better you'll be able to refine your search criteria. So depending on your experience level, you'll want to sift through as many prospective investments as you can manage.

The good news is that while property listings are a great place to start, this is just the tip of the iceberg—there are a lot more ways to find prospective investment properties than most people realize.

BROKERS

Broker listings are a great way to begin, and you can typically find many of these on websites like LoopNet.com, or even on your local multiple listing service (MLS) website. Some listings on LoopNet.com even include full financials, which can be a good resource for novice investors who want to start running some real numbers to educate themselves without imposing on a broker prematurely.

A good broker can be one of an investor's most important allies. Brokers are an excellent resource for information, for prospective acquisition candidates, and for securing tenants. In my experience, brokers are very important and provide a valuable service, both for new and seasoned investors. For the most part, they work hard to earn their commissions. I recommend cultivating relationships with brokers and always treating them fairly.

You can start off on the right foot by being respectful of a broker's time. One way to do this is to at least drive by a property on your own before you press for too much information or schedule a showing. In my experience, driving by a property (or walking its vicinity) is a quick and easy way to get a feel for it. A drive-by will allow you to immediately rule out more than half the properties you're interested in. If a property passes muster, you can reach out for further information and then eventually schedule a showing. Viewing a property can also be an imposition on the tenants. So be considerate and don't schedule a bunch of showings before you do your homework.

Establishing good broker relationships is also important because a broker will often present new property listings to select investors before advertising them publicly. In some cases, sellers don't want anyone to know their property is for sale. But more frequently, the broker wants to find their own buyer directly so that they can earn the full commission. If a property is advertised and another broker brings a buyer, then the commission would need to be shared. But if the broker finds their own buyer and represents both the buyer and the seller, they keep the whole thing. So there is a pretty strong incentive to sit on the listing for a while.

As valuable as a good broker can be, relying on broker listings is only scratching the surface. The more experience you gain, the more you'll learn to efficiently identify and evaluate prospective investments on your own. This reduces your dependence on brokers, though brokers remain important.

EXPANDING YOUR LEAD SOURCES

Like most investors, I started off working primarily with brokers to find properties and have progressively done more and more research on my own. This is because I have learned that only considering properties that are listed for sale through brokers is too limiting. While you should certainly monitor all the listings and you can occasionally find good properties that way, I have found that the best properties usually aren't publicly advertised as being for sale.

Finding the right property is a lot like finding the best person to marry. If you're single, would you only go out with people who have posted profiles on a dating website? The best prospective partners, just like the best prospective properties, aren't necessarily advertising their availability with a sign or website. Sure, you might find a fantastic partner online, but aren't you better off considering all your options?

The goal is to explore as many potential opportunities as possible, thereby putting yourself in a position to make the best decision. Never limit your options in real estate, or in life for that matter.

What many people don't realize is that the most common way opportunities are lost is through inaction. You should always be taking steps to open more doors—putting yourself in a position to then make the best decision you can. Inaction will mean the option never presents itself, and the decision is never yours to make. If you want to succeed, you have to work to keep as many doors open as possible so you can decide which ones you want to walk through.

In my experience, everything is for sale, and everyone is a seller. It's just a matter of how motivated the seller is. The first priority should be to identify the best properties. If it's not listed for sale, you can check the tax records to determine who the owner is. Then, reach out to them and try to establish a relationship. If the owner isn't motivated to sell at that time, you want to be the first person they call when they change their mind.

DIRECTLY APPROACHING PROPERTY OWNERS

The prospect of approaching an owner about selling can be intimidating for some people. But what's the worst thing that can happen? They can be rude and say no? Most owners are receptive to inquiries if you present yourself in the right way. It's all in the details.

How do you think an owner will react if you approach them and say: "I noticed this place is getting run-down and you're not taking very good care of it. Since you haven't been able to lease it, I was wondering if you'd want to sell it to me?" Pretty good way to get hung up on or a door slammed in your face.

On the other hand, picture this: "Hi, my name is Sally and I'm a real estate investor. I just wanted to let you know that I really like your property. I think it's in a great location and (fill in the blank here with any suitable compliment). I just wanted you to know that if you decide to explore the idea of selling, I'd be interested. Have you considered selling at all? Would it be OK if I leave my contact information with you in case you ever change your mind?"

You're much more likely to get somewhere with a prospective seller if you're complimentary and direct, but not pushy. When you're contacting somebody "cold" to express an interest in purchasing his or her property, it is not an appropriate time to say anything negative about it. If you need a nice way to communicate that it's run-down or not being cared for, then just tell them you think that the property has a lot of potential.

Remember, you're approaching them. They're not coming to you. It's somewhat different when a seller is highly motivated. Though in the end, they're likely already aware of their property's strong and weak points, and probably know more than you do. Going out of your way to point out problems isn't necessarily going to get you a better price.

You need to establish a rapport with the owner or their representative—particularly if it is a local owner. You can certainly be a little more direct if the seller is a larger, out-of-town entity. Such owners tend to be less emotionally invested in their assets.

Likewise, you can be more direct when working through a broker. Good brokers tend to have strong people skills and are adept at phrasing things the right way when relaying your messages. Tact is a prerequisite for success in their profession.

Whether you're handling an inquiry yourself or through a broker, it's also important to make sure that you are communicating with the actual ownership entity. Most investment properties are being taken care of by a property management company—and it's often not in their best interest that the property sell. They've already won the business of the current owner and might not want their management contract to be put at risk by a sale. Unless you have an established relationship with a property manager, you cannot rely on them to relay your interest to the actual owner.

WORD OF MOUTH

Word of mouth is perhaps the most effective way to locate a prospective property aside from getting leads through brokers or directly approaching owners. An investor can quickly build relationships with a large team of partners who might know of owners interested in selling.

Leads can come from real estate attorneys, accountants, lenders, contractors, fellow investors, architects and engineers, tenants, government officials, and many, many others. For a full list of partners that might be of assistance, refer to Appendix B. The more people who know you're looking, the more leads you'll get.

AUCTIONS

Auctions are another potential source for investment properties, though buying at auction can be risky and make financing tricky. Most auctions require proof of sufficient funds, a significant down payment at the time of the auction, and they have a short window for closing. The most common requirement is for a closing within 30 days, which is generally not long enough to go through the traditional bank lending process.

But if the price is low enough and you're able to secure the resources, auctions can be a source of great bargains. Personally, I did not venture into auctions until I had established a moderately sized portfolio and gained significant experience.

The key to buying properties at auction is to exercise an extraordinary level of caution. Frequently, properties that are up for auction have limited information available and restricted access, and in some cases, no access at all. Compound that with the fact that most auction properties are in some level of distress to begin with, and the associated risk can be extremely high.

If you're going to purchase a property at auction, you need to do as much research as possible and assume the worst with regard to any unknowns. Be overly conservative in every respect. If you can't access the property, recognize that you might find mold, major structural problems, or even environmental contamination.

To date, I've had mixed results with auctions. For my first auction property, I remained cautious and took a very limited risk. It was a local, five-unit apartment building that I purchased through the Internet auction site Hubzu. The only reason I knew about the online auction was that I saw a sign in the front yard while driving by. I promptly pulled over and took a photo of the sign so I could go home and research it further.

A valuable resource for researching an investment property is to look at the real property tax information, which in many areas is freely available on the public website of the local tax jurisdiction. The real property tax information can provide you with a wide range of data, including the zoning, acreage, square footage, sales history, etc. You can often view the tax map and even look up information on surrounding parcels.

In the case of this particular auction property, I was intimately familiar with the neighborhood, and as I studied the property's tax map, I confirmed my suspicion that three sides of the parcel bordered a large, planned future development project. Even though the property was in terrible condition and had a tarp covering a section of missing roof, it was strategically located and would soon be worth more due to the development.

Studying the auction listing, I found out that the property was listed as a real estate owned (REO) property, which means a bank owned it. In this instance, the auction site was selling it on behalf of the bank, and the bank had the final say over whether to sell the property at the highest bid. I decided to give it a try. As it turns out,

I was the only person who ended up bidding on the property and, while my $20K winning bid was rejected, I did get a counteroffer from the bank, and negotiated a purchase price of $24K.

While such a purchase was well outside of my normal investment strategy, I decided it was too good of an opportunity to pass up. Even though the property was in terrible condition, it was strategically located, and the purchase price was about $100K below the assessed value.

The cost of renovating the property was too high to meet my investment criteria. So, after closing, I listed the property for sale with a local Realtor at $99K. Six months later, I ended up selling it for $60K to the developer of the neighboring property, who proceeded to demolish the apartment building to create more parking for their project.

I don't generally flip properties and much prefer to buy and hold, but I deemed this to be a very calculated and low-risk opportunity due to the location. And my backup plan was to renovate the property and lease it out. The return would have been low, but I wouldn't have lost money. In the end, it was my strong knowledge of the local market dynamics and the planned project that made the difference.

My success at the first auction prompted me to look for bigger opportunities, and I later ended up purchasing two larger multi-family properties at foreclosure auction with mixed results. One of the properties was the Solar Building, which I introduced in Chapter 1 and whose story continues in subsequent chapters. The second multifamily property was a nightmare that took more than two years to renovate and cost us far more than we will ever get back. It was affectionately known around the office as "the money pit." Every time we opened something up, we found more and more serious issues. We ended up needing to replace all the mechanicals, and uncovered a variety of environmental problems that had to be remediated.

The property consisted of two apartment buildings housing 28 units, and in the end we decided that the problems were so extensive that we had the smaller of the two buildings demolished.

It was rewarding to renovate the larger apartment building, and I'm proud of what it is today, but it was a terrible investment and poor judgment on my part. I'm fortunate that this happened after I had already built up a sizable portfolio. If it had been one of my first investments, it may very well have been my last.

In retrospect, I realize I had made two major mistakes. First, my earlier successes made me overconfident and careless. Coming right on the heels of a successful turnaround, I didn't do as much due diligence or account for enough of the unknowns. The biggest gap in my research was related to the mechanical and structural elements of the building. There were far more extensive problems than I anticipated. My optimism surrounding the project was reflected in the assumptions I made, and my cost estimates for renovation were way, way too low.

A contributing factor was the inherent risk associated with most foreclosure auctions that I mentioned earlier—we had very limited physical access to the property ahead of time. I had actually managed to do a quick walk-through, but was unable to conduct a proper inspection. In a case like this, if you're going to take a chance, my experience reinforces the need to be prepared for the worst-case scenario in regard to what you might find inside the building or behind the walls.

> *"If you're not making mistakes, then you're not doing anything. I'm positive that a doer makes mistakes."*
> —JOHN WOODEN

The second mistake I made was not selling the property and limiting my losses as soon as the scope of the problems became evident. In my defense, the news trickled in over time. So I was like that proverbial frog sitting in the pot of water as it slowly heated up. I didn't notice how boiling hot the water was until I was cooked. Most importantly, this was a situation I never should have found myself in to begin with. If I hadn't been overly optimistic with my assumptions before the auction, the whole disaster could have been avoided.

BUILDING A PIPELINE

Finding investment properties, regardless of the source, is very similar to a sales pipeline in business. The idea is that you have a large hopper, and you drop a whole lot of leads in there. As leads work their way through your evaluation processes, most will be filtered out.

> "It's not given to human beings to have such talent that they can just know everything about everything all the time. But it is given to human beings who work hard at it—who look and sift the world for a mispriced bet—that they can occasionally find one."
> —CHARLIE MUNGER

As an example, maybe 1 out of every 10 prospective properties you find will be worth analyzing. And maybe 1 out of 10 properties you analyze will be worth putting an offer in on. And maybe 1 out of 10 properties you put an offer in on will result in a purchase agreement. And maybe half of the properties with a purchase agreement will result in a closing.

Working in reverse, you can quickly calculate that you'll have to look at *2,000* prospective properties before you can expect to purchase the right one. Obviously, that takes a lot of effort.

2,000 Prospective Properties
200 Worth Analyzing
20 Offers
2 Purchase Agreements
1 Closing

If you have the discipline and perseverance to look at 2,000 properties before you purchase the right one, that's a good indication you've got what it takes to successfully grow a commercial real estate portfolio.

> *"Effort only fully releases its reward after a person refuses to quit."*
> —NAPOLEON HILL

If you're still motivated, it's time to roll up your sleeves, get beating the bushes for prospective properties, and learn how to analyze them.

THE SOLAR BUILDING PROJECT: PART III

 Two months after we saw the Solar Building foreclosure auction advertised in the local newspaper, and 30 days after submitting the winning bid, I attended the closing. Walking out of the attorney's office and heading back to my office, I was nervous but excited. Yes, the investor side of me had done my homework and saw a chance to add more value than ever before. But the sliver of fear lingered.

Once I got back to our office, I reviewed our new safety rules with the staff. Under no circumstances was anyone to enter the building alone. I passed around pepper spray to my employees. I had purchased pink ones for the ladies and black ones for the men. Yes, I had color-coordinated the pepper spray canisters. Nobody could accuse me of being thoughtless. Mentally, I added this ceremony to the long list of things I never imagined I'd be doing as a real estate investor.

Not wanting to deal with this scary property, my staff had unanimously voted in favor of keeping the existing management firm in

> *"If it scares you, it might be a good thing to try."*
> —SETH GODIN

place. But unfortunately for them, I held veto power and, though I seldom used it, I did so in this case. The Solar Building needed dramatic change and in order to accomplish that we needed to be hands-on. We would manage it in-house.

Then I nearly caused a revolt among the team by announcing that, not only were we going to manage the property ourselves, but we were also going to relocate our company office into one of the vacant commercial spaces on the ground floor! It was to be a test of wills, and while I had no way of knowing it at the time, the first 24 hours of ownership was going to shake my foundations and make me question my decision. There was no way I could have imagined what was coming our way. To be continued...

KEY POINTS

- ▶ Once an investor has picked a specific geographic target market and determined what kind of property they are interested in, the goal shifts to identifying specific properties for potential acquisition. In order to do this you need to cast a wide net.
- ▶ It is important to establish good relationships with area brokers. They provide a valuable service and can be a great source of information, properties, and tenants.
- ▶ Investors should also generate leads through word of mouth, auctions, and even creating their own off-market opportunities by directly approaching property owners.
- ▶ An investor needs to be highly motivated and persistent. In most instances, a large quantity of properties will need to be evaluated before the right one is eventually acquired.

CHAPTER 6

ANALYZING PROPERTIES

"Facts do not cease to exist because they are ignored."
—ALDOUS HUXLEY

"The ultimate authority must always rest with the individual's
own reason and critical analysis."
—DALAI LAMA

■

ONCE YOU'VE IDENTIFIED A prospective property, it's time to dig in and do some analysis, both quantitative and qualitative. It's extremely important to evaluate the properties you're considering, and the most efficient way to do this is in phases.

You can start with a quick, broad-brush review as an initial screen and then progress into more thorough analysis when you're considering making an offer. You'll do an even more detailed analysis once the property is under contract and you enter what is called the due diligence phase.

INITIAL SCREENING

In most markets, it's not feasible to analyze every single property, so you need to narrow things down a bit. The first broad-brush screening is generally qualitative, including confirmation that the property fits the criteria you have established with regard to its location, type, class, etc. This can also include a visual investigation, perhaps starting with a review of the property and tour of the immediately surrounding area.

If you are not nearby or not familiar with the specific area and property, you can do your first look with satellite images and Google Street View, followed by a drive-by. You very well may not know what you're looking for until you find it. And while the property might look fine to you, what's located next door (or even a few doors down) may not be.

While this initial screening might be brief, it would cover a range of factors that can affect your decision to continue pursuing a property. Is it well located? Does it have enough parking? What maintenance issues are readily evident? How difficult will it be to maintain? Make sure to analyze a property both in terms of your own goals, and through the eyes of a tenant.

For example, when considering apartments, I always like to see a lot of units under one roof, preferably with a shared entry door and lobby. Why? From experience I've found that this configuration can create economies when turning a property around. I can make a difference to all the tenants by installing one beautiful new door, one state-of-the-art key fob system, refurbishing one lobby, etc. This was the case in the Solar Building, where 70 tenants shared a single point of entry. Contrast that to another one of my properties that also has 70 units, but in this case they are spread out in nine buildings. Each building has its own entry door, lobby, front walkway, green space, etc., and any upgrades we make to the common areas cost literally nine times as much.

So for me, noticing a lot of units under one roof would weigh in a property's favor in my initial screening. This is a personal preference. All things equal, I'd be more likely to move forward and devote more effort to evaluating it. That said, other characteristics could make me take a pass and move on. For example, if the building were in the wrong part of town, it would most likely rule a property out regardless.

Additional criteria for screening properties are covered in later chapters. But over time, you'll learn to identify your own preferences and know specifically what to look for. This is an exercise in refining your own criteria, what you're comfortable with, and determining whether a property fits your needs and "feels" right for you.

Initially filtering properties in this way is not only necessary from a practical standpoint, but it will help ensure you're not wasting your time, or the time of a broker or seller, by poring over a property that never stood a chance. You've effectively increased the seriousness of any inquiries you make.

> *"Not everything that can be counted counts, and not everything that counts can be counted."*
> —WILLIAM BRUCE CAMERON

What's next depends on where your lead came from. If the property isn't for sale, you'll attempt to put it in play by reaching out to the owner. If the prospective property is for sale, you'll contact the broker or other intermediary who brought it to you in order to secure enough additional information. This is the point at which you will conduct your initial financial analysis.

RUNNING THE NUMBERS

Once a property passes your initial screening it's important to run the numbers to determine if it would be a solid financial investment. Numbers aren't the only thing that matters, but they're extremely important. Best to know ahead of time if a property is a sinking ship so you can avoid getting on board.

Over time you'll get better at running financials and better at predicting how they will look before you even crack open a spreadsheet. That said, properties can be deceiving even to the trained eye. After financially modeling thousands of properties, I am still sometimes surprised by the results. There are properties out there that look, smell, and feel like they will be solid investments, but then the numbers tell you otherwise. And the reverse is also true.

The specific number you'll be most interested in calculating is the net operating income (NOI), which was introduced in Chapter

1. Once you have the NOI, you can apply a cap rate that is appropriate for the type of property and location. Cap rates are a moving target, but if you talk with investors and brokers in your area, you should be able to develop a pretty good knowledge of what cap rates similar properties are commanding.

Your knowledge of cap rates will also improve as you analyze more properties in your target market. Remember that your cap rate determines your price. Your risk goes up when you overpay for a property. This means you need to get a handle on local cap rates, which is another example of where relationships with good commercial real estate brokers can be a valuable asset.

PROFORMAS

You may recall from Chapter 1 that you calculate NOI by adding up income and subtracting expenses. Properties listed through a broker will often have these calculations prepared for you, including the cap rate used to arrive at the asking price. But more often than not, a property prospectus is based on "proforma" calculations.

Proformas are basically future projections of a property's financials, *not* actual financials. When proformas are provided by a seller (or their broker) they are generally fictitious attempts to portray an overly rosy future. *As a buyer, you should commit to only valuing prospective investment properties based on their actual current financial situation.*

Seller proformas often show occupancy levels that are higher than a property has been able to sustain in the past, or expenses that are lower than have actually been experienced. A seller shouldn't expect you to pay for improvements that haven't been made.

For example, if a seller says that occupancy can be raised (and shows that higher occupancy in their proforma), you shouldn't have to pay for it in advance. If it were that easy to boost occupancy, the seller should go ahead make it happen. Then the property can legitimately merit the price reflecting that scenario.

Recognize a proforma for what it really is—the seller's attempt to demonstrate as much future *potential* value as possible. To do an accurate valuation of a prospective investment property, I recommend using a current rent roll to project your income, and actual historical expenses to project your expenses, but *not* seller proformas.

INCOME

The first thing to request in order to accurately gauge a property's income is a rent roll. A rent roll is a list of tenants and how much rent they are paying. Asking for a rent roll is a reasonable request— one that should be expected and accommodated by most sellers. Some sellers may require that you sign a confidentiality agreement beforehand, but most will be prepared to readily hand it over.

The information recorded on a rent roll can vary, but in addition to rent, it will frequently include lease information such as start and end dates, whether there are renewal options, and whether the tenant is responsible for additional charges such as utilities.

Actual historical income information is valuable for providing support and context, but a rent roll is the best measure of current income and thus the most accurate way to determine a property's current value. If the rent roll reflects monthly rent, convert it to an annual basis for your NOI calculation, including any other income derived from a property besides just a tenant's base rent.

In Chapter 1, we reviewed an example of a 30-unit apartment building that walks through the calculation of NOI at a high level. In calculating NOI, it is important to include all ongoing income streams and operating expenses. At this stage, an investor is primarily concerned with current income levels. Later on, it will be important to also look at historical income dating back as much as two to three years to provide some context. It's important to know if income is on an upward or downward trend, so you can figure out why.

Examples of income that might be present when analyzing an apartment building include:

- Rent
- Late fees
- Pet fees, including non-refundable deposits and extra rental charges
- Forfeited security deposits
- Laundry or vending income
- Revenue sharing with cable or Internet providers
- Parking
- Application fees
- Bad check fees
- Utility reimbursement
- Storage unit fees
- Co-op maintenance fees

Income information is typically provided for at least one year since some of these income sources such as late fees and forfeited security deposits can fluctuate wildly from month to month. Averaged out over a yearlong period you should be able to get a fair handle on things though because such income tends to be more consistent year over year.

For a commercial property, depending on how the lease is structured, you might also have tenant reimbursements for things like property taxes, insurance, and common area maintenance (CAM). CAM generally includes maintenance associated with the inside and outside common areas such as snow removal, landscaping, parking lot maintenance, and utility bills for lighting or heating and cooling of common areas.

These types of shared expenses are sometimes passed on to tenants on a pro rata basis, which involves allocating them to a tenant in proportion to the fraction of square footage that they occupy in the property. The tenant reimbursements are then counted as income, so that when we calculate NOI they will offset the corresponding expenses.

EXPENSES

Unlike income, expenses can be difficult to measure by simply looking at the snapshot of a single point in time. Expenses are also too easy for a seller to manipulate over the short term, so you'll want to look over longer periods.

The best way to gauge current annual expenses is to get copies of the property's *actual* expenses for the trailing 12 months. You should also get copies of annual expenses for the prior two years, if available, in order to provide some context and determine whether the property has changed significantly over the recent past.

In cases where the trailing 12 months is not available, you can instead try to secure the actual year-to-date expenses, especially if you're in the later half of a calendar year. If you elect to prorate year-to-date expenses so as to convert them to annual numbers, just remember to account for seasonal expenses that may not yet have been incurred at that point in time, or were already fully incurred prior in the year.

For example, let's say you're at the midpoint of a year and you decide to use year-to-date actual expenses as the basis for your estimate. In order to prorate the expenses into annual numbers, you would have to double them. But if the property tax was already paid in full in the first half of the year, it wouldn't make sense to double that number. Likewise if it's paid in the second half of the year, you wouldn't estimate it at zero. Depending on climate, seasonal expenses such as snow removal, winter heating bills, and summer cooling are other examples of expenses that are not typically incurred equally each month throughout the year. It's preferable to analyze the trailing 12 months' expenses when possible, so you can avoid any potential blind spots like these.

An important thing to remember in running any numbers is to always think critically and apply a healthy dose of common sense. Too many people start plugging numbers into a spreadsheet without using sound judgment and thinking about what they actually represent.

Once you total your current annual income and expenses, you'll be ready to calculate your NOI. Remember to exclude any debt payments from your expenses when valuing your property. Debt should be analyzed separately.

Expenses might include such things as:

- ► Property management fees
- ► Common utilities
- ► Landscaping
- ► Snow removal
- ► Insurance
- ► Property taxes
- ► Repairs and maintenance
- ► Legal fees
- ► Advertising

BUYER'S PROFORMA

In addition to analyzing current income and expenses, you should create your own proforma. Your buyer's proforma is basically your vision of what the income and expenses will look like in the future.

Here you are giving consideration to how you might make improvements, whether they be physical or operational. What are the changes you plan to make and how will that affect the income and expenses? What will the NOI be and how much will the property be worth later? How much value do you expect to create? Specific strategies for adding value are covered in detail in a later chapter, but you'll start to formulate these ideas as early as possible.

Take particular note of property taxes at this stage. It is highly advisable to look up the real property data for the parcel(s) to see what the assessed full market value is. If the proposed purchase price is higher or lower, you should prorate the current property taxes to reflect an eventual reassessment to the purchase price.

Say, for example, you are looking at a property appraised at

$250K with current annual property taxes of $10K per year. If you intend to purchase this property for $275K, which is 10% higher than the assessed value, then you can expect that your property taxes will eventually follow suit and also rise 10%. So your buyer's proforma should reflect property taxes of $11K per year, not $10K. In cases where a property's current assessment is highly inaccurate, adjusting the property taxes in this manner can sometimes have a dramatic effect on valuation—an affect that is magnified in areas with high property tax rates.

Some of your estimates may be less easy to calculate, and a fair amount of judgment may come into play. When creating a proforma, strive to keep the future income and expenses as objective as possible. There are a variety of reasons, emotional and otherwise, that an investor might be predisposed in favor of or against a property. Like most analyses, the creation of a real estate proforma involves numerous assumptions, so there is ample opportunity for bias to creep in if you allow it. As a professor of mine used to say, "If you torture the data enough, it will tell you anything you want to hear."

There is every opportunity to reject or accept a property for qualitative reasons. But don't twist the numbers to rationalize your predispositions. If you're going to accept or reject a property for other reasons, that is perfectly fine, but try to keep the numbers clean and do so with as accurate a financial picture as possible.

NET OPERATING INCOME

Once you have nailed down both the current and future income and expenses, you are in a position to look at the NOI. Now you can apply a cap rate to arrive at a fair price for the property. You can also look at the future value of the property to gauge how much upside potential there is.

The following is a sample analysis, done for a small office building with full gross leases. A "full gross lease" means that most of the major costs of owning and operating a property such as insurance, property taxes, and CAM are covered by the landlord and not billed back to the tenants.

This example starts with an analysis of the current income and actual expenses, in order to arrive at a valuation. In the next column is a buyer's proforma, which includes projections for future income and expenses.

INTERPRETING THE ANALYSIS

There is a story to be told in the adjacent example. In its current state, the property should be valued at approximately $277K. But you can see from the proforma that the investor has some improvements planned. This includes a boost in income resulting from a scheduled rent increase, and the lease-up of a space that is currently vacant. If implemented successfully, these steps can raise the NOI and create value after closing.

Looking through the expenses, you can see that there are steps planned to further improve NOI by making some operational changes. The investor has actually taken the time to secure vendor quotes for some of the routine maintenance. Based on these quotes, the cost of things like cleaning, landscaping, snow removal, and trash removal can be reduced. The investor also has plans to implement some conservation measures that will reduce utility consumption by 18% to 25%, a realistic goal for many older properties.

Offsetting part of these savings, there are some expenses this investor expects to be higher after closing, such as property management fees (something that could be avoided altogether and further boost cash flow if the investor is willing to do it himself). In sum, the investor is projecting an increase in NOI of about $17K, resulting in substantially improved cash flow and a jump in valuation of more than $180K.

If your analysis uncovers value that hasn't been unlocked yet such as in this scenario, that is good. That's where you can make a great return. But when valuing an income property, the price should be based on actual numbers and not your projections. This

INCOME	CURRENT MONTHLY RENT	BUYER'S PROFORMA	NOTES
Premium Financial	$ 1,400	$ 1,449	Scheduled 3.5% Rent Bump
ABC Insurance	$ 875	$ 906	Scheduled 3.5% Rent Bump
Language Center	$ 1,200	$ 1,242	Scheduled 3.5% Rent Bump
Counseling Professionals	$ 1,600	$ 1,656	Scheduled 3.5% Rent Bump
VACANT 1 (1250 SF)	$ 0	$ 1,563	Vacant Suite to Be Rented @ $15/SF
Total Monthly Rent	$ 5,075	$ 6,815	
Vacancy Loss	10%	$ (682)	
ANNUAL RENT	$ 60,900	$ 73,603	

EXPENSES	PRIOR YEAR ACTUAL	PROFORMA	
Cleaning and Cleaning Supplies	$ 2,199	$ 1,600	Proforma Based on ABC Cleaning Quote
Insurance	$ 1,700	$ 1,700	Keep Same Provider and Coverage
Landscaping	$ 1,645	$ 1,250	Proforma Based on Bob's Landscaping Quote
Professional Fees	$ 500	$ 800	Estimate for Legal and Accounting
Property Management	$ 1,827	$ 2,944	Proforma Based on Management Company Quote
Repairs and Maintenance	$ 7,600	$ 7,360	Estimated @ 10% Revenue
Snow Removal	$ 1,750	$ 1,500	Proforma Based on Bob's Quote
Taxes	$ 2,444	$ 2,566	Assume Reassess @ Sale Price
Trash Removal	$ 2,400	$ 1,800	Proforma Based on Timmy Trash Quote
Gas and Electric	$ 11,337	$ 8,503	Projected 25% Reduction—Energy Upgrades
Water	$ 2,576	$ 2,112	Projected 18% Reduction—Conservation Upgrades
ANNUAL EXPENSES	$ 35,977	$ 32,135	
NOI	$ 24,923	$ 41,468	
VALUE @ 9% CAP RATE	$ 276,917	$ 460,758	
Purchase Price	$ 275,000	$ 275,000	
Closing Costs	$ 5,500	$ 5,500	
Total Investment/Cost	$ 280,500	$ 280,500	
Cash (15% + Closing Costs)	$ 47,575	$ 47,575	
Bank Loan (70%)	$ 192,500	$ 192,500	
Seller Loan (15%)	$ 41,250	$ 41,250	
Total Debt	$ 233,750	$ 233,750	
Term (years)	20	20	
Interest Rate	5.50%	5.50%	
Annual Debt Service	$ 19,295	$ 19,295	
DSCR	1.29	2.15	
ANNUAL CASH FLOW	$ 5,627	$ 22,173	
CASH-ON-CASH RETURN	11.8%	46.6%	

is tricky, because at the same time, you should be closely looking for potential ways to boost NOI and thereby add value. You *are* looking for that potential. But you should not be expected to pay for anything that isn't there yet.

What you can and should definitely do is prioritize potential acquisitions where you are able to identify value-creation opportunities ahead of time. In other words, prioritize "value-add" opportunities. So-called value-add opportunities are ways that an investor can boost income or reduce expenses in order to raise NOI, thereby boosting the value of the property. Some people call this "forced appreciation" and you will find a full chapter dedicated to this important concept later in the book.

When evaluating prospective properties, value-add opportunities should be a significant part of the "go" versus "no go" decision. That said, there is likely a range of cap rates that falls within your desired investment criteria, and value-add opportunities, in addition to influencing your decision about whether to move forward, might push you to different points within that range.

There is obviously a point at which a refusal to recognize the value of future potential breaks down. A well-located and desirable but vacant property, for example, is usually worth more than zero. But unless you secure tenants before an acquisition, it might result in negative cash flow for an indefinite period of time and not be the best investment for somebody new to commercial real estate.

Again, I can't overstate the importance of knowing the market that you choose to invest in. This applies to knowing the cap rate, as well as all those intangibles that can only come from experiencing a place on a day-to-day basis. Intimate familiarity at the local level is one of the greatest advantages you can leverage as a small investor!

DEBT SERVICE COVERAGE

To mitigate your risk as a small investor, I recommend only acquiring properties with an established strong cash flow and ample debt service coverage. You want properties that will allow you to reinvest cash flow in perpetuity and also provide you with a cushion for when there are setbacks.

"Debt service" is a just a fancy name for paying your mortgage. And a debt service coverage ratio (DSCR) is calculated by estimating how much net operating income you will generate in a year relative to your total mortgage payments. Banks use this to see how much cushion you have to pay them if there are unanticipated fluctuations in income. The higher the DSCR, the more comfortable they are lending to you.

Debt Service Coverage Ratio = NOI / Mortgage Payments

Lenders typically like to see a minimum DSCR of 1.25x. When considering a property, you should calculate this for your own knowledge too. It's important that you're confident you'll generate enough cash flow to cover the mortgage, even after you set aside money for everything else. If a property is too close to or below 1.25x, it should alarm you just as much as it would alarm a lender!

If you review the sample analysis earlier in this chapter, you'll see that the DSCR starts off at 1.29x, which is somewhat concerning. What if you unexpectedly lose a tenant or have some other setback? You need to use your best judgment and run some scenarios to get comfortable. On the positive side, this investor has identified ways to raise the DSCR above 2.0x in the near future, which is a wonderful thing.

Another strategy to mitigate the risk of your DSCR dropping too low is to look for income that is spread across as many tenants as possible. Ideally this means you have rent coming from multiple sources, and you try to avoid properties where a high percentage of the income is dependent on one or two tenants because your risk would be so concentrated. Say, for example, 60% of a property's rent comes from one tenant. What happens if that tenant goes out of business?

Even with a strong lease you can sometimes lose a tenant. Maybe the owner dies or goes to jail. Or packs up in the middle of the night and moves to Thailand. Unexpected things happen. The fewer tenants you have, the more it's going to hurt to lose one. This is particularly true when you are dealing with tenants that are locally owned businesses.

National tenants can carry far lower risk, particularly if they have a longer-term lease and a corporate guarantee. But even that doesn't mean you won't lose them. Large companies go out of business all the time.

So be cautious of properties that are overly dependent on a single tenant, particularly when your portfolio isn't large enough to carry a vacant property while you scramble to fill it back up. In general, the more tenants you have, and the more equally spread out your income is among tenants, the better off you are. Put your eggs into multiple baskets.

Depending on your risk tolerance, you should try to ensure you are able to keep a property afloat (DSCR above 1.0) with 30% to 40% vacancy. Run the numbers ahead of time, and figure out whether you'll be able to pay the bills if you lose your largest tenant. How about your largest two? It's important to measure your risks ahead of time and understand what your exposure is before making a final decision.

As mentioned earlier, the diversity of the income is one of the appeals of apartments. A 25-unit apartment building, for example, typically has a relatively equal distribution of income among the tenants. Most likely, each individual tenant will be contributing 3% to 5% of the income.

THE NEXT LEVEL: DUE DILIGENCE

When doing your initial valuation and constructing proformas, it's fine to rely on data provided by the seller. But by the time you're ready to put a property under contract and enter your due diligence phase (inspection period that starts after you have a signed purchase agreement), you'll want to do more thorough research and make your calculations as accurate as possible.

Keeping rough estimates is a risk you should try to mitigate by getting more solid information. When you're doing serious due diligence, take away as many unknowns as possible. This includes closely scrutinizing all information provided by the seller—look for inconsistencies and verify as much as possible.

Verifying Income

To verify income, I recommend requesting the trailing 12 months of *actual* income and then comparing it to the rent roll. This will allow you to see the actual collections versus what is shown on the rent roll, which will reflect what was scheduled. A rent roll tells you what *can* be collected but not what *actually is*. By reviewing actual income, you can also see if there are concessions, bad debt (tenants not paying rent), or notorious late collections.

Concessions are particularly easy to hide on a rent roll. For example, a rent roll for an apartment building might show that all of the tenants are paying $800 per month in rent. But if each of the tenants was given three months of free rent and a large-screen TV when they moved in, that needs to be factored in to your income projections. When excessive concessions are offered, it can distort the picture created by a rent roll and should raise a red flag. It calls into question whether the rents and occupancy are sustainable at current levels.

The second way to vet the rent roll and nail down income is to request copies of all the tenant leases, and then carefully cross-checking the information in the leases with the data in the rent roll. In my experience there are discrepancies more times than not, frequently unintentional but not always. On a surprising number of occasions I have discovered landlords accidentally undercharging tenants. This is most often due to a landlord's poor record keeping where they miss scheduled rent increases. An owner might also strike a verbal agreement with a tenant that if they pay early they get a discount. In cases like these you can add value to a property just by charging the rent defined in the lease!

As mentioned in the introduction, when I bought my first property, I renegotiated the price multiple times during due diligence (after the initial agreement was signed and prior to closing). This renegotiation was based on evidence that the rent roll provided to me by the seller was completely inaccurate and, in some cases, fictitious. The more I dug, the more I found. Not only did the leases not add up, but during my inspection I noticed that some of the spaces that were supposedly leased were actually vacant!

In most cases, I try to avoid renegotiating a deal after there is a signed purchase agreement. You generally expect to find a few surprises during due diligence, but unless it's really major, it's bad form to keep going back and trying to renegotiate. Some people in the industry call this "retrading." Retrading is frowned upon and brokers don't like it. Try to honor your agreements when possible or it can tarnish your reputation. In this particular case, there were numerous errors and some were pretty egregious so I felt justified. My broker agreed.

Verifying Expenses

The expenses provided by a seller can be just as tricky to evaluate as the income because they are relatively easy to manipulate over the short term. Knowing they are going to list a property for sale, some landlords will just stop making repairs or cut back on routine expenses such as landscaping, paint, etc. This not only distorts the financial picture but leaves a buyer with a pile of deferred maintenance after closing. So you should always use actuals and look over longer periods of time—preferably at least the current year-to-date and the prior two full calendar years. A good rule of thumb is to question any expenses that reflect a change of greater than 5% from the prior year.

When a seller suppresses actual expenses over longer periods of time by deferring routine maintenance, it is also usually evident through a physical inspection. With some experience you will get a better feel for when numbers just look "off," but you can also note signs of deferred maintenance by paying close attention during an initial walk-through and later property inspection.

Examples of things you might notice include anything from overgrown landscaping and peeling paint to cracked windowpanes and stained ceiling tiles. You might see expired inspection tags on fire extinguishers, elevators, or boilers. Basically, anything that hints at an owner's reluctance to spend the money necessary to maintain the property at a level appropriate for its class.

The more serious you get about a property, the more deeply you should dig in. On the expense side, this means trying to secure copies of bills to back up the expenses. You should also consider getting actual vendor quotes of your own.

In many ways, by the time you're done with your due diligence, your analysis of a property starts to take on the same quality as a bank's underwriting process, which occurs when they vet your application for financing.

Though "underwriting" is a banking term, many investors refer to their own due diligence as underwriting. There is a lot to consider when underwriting a property, and some factors are unique to the specific type of commercial real estate you're evaluating. For more depth, I recommend a review of Appendix C, which provides a good overview of each property type and valuable insights into a bank's considerations when evaluating a commercial loan application.

You can use many of the same criteria to vet your own purchase.

LIMITATIONS OF ANALYTICS

While financial analysis is important, it's equally important to look at considerations that are less easily quantified. As I mentioned earlier, look at the surroundings, and use your intuition and good judgment. There is a lot more to a property than numbers. There are limits to any quantitative analysis, and the math needs to be given some broader context.

To facilitate this more qualitative and intuitive assessment, you should schedule a showing of the property—and ideally more than one. Your initial screening may have helped you get a rough idea of issues on the exterior and the property's surroundings, but you still need to take a close look at the interior before you submit an offer.

> *"Follow your instincts. That's where true wisdom manifests itself."*
> —OPRAH WINFREY

Once I've reviewed a property's numbers and reached a point where I'm considering putting in an offer, I invite a few people whose experience and judgment I trust to walk through the property with me. A fresh set of eyes, or multiple sets, particularly those practiced at maintaining or leasing similar properties, can be invaluable. You may also bring along a contractor.

It might seem odd that I do my initial financial analysis prior to a walk-through, but this is an investment property so the underlying numbers are a prerequisite. The preliminary financial analysis is also something I can do from my office, gathering information via phone and email. Based on these initial findings, I can then determine whether to impose on the owner, broker (if one is involved), and tenants for a walk-through.

Regardless of the timing, walk-throughs are a critical part of analyzing a property. Without fail, details will be noticed and points will be raised that you'd thus far failed to fully consider. Things that never show up in your spreadsheet! The end result can sometimes dramatically change your level of interest or perceived value of a property. Examples of serious things you might notice would be a bad roof, outdated electrical, asbestos, or major safety issues.

You don't need to panic if you lack the requisite knowledge to spot these, or that you may have missed something during your walk-through. A purchase agreement should always include a due diligence period that gives you a chance to do a more thorough inspection after the property is under contract. This is the point at which you can hire a professional inspector or bring contractors through to take a closer look and try to find anything you might have missed.

That doesn't mean you shouldn't do the recommended research and walk-through. It's worth the extra effort to try to be as informed as reasonably possible before making an offer. It's always messy and uncomfortable to be in a situation where you're trying to renegotiate a contract based on something that was already disclosed or would be obvious to a casual observer but you didn't notice. These types of situations can erode trust and cause deals to fall apart. You're much better off doing your homework and submitting an offer that is based on a careful and thoughtful analysis.

KEY POINTS

- An initial qualitative property screen might confirm that the property fits the criteria you have established with regard to its location, type, condition, class, etc. A virtual or on-site cursory visual survey can help garner additional insights.
- Current income and actual historical expense should be used to arrive at an NOI for valuation purposes. This should be supplemented by creation of a proforma in order to assess future potential.
- Prioritize projects where you identify value-add opportunities, but resist overpaying for unrealized potential.
- Look for properties with a strong, diversified cash flow that will provide you with ample debt service coverage. This will allow you to reinvest cash flow and provide you with a margin of safety.

CHAPTER 7

STRUCTURING DEALS CREATIVELY

"Creativity is one of the last remaining legal ways of gaining an unfair advantage over the competition."

—ED MCCABE

"There are no rules here. We're trying to accomplish something."

—THOMAS EDISON

■

N THE LIFECYCLE OF a project, the initial acquisition is likely to be the stage where the most cash is at stake. In the real estate investment community, there's a popular saying that "you make money when you buy, not when you sell." This adage is frequently intended to emphasize the importance of paying the right purchase price, but it's also applicable to the amount of cash you put into the deal.

The cash you put into an acquisition has a dramatic effect on your cash-on-cash return, or the amount of cash you get back relative to the amount of cash you put in. This is where the structure of the deal comes into play. When I say "structure of the deal," I'm talking about the combination and sources of cash and debt that will be used to pay for the property and the closing costs.

Exactly how you choose to structure a deal can have a significant impact on how much cash you need to contribute at closing. This means taking a hard look at how you're going to finance the acquisition, and also how you can manipulate all the factors that influence the amount of cash required at closing.

Efforts to reduce the cash required at closing are ultimately designed to secure the maximum value with the least amount of cash while balancing risk.

An investor is well advised to be thoughtful when choosing which projects make the most sense for minimizing cash injection. There are costs and risks associated with most creative financing strategies, and that needs to be considered as you pursue the ideas presented in this chapter. This is particularly true when you employ strategies involving high levels of debt. You should have a clear plan to boost income after closing so as to make sure you can achieve a healthy DSCR and comfortably make your mortgage payments. The more concrete and bulletproof the plan to boost NOI, the more aggressive you can be with your borrowing.

Ideally, you will identify ways to creatively structure deals so as to minimize cash outlay at closing, boost post-acquisition cash flow, and maximize cash-on-cash return. I've done several deals that have required less than 5% of the purchase price to close. In such a case as this, $50K could buy you a $1M property. So far, I've done two commercial deals with no money down.

The possible ways that an investor might structure deals is only limited by their own creativity. Nothing is off the table. Every investment is a puzzle, and you just need to make all the pieces fit.

> *"It takes as much imagination to create debt as to create income."*
> —LEONARD ORR

 What follows are some of the more commonly employed techniques that investors use to reduce the amount of cash required at closing when acquiring apartments or commercial real estate.

SELLER FINANCING

While not particularly common, there are some commercial properties to be found where the seller has no debt and is willing to extend financing to the buyer.

In a situation such as this, the seller basically becomes the bank. You can negotiate terms, but you're borrowing from the seller and make loan payments to them after the acquisition just like you would to the bank.

In order for a seller to finance your purchase without any bank involvement, the following conditions would need to be met:

1. The seller would need to own the property free and clear, or at least have a debt level low enough that they can either pay it off from their own resources or through your down payment.
2. The seller would need to agree to the concept and terms of seller financing.

It is definitely possible to uncover properties where the above criteria are met, but it is not a particularly common situation. Thus far, I have only completed one commercial real estate deal that fulfilled both of the above criteria. But it was a good project, and I'll certainly seek to do it again when the situation allows.

Usually, the seller will still expect you to put some cash down at closing, though the amount is negotiable and can vary widely. In some cases, motivated sellers might extend 100% financing, though this is unlikely, with the exception of situations where the buyer is a trusted or known commodity.

It is common for seller financing to include a "balloon payment." This means that after a specified period of time, usually 3 to 10 years, the remaining unpaid balance of the loan will come due, typically necessitating a refinance.

For value-add investors, seller financing with a balloon payment may still be an attractive option because it can provide the time necessary to take over the property and add enough value to secure traditional bank financing down the road. There is risk involved, however. You need to make sure the balloon payment isn't due too quickly for you to execute a turnaround and secure alternative financing. Otherwise you face potential foreclosure and loss of the property.

COMBINING BANK FINANCING AND SELLER FINANCING

While sellers don't often own commercial properties outright, it is *much* more common for them to have a mortgage and to have also built up enough equity to help the buyer with a small loan.

In this scenario, a significantly greater number of commercial real estate owners are willing to extend a modest amount of owner financing, equal to say 5% to 25% of the purchase price. The balance of the purchase price would then be covered through a combination of cash and conventional bank financing, allowing the seller to still pay off their debt and partially cash out at the same time.

You might apply for bank financing to cover 70% to 75% of the sale price, for example, and use seller financing for another 5% to 15%. Or you can split it any other way you see fit, as long as you can convince the seller and the bank to agree.

This debt combination is an effective strategy that I have used on multiple occasions. For those ensconced in the industry it is not considered unusual. Sellers are often receptive to small loans of 5% to 10% if they have enough equity and it suits their purposes.

You might wonder what would motivate a seller to extend owner financing. There are a variety of reasons why they may be open to the idea, including the following:

▶ It is more important to the seller to get the highest possible price for their property than to completely cash out at the time of the sale.
▶ The seller feels a sense of security in the underlying property as collateral for their loan. They know that if you don't pay them back as agreed, they can take possession of the property.
▶ The seller wants to sell but has concerns about how to reinvest the money afterward—the idea of earning interest appeals to them.
▶ The seller's property has increased in value (or it has been fully depreciated). In this case, the seller may be concerned

about the capital gains tax implications of cashing out all at once and is thus intrigued by the possibility of avoiding a large tax hit at the time of the sale. Owner financing spreads payments out and can allow them to spread the gains across multiple years, thereby dropping their income into a lower bracket and reducing their tax burden.

► The seller is highly motivated to part with the property for personal reasons, such as a need to relocate, a medical emergency, or other change in their personal situation. Their dire situation makes them more open to any concessions or arrangements.

► The seller is living off the property income, and the idea of continuing to get a check in the mail every month appeals to them and gives them a sense of comfort.

► The seller doesn't already have specific plans for the proceeds of the sale. (In commercial real estate, some sellers plan on doing something called a 1031 Exchange, which allows them to transfer their equity into a similar property to avoid the tax implications. Such a seller would not be a good candidate for seller financing.)

► The seller has a personal attachment to the property and is motivated to help make sure that the property goes into the right hands.

► The seller holds the buyer in high regard and is motivated by the idea of helping the buyer to be successful.

There are of course other reasons, but these are some of the more common ones. One thing I've learned through experience, though, is to never presume that you understand a seller's motivations. It's best to ask questions, but to mostly listen. The better you understand the seller's situation, the better positioned you are to craft a deal that will best fit the needs of both parties.

I have found that an effective way to approach the seller financing component is to offer a low price initially without seller financing, and then wait to add the seller financing in later when you give a higher counter during negotiations.

This gives the seller the impression that you don't need owner financing to do the deal and thus creates an image of a strong buyer—somebody they might be more comfortable lending to. It also helps them rationalize extending a small loan in exchange for getting a higher price on their property than they would have otherwise been able to secure.

In this scenario, you can often ask for preferred terms on the seller financing—a very low interest rate and a long amortization period, which is important for reducing monthly payments. You could also seek a no-interest loan, or interest-only payments. These kinds of preferred terms can dramatically improve a property's cash flow, boosting your debt service coverage, and managing risk by giving you a little more breathing room.

Remember, there are no rules when negotiating seller financing and everything within reason is generally open for discussion. This includes the amortization period, the interest rate, whether there is a balloon payment and when, whether payments are interest only, etc. You are only limited by your own creativity and the willingness of the seller.

MASTER LEASE AGREEMENTS

Another technique available to commercial investors is the master lease agreement. Though a little more complicated, the master lease agreement can be an effective way for an investor to get complete control of a commercial property with a limited amount of cash.

Basically, a master lease agreement provides the investor with "equitable title." In other words, you get all the rights typically associated with ownership, including the right to rent it out, keep the cash flow, and reap any tax benefits. You don't actually own the property, but the agreement typically gives you the right to acquire the property outright under specific terms at a defined point in the future. In exchange, you make a monthly lease payment to the owner, who in turn uses those payments to pay their mortgage.

Master lease agreements can be a particularly useful strategy for investors with limited resources or when more traditional financing is not a viable option. This might include situations where you are acquiring a distressed property whose cash flow wouldn't meet a bank's lending criteria.

For a value-add investor, a master lease agreement is an ideal situation because the final acquisition price is locked in, so the term of the lease can be used to increase the value of the property. Ideally, during this time period you can create enough new equity to conclude the transaction with 100% bank financing. For example, let's say you negotiate a master lease agreement with the option to purchase a property for $750K. Over the term of the agreement you make enough improvements to achieve an appraised value of $1M. Now you secure a commercial bank loan for 75% of the appraised value, which will cover the entire purchase price of the acquisition! In this case your hard work has created equity of $250K, allowing you to purchase the property with no cash.

A seller typically needs to be pretty motivated to accept a master lease agreement, or else be desirous of dodging a large early payoff penalty on their mortgage. But in situations where a seller is having major issues with a property, a master lease agreement can sometimes be an attractive option.

For the most part, a seller's motivations for a lease agreement are very similar to those that would make them open to owner financing. These include a wide range of potential personal issues, or deferring the tax consequences of a sale.

If the seller is carrying a mortgage, this can sometimes be a stumbling block because many mortgages include language that prohibits master lease agreements. This language is often found in a "due on sale" clause. Even though you're not actually consummating a sale at the time, due on sale provisions can be triggered by the granting of rights conveyed through a master lease agreement.

I have not used this strategy, but I am familiar with multiple projects where it was employed, with various outcomes. Because of how complicated master lease arrangements can be, they may not be the best option for inexperienced investors. That said, it's a technique that has been around for a while and many investors have executed master lease agreements successfully.

Whenever negotiating a master lease agreement, the buyer should rely heavily on their real estate attorney, and preferably one with experience in this particular area. When an underlying mortgage is involved, provisions should always be made to make 100% certain that the seller is in fact making their mortgage payments throughout the term of the master lease agreement. This may involve setting up a third-party escrow. Otherwise the property could actually end up in foreclosure without your knowledge! This exact situation is what precipitated the legal quagmire that culminated with the Solar Building going on the auction block.

ASSUMING THE SELLER'S MORTGAGE

On more than one occasion I have agreed to assume the seller's mortgage as part of an acquisition. Assuming a seller's mortgage involves accepting liability for all the terms imposed, including the interest rate and payment obligations. The assumption usually needs to be approved by the seller's current lender. In some instances, an assumption can allow a buyer to avoid having to obtain their own mortgage.

As an example, say you're acquiring a commercial property for a price of $500K. In the course of negotiations, you learn that the seller has an existing mortgage with an outstanding principle of $450K. You might offer to assume the seller's $450K mortgage, and then pay the remaining $50K in cash.

A mortgage assumption can sometimes be a real win-win situation for both the buyer and the seller. It can be an attractive option for the buyer if the terms are favorable, or if it reduces the amount of cash required at closing. Assuming the seller's mortgage can usually only save cash if the seller's mortgage balance is greater than 75% of the proposed purchase price. Or, if the mortgage balance is lower than 75% of the purchase price, you could potentially combine a mortgage assumption with seller financing so that the combined debt exceeds 75%.

From the seller's perspective, an assumption can sometimes allow them to avoid steep early payoff penalties that are common in commercial mortgages. This is particularly true if the commercial mortgage is a conduit loan, which means it has been bundled up and sold as part of a commercial mortgage-backed security (CMBS). In such cases, it wouldn't be unusual to find a $1M loan with a prepayment penalty as high as $100K or $200K if it is prepaid well in advance of its maturity date. In this case, if you can save the seller $100K to $200K by assuming their mortgage, you can often negotiate a much better purchase price, or even agree to split the savings with the seller.

Agreeing to assume a mortgage does have its downsides, however. The biggest one being that, depending on the lender and terms of the mortgage, it can be a lengthy and sometimes costly process, with no guarantee you're going to be approved. The terms of the mortgage may be better or worse than you can secure yourself—it really all depends on the specific circumstance.

Exploring the feasibility of a mortgage assumption requires the cooperation of the seller and some motivation on their part. But it's a legitimate option in the right circumstances and, as discussed in the introduction, was how I financed my first commercial property.

WRAPAROUND MORTGAGE

An alternative form of financing that is far less common is something called a wraparound mortgage. With a wraparound mortgage (or a "wrap"), the seller keeps their existing mortgage in place after the sale—they don't pay it off, and they keep it in their own name. But as part of the terms of the sale, the seller extends the buyer owner financing for a larger amount than their underlying mortgage amount. In effect, this makes the buyer responsible for the seller's mortgage moving forward, plus some additional debt. Basically, the seller is "wrapping" around the existing mortgage with owner financing.

Say, for example, you'd like to purchase a property for $100K and the seller has an existing mortgage of $60K that they agree to keep in their name. The seller may wrap the $60K mortgage with another $30K of owner financing, and thereby extend a total financing package to you of $90K. In this situation, you would then contribute the remaining balance of $10K in cash. You would actually own 100% of the property, even though the seller still has their own mortgage on it. The seller would collect monthly mortgage payments from you on the $90K wrap, and then in turn make the required payments on their underlying $60K bank mortgage.

As you might imagine, the seller is likely to have reservations about transferring ownership of the property while keeping the bank mortgage in their name, knowing that their credit could be at risk if everything heads south. But getting a higher price for the property can sometimes offset these concerns, as can the lure of collecting interest payments that are higher than what they pay on their underlying debt.

As with master leases, wraparound mortgages can be complicated and involve some risk. They are often prohibited under the terms of the seller's mortgage and you'll want to seek the assistance of an attorney with relevant experience in these matters. You'll also want to ensure there are provisions put in place to guarantee that the seller is using part of the monthly payments you send them to make their underlying mortgage payments.

SYNDICATION

All of the strategies in this chapter are designed to help you structure a deal with maximum value using the least amount of cash while balancing risk. In an ideal situation, you would use your own cash to pay for whatever down payment is due. The greatest benefit of this approach is that you retain full control of the project, and are positioned to reap 100% of the return on your investment of funds and hard work.

So what do you do when you don't have enough cash? Or maybe no cash at all? In lieu of securing funds through debt, investors can also raise funds through equity. This approach, commonly referred to as syndication, involves the allocation of partial ownership to other investors in exchange for their cash contributions into a specific project, or into an investment fund that will be deployed in projects yet to be identified. It's the same basic principle used by many large investors, including the one in wingtip shoes depicted in Chapter 4.

The exact terms defining how investors are rewarded, and how you can profit from pulling such a deal together, can vary widely. Some common features of a syndicated deal include the following:

- ▶ **Equity Participation:** As the person who pulls the whole syndication deal together, you can set aside a portion of the project ownership for yourself. The amount of this equity can vary widely, but might typically be somewhere in the 10% to 30% range. It might also be stepped, whereby you have low equity until the participating investors achieve a certain return, at which time your equity would increase to a predefined level.

- ▶ **Profit Participation:** In exchange for their equity participation, cash investors might get a preferred return of 7% to 12%. In other words, you won't get any profits at all until this level is realized by your investors. Then, once this threshold is cleared, additional profit over that level can be proportioned between you and your investors according to whatever split was agreed to. This is a great way to share the risk and reward with your investors.

- ▶ **Acquisition Fees:** As a syndicator you can incorporate a fee in exchange for finding a property, conducting the due diligence, working with lenders, and shepherding the deal through closing, etc. Acquisition fees can be a flat amount but are more commonly structured as a percentage of the purchase price, and typically range from 1% to 3%. They are paid out in cash at closing. My personal recommendation would be to stay on the lower end of the percentage range so as not to get too greedy. It's a lot of work to pull a deal like this together so acquisition fees are justified, but you're already getting equity participation and need to be fair to your investors, who are placing their faith in you and taking a risk by putting in the cash.

▶ **Asset Management Fees**: Most syndicated deals involve property management by a third party. But somebody needs to "manage the manager" and provide the oversight necessary on an ongoing basis to ensure that your investment team's interests are being watched out for. There is also administrative work to be done related to management of the investment entity, including regular communication and reporting. As the asset manager you can justifiably collect a monthly fee for this responsibility, which is typically equal to no more than 1% of the project's gross income.

Structuring and managing a syndication deal can be complicated for those without experience and it is not a path that I have yet elected to follow. If you decide to take this approach, you would be wise to seek the help of a real estate attorney who has experience specifically with these types of deal structures.

The clear advantage of syndicating a project (or fund) is that you can put in less cash and thus potentially acquire a property that is much larger than would be possible on your own. However, there can be significant downsides to syndication, including:

▶ Lack of flexibility with regard to deferring owner draws or reinvestment back into the project. Passive investors in commercial real estate projects tend to want a defined return on a specific timeline agreed to in advance.

▶ Higher legal fees resulting from complexity of the legal entity and the need for more agreements. You may also need to pay for the creation of a private placement memorandum (PPM) to comply with SEC regulations.

► The more parties that are involved, the higher the chance of disagreements arising.

► Lower profits resulting from both the division of owner distributions and higher costs.

► Administrative burden resulting from managing investors and reporting.

► The need to identify an exit strategy up front. Most syndicated deals or funds have a set time period for the capital to be deployed and paid back.

GRANTS

Given the challenges associated with borrowing or raising money, the idea of securing a grant can be very appealing.

Novice real estate investors sometimes operate under the illusion that there are numerous grants that are readily available to help finance their projects. The reality is that while there are grants, tax breaks, and other forms of government subsidies out there, the process for securing them can sometimes be lengthy, complicated, and political. The companies who rely on large grants and tax credits for their development projects usually have experience and expertise in securing such funds. They invest heavily in cultivating relationships with the right people.

Grants and other government assistance programs are also typically earmarked for development projects that meet a specific need, such as affordable housing, job creation, or other advantageous community projects that might not otherwise attract private investment. And they almost never cover enough of the project cost to eliminate the need for bank financing.

All that said, grants can be a great source of project financing if you can successfully secure them. And they work well for many investors. You just need to recognize that they can put you in a much more precarious position since you are dependent on other parties and factors outside of your control. So do your homework. Government subsidies of any type introduce another element of risk, can dramatically lengthen the duration of a project, and often come with contingencies that can increase your project's costs.

The Lincoln Building

Out of all my investments to date, there is only one for which I sought grants. The property is called the Lincoln Building, and it is a prominent five-story downtown commercial building whose condition had dramatically deteriorated under prior ownership.

A financial analysis showed that the costs associated with renovating the Lincoln Building would be too high to support bank financing—without assistance the project would lose money, even if it were fully leased at market rental rates. In order to break even we would need to secure grant money for about 20% of the $13M renovation cost.

Despite the financial risks, I really liked the building and didn't want to see it torn down. A well-respected contractor shared my sentiment, so we decided to do a 50/50 joint venture (my only partnership to date) and together we purchased the property. We knew the grants and tax credits were out there to help with such a project because we had seen other developers secure them successfully, and we were confident we could do the same.

In hindsight we were naive. After nearly four years of lobbying and applying for grants, we have had limited success. Our team has invested thousands of hours of time, but despite our best efforts, the total amount of grants secured so far amounts to less than 5% of the total project cost, and most of these funds came with strings attached.

The smaller grants have allowed us to get started and covered about half of the costs associated with restoring the facade and renovating some ground-floor commercial spaces. But as I write this, the property remains mostly vacant, and the work necessary to halt further deterioration and stabilize the property has been costly. In the meantime, we continue to incur carrying costs such as property taxes, insurance, utilities, and routine maintenance.

Nonetheless, we remain committed to the project and forge ahead. Renovation continues, and we're cautiously optimistic about our latest grant applications.[7] While the Lincoln Building project is unlikely to be profitable, we saved a prominent, historical building in our downtown, so in that sense it's a project we can take pride in.

ALEXA MURRAY

The motivations behind this high-profile project were in part altruistic, but my partner and I certainly never expected to lose so much money. It's been a hard lesson. My biggest mistake was assuming grants could be easily secured. I also bought the property without adequate cash flow to support redevelopment efforts. The bottom line is that I strayed too far from the sound principles that have made me successful in real estate.

---

7 Update: The project was later awarded $950K in economic development grants.

Despite the project's bleak financial outlook, the Lincoln Building has been a valuable learning experience. It has prompted me to recommit to the principles espoused in this book and focus on privately funded projects with stronger fundamentals.

> *"What is defeat? Nothing but education. Nothing but the first step to something better."*
> —WENDELL PHILLIPS

CLOSING COSTS AND CREDITS

In addition to creative financing structures, there are a variety of ways that you might negotiate closing costs and credits to reduce the amount of cash you need to close. In my experience, sellers tend to be a lot more focused on the top-line dollar amount of an offer than they are on smaller credits and who pays for each aspect of closing. But cash is cash, and every dollar you save today is important, regardless of whether it comes from a lower purchase price, a lower down payment, or reduced closing costs. And if a seller believes that giving the buyer a credit allows them to get a more competitive top-line offer or helps get a deal done, such concessions can be agreeable to both parties.

Maintenance or Replacement Credits

Older properties often have a ton of deferred maintenance—especially value-add properties. In these cases, you can incorporate a clause in the purchase offer that gives you a deferred maintenance credit from the seller at closing in exchange for accepting the property "as is." You can actually use this approach even if you're unaware of any significant deferred maintenance items. Chances are, there is something that will need work after closing.

A word of caution if you elect to utilize this approach: before accepting a property as is, you'll want to have the property thoroughly inspected. But this inspection can still come after you secure a signed purchase agreement. Just make sure there is a contingency allowing you a period of time to conduct the inspection with the option to walk away if you're unsatisfied.

A deferred maintenance credit can be any amount, though I've seen it as high as 5% to 10% of the purchase price. Whether or not this credit would reduce the purchase price used by the bank in determining your loan amount depends in large part on your lender's policies. Most of the time, if the dollar amount is 3% or less, it wouldn't change the purchase price, but would instead reduce the amount of cash you would need to close.

You don't have to specifically spell out what the credit is for, but that is an option. In that case, you would quantify a credit amount to be provided by the seller at closing that is sufficient to correct a particular deficiency, such as an aging roof or parking lot. You might get a credit adequate for a roof replacement, but the funds can be used however you wish. Perhaps a few small repairs can be done to defer a full replacement until a future year. Unless a lender dictates otherwise, this is your choice as a buyer.

Escrow and Reserve Accounts

On several occasions, including on my first acquisition, I have successfully negotiated a credit equal to the balance of the seller's escrow or reserve accounts at closing. Escrow and reserve accounts are set up and maintained by banks on most commercial loans. They collect funds from the borrower with each mortgage payment and set them aside in escrow accounts for such purposes as paying property taxes, paying insurance bills, making improvements, or major repairs. They are sort of like bank-imposed and bank-managed savings accounts to make sure the money is set aside for future needs.

Smaller banks are less likely to require escrow and reserve accounts, but large lenders usually insist on them. A typical commercial loan will have a reserve account for capital improvements, and escrow accounts for property taxes and insurance. There are many other types of reserve accounts out there, but these are the most common types.

If the seller of a property has owned it for a while, their reserve account balances can sometimes have grown rather large. As the buyer, these large escrows are usually not consequential because they are governed by the seller's lender. But that changes if you are assuming the seller's mortgage because when the seller's bank approves the assumption, the approval is likely to include a contingency requiring you to replace the full balances in these accounts, which can require a large infusion of cash that you will otherwise have to come up with on your own. To help offset this, you can request a closing credit from the seller equal to the balance of the reserve account.

If you are not going to be assuming the seller's mortgage, you can still request this concession. One tactic I have used is to request a credit in the amount of the seller's replacement reserve in order to offset deferred maintenance. The rationale here would be that the money the seller has set aside over the years was deemed by their lender to be an adequate amount to properly maintain the property. In theory its accumulation would be sufficient to offset a property's physical deficiencies.

It can be difficult to make a strong push for the seller's escrow account since it doesn't really benefit the seller, other than to help get a deal in place. But if you have a motivated seller, everything is on the table, escrow accounts included. It's also a concession that seems to be less scrutinized by very large sellers, who might be responsible for sizable portfolios and may not be concerned about this level of detail.

Prorated Rent

One of the easiest ways to reduce the amount of cash you need to come up with at closing is simply to schedule your closing early in the month. Most purchase agreements include language that gives you a credit for prorated rents at closing. So if you close early in the month, you'll get a credit for most of that month's rent. This can sometimes give you about 2% of the purchase price.

Try to avoid scheduling the closing for the first few days of the month, however, as rent may not have come in yet. All things equal, I usually try to get a closing date between the 5th and the 10th so that I get at least two-thirds of the month's rent at closing.

Security Deposits

You will also get a credit at closing for all the tenant security deposits that the seller holds, which can sometimes equate to another 2% of the purchase price. Commercial security deposit funds are not regulated the same way as residential security deposits.

In most states, landlords are required to keep apartment security deposits in separate, interest-bearing accounts, so while these funds are transferred to your care at closing, they are technically owned by the tenants and you can't legally use them. But commercial security deposits that are transferred to the buyer at closing are different. They can be comingled with other funds in your operating account and used for any purpose.

Just remember that while you can deploy commercial security deposits to cover closing costs, it is technically debt. You'll have to pay the deposit money back to the tenant if and when they leave and fulfill their obligations under the terms of the lease. And if you eventually sell the property, you'll have to convey the deposit amounts to the buyer. But the commercial security deposits you get at closing are basically equivalent to a no-interest, no-payment loan of indefinite term.

You don't have to negotiate the receipt of these security deposits, but you should review the tenant leases to make sure you're getting all you're entitled to. Commercial security deposits can represent a significant credit that many investors overlook when trying to determine how much cash they will need to come up with at closing.

Closing Costs

There are numerous closing costs that can be paid by either party. Interestingly, what is conventional, or traditionally paid by each party can be specific by state, region, or even municipality. Regardless of convention, everything is negotiable. An attorney should be able to help you navigate these waters.

The idea is to consider pushing some of the closing costs onto the seller. Examples include survey costs, mortgage tax, and even legal costs. Alternatively a fixed dollar amount closing cost credit can be included in the purchase agreement without defining the specific costs that it will cover.

NEGOTIATING THE DEAL

Any creative deal structure you might choose to employ needs to be carefully thought through ahead of time. Many of them need to be accounted for in structuring the initial purchase offer or, if not up front, at least at some point during the negotiation. Part of this process involves getting a sense of what is important to a seller and what they might be open to.

Using a combination of one, two, or even three of the strategies introduced in this chapter can save you a lot of money at closing. But you need to strike a balance and feel each situation out to determine when they are appropriate. If you try to incorporate too many strategies at once, or do it in the wrong situation, you risk alienating the seller. If you are excessive, it might even make them angry.

Typically the extent to which you can leverage strategies to minimize your cash outlay will boil down to a combination of how motivated the seller is and what constraints they might be operating under. Also, if the seller is more experienced in commercial real estate, they might be more comfortable and open to creative financing structures.

Always learn as much as you can about the seller, and then make a concerted effort to put yourself in their shoes. What is there for them to like about the deal? Are you offering a compelling price? Saving them money on an early payoff penalty on their loan? Helping them avoid taxes on capital gains? How can both parties win? These are the types of questions you should be asking yourself as you craft your offer and negotiate.

You should be able to clearly explain why the deal structure you might propose would be of interest or benefit to the seller. If you can't, that isn't a good sign.

Several of the most promising creative financing strategies depend on the seller's debt situation, including owner financing and assuming a seller's mortgage. If and when you can get it, knowledge of the seller's motivations and debt situation is extremely valuable because it will allow you to propose viable and mutually beneficial deals. An experienced broker can help you mine for this information tactfully and navigate any of the objections or issues that might arise when communicating with a seller.

In terms of negotiation strategy, I mentioned earlier that it can sometimes be effective to make an initial offer low enough to seek creative financing solutions or concessions as your price point rises in negotiation. For example, maybe in your initial offer you include an owner financing element, but you limit it to only 5% of the purchase price, with 75% bank financing. This helps the seller get comfortable with the idea, and raises fewer red flags than if you had led with an offer asking for the moon. Trying right out of the gate to structure an offer where you're putting in almost no cash is not a good way to inspire confidence in a seller (or broker) that you're a serious buyer.

As negotiations proceed and you raise your price point, you are then in a better position to ask for more. Hopefully, the seller has already decided that a small piece of owner financing is OK, so when it goes to 10%, and maybe later 15% or 20%, that doesn't seem like such a big deal.

There is a tendency for some sellers to be very locked in on getting their desired sales price, and less focused on the terms. Psychology comes into play here. The fact that there might be a $20K credit in the closing adjustments, for example, might be completely overshadowed by the fact that a certain target number they had in mind for the sale is in bold print at the top of the purchase agreement.

As the buyer, it's not often that you can get everything you want. But you can usually get some things. Successful execution depends heavily on matching up the best strategy with the seller's needs and desires. You want to create a structure where both parties are happy.

CAUTION

This is an appropriate time to reinforce two points. First, never enter into any financial agreements without the assistance of a qualified professional. An experienced and qualified commercial real estate attorney doesn't come cheap, but they're worth it when you consider the consequences of either doing it on your own or using the wrong person. If you enter into a bad agreement the consequences can be disastrous.

 The second point is a reiteration of the warning in Chapter 1 to avoid overleveraging. It is absolutely critical that you not overextend yourself. *Just because you find a situation where you can put in low cash at closing doesn't mean it's always the right thing to do. Sound judgment needs to prevail.*

There is great risk involved when you take on debt, so you need to be very careful. Because I'm laser-focused on acquiring the most promising value-add properties, I'm comfortable employing techniques that involve higher debt levels. This kind of value-add approach, if done carefully, can allow an investor to create enough equity to satisfactorily offset their debt. But again, it's critical to find that equilibrium and not burden yourself with too much debt.

While I have successfully employed most techniques in this chapter, I have also walked away from opportunities to use owner financing because I wasn't able to identify enough opportunities to add value, or I didn't want to take on the higher risk associated with the debt. A wise investor needs to be prepared to do the same thing, whether it's due to higher risk or the possibility of depleting all of their personal savings. Don't get caught up in the "dream" of a particular property. Walk away from deals that will overextend your resources.

KEY POINTS

- ▶ Investors can sometimes identify ways to creatively structure deals so as to minimize cash outlay at closing, boost post-acquisition cash flow, and maximize cash-on-cash return.
- ▶ Owner financing, either alone or in combination with bank financing, can sometimes provide a vehicle by which an investor can reduce the size of their down payment.
- ▶ Cash outlay can be minimized through a wide variety of other strategies, including mortgage assumptions, deferred maintenance credits, escrow and reserve accounts, prorated rent, security deposits, sharing closing costs, and syndicating deals.
- ▶ It's critical to avoid burdening yourself with too much debt. A wise investor should walk away from any deals that will overextend their resources.

CHAPTER 8

WORKING WITH BANKS

"I have always been afraid of banks."
—ANDREW JACKSON

"It's easy to get a loan unless you need it."
—NORMAN RALPH AUGUSTINE

■

"**HI, THIS IS BRIAN** Murray with Washington Street Properties. I'm calling regarding our mortgage on 215 Washington Street, in Watertown, New York. I submitted a request for a reimbursement from the replacement reserve account, and I haven't heard anything back. I completed all of the paperwork required and submitted the entire package seven weeks ago. This is the fifth time I've called. I was wondering if you could please help me out?"

"Hi, Mr. Murray. Let me put you on hold while I look into this."

Ten minutes later…

"Thank you for holding, Mr. Murray. Your application was reviewed last week, but it was rejected. It appears that the application was complete, but I'm afraid the rent roll and financials were not recent enough. They can't be more than 30 days old."

Hmm… how was I to respond to this without completely alienating my sole point of contact at the bank? I tried hard not to let my frustration get the better of me.

"OK, well, those documents were current when I submitted them. I'm not sure how I'm supposed to provide rent rolls and financials that are less than 30 days old when it takes the bank seven weeks to review them. Do you have any suggestions? This keeps happening and I really need the money. I fronted all the cash to make the improvement, but I can't seem to get reimbursed from the reserve account. I understand you control the escrow accounts, but this is my money, and I need access to it."

Despite my best efforts at restraint, my frustration was creeping through.

"I'm sorry, Mr. Murray. All I can tell you is to resubmit the package with the current rent roll and financial information and we'll process it as soon as we can. But I can't make any promises—we get a lot of requests and there is a backlog right now."

I wish I could say conversations like this weren't a regular occurrence when I started my real estate business. My first commercial mortgage, which I assumed from the seller, began to feel like a noose that was slowly tightening around my neck.

Yes, I was very excited to have assumed the mortgage. But this particular mortgage had numerous "reserve accounts" that I paid into every month—many more than normal. These reserve accounts held money that the bank collected and set aside to ensure that all of the property's financial obligations could be met. The accounts included a property tax escrow, an insurance escrow, a debt service escrow (to cover any missed mortgage payments), a replacement reserve (to reimburse me for approved capital improvements), and a tenant improvement reserve (to reimburse me for build-out of tenant spaces).

These were all well and good, if only I could access the funds when I was entitled to them. There was a defined process for funds to be released, but the bank did everything they could to complicate this and keep control of the money. At one point, there was enough money in the tax escrow to pay my property taxes for the next five years, yet they refused to reduce my monthly tax escrow payments!

There was no easy way to challenge this. I didn't have the resources to wage a legal battle against a corporate titan. And even if I did, commercial borrowers aren't protected by the kinds of laws designed to help residential borrows. On top of that, there were

1,000 different things the bank could easily do to cause me more problems than they already were. I was like a small insect to them, and I didn't particularly want to end up on the windshield.

To top it all off, I would incur a hefty penalty if I paid the note off early. Even so, after dealing with

> *"The borrower is servant to the lender."*
> —PROVERBS 22:7

these shenanigans for more than a year, I began to fantasize about getting rid of this albatross that they called a mortgage. I made it my mission to refinance.

Over the course of the next two years, I wasted literally thousands of hours trying in vain to borrow money and pay this mortgage off. My timing was terrible. Not only was I a new investor with a property that wasn't "seasoned," but I was also trying to borrow money during the worst lending environment in decades.

TURNING THE CORNER

Eventually, I purchased my second property with owner financing, sidestepping the need for a bank at all. I leased up all the vacant spaces in my two properties and persisted in creating value. The lending environment began to thaw, and a bank eventually said yes, not just to refinancing my two mortgages, but also to taking some cash out for the acquisition of additional properties. All of the money tied up in all those pesky reserve accounts would finally be released.

I learned a funny thing about the magic of a bank saying yes. Not only is it a big hallelujah moment for the borrower, but it can also make you look all new and shiny to other potential lenders. It was my attorney who actually suggested that I visit a local bank who hadn't expressed interest in the past. "They're big competitors," he said. "You should stop in to see them and let them know you have a commitment from the other bank."

Turns out, his advice was monumental. Once the local bank realized I was about to borrow from a competitor, they moved quickly, and I was offered better terms. This was a pivotal moment for my business and the beginning of a long and mutually beneficial relationship with this local bank.

Those first few years of dealing with mortgage brokers and banks permanently changed my view of the lending landscape in commercial real estate. I was humbled and learned a lot of hard lessons that won't soon be forgotten.

If I hadn't been through this experience, I'm not sure I would appreciate just how important it is to have a good relationship with the bank. I am enormously grateful every time a bank (or anyone else) lends me money. What does that translate to, from a practical standpoint?

Well, for one thing, I would eat ramen noodles three meals a day and live in my truck before I would miss a mortgage payment. To this day I still do business with that same local bank that helped me refinance that beastly mortgage that I assumed on my first property. Since my first closing with them, I've made thousands of mortgage payments to them, and not a single one has been late.

> *"If you think nobody cares about you, try missing a couple of payments."*
> —STEVEN WRIGHT

This particular local bank has been an exceptional partner and will always be my first choice, though I have since diversified my debt by spreading it across multiple lenders, just in case any problems emerge. As your portfolio grows, I think it's a good idea to manage risk by establishing credit and relationships with more than one lender. A bank might be acquired, sell their loans, change their policies, or exit entire lines of their business. If it's a small bank, they might eventually reach their risk exposure limit with you.

As we learned in Chapter 1, our rocket fuel is comprised of cash with the right blend of leverage and compounding. Leverage is a fancy way of saying debt, and while debt can come from a variety of sources, a major portion of it is likely going to have to come from one or more banks.

The information in this chapter is intended to help you get a better understanding of how bank financing works so that you're in a better position to navigate the process. If you follow the steps provided, you will be better prepared and make the best possible impression. The goal is to submit the strongest application you can to start your relationship with a bank off on the right foot, to improve your likelihood of not only getting a mortgage but also securing the most favorable terms.

Longer term, every small investor should work hard to cultivate positive relationships with lenders and show them sincere respect. You can do this by learning to look at debt from the bank's perspective, and understand what they can and can't do. And always be immensely grateful if you have somebody willing to lend to you on good terms. It's hard enough to get somebody to lend money to you at all. But if you can find a bank that works with you instead of against you, that is gold. A good lender is one of the most valuable business partners you can have.

APPLYING FOR FINANCING

Securing a commercial mortgage from a bank can be a fairly onerous process. It starts off with an application. The documentation and information required can vary significantly depending on the lender, and it can sometimes be substantial. A commercial mortgage application goes well beyond what the average person might experience when buying a single-family home. Borrowing for commercial real estate is more akin to applying for a business loan. So instead of just vetting you, the bank is also evaluating all aspects of the underlying business investment—the commercial real estate.

In general, the core information that you should expect to provide to the lender includes the following:

- ▶ Bank-specific application form
- ▶ Executive summary or project overview
- ▶ Current rent roll
- ▶ Actual historical financials (typically prior two to three years and current year-to-date or trailing 12 months)

- Copy of lease(s)
- Copy of purchase agreement and amendments
- Proforma financials
- Personal financial statement
- Real estate schedule
- Business financial statements
- State and federal tax returns

Whether it's required or not, I will typically invest a significant amount of time developing a project summary for the bank. This basically amounts to a short business plan. I include a qualitative description of the project, including the particulars and a narrative that explains the financials.

In most cases, you won't have the opportunity to make an in-person presentation "selling" your project to the bank. Your project summary allows you to make a positive impression, communicate the details of your plans, and explain all of your assumptions. It is in large part your first impression and should be meticulously prepared.

Imagine that anybody who reads your project summary is going to be asked to describe it in one word. Prepare that document with the goal of ensuring that that one word is "professional." If the reader were asked for further one-word adjectives, we'd be looking for things like "compelling" and "thorough." If the document were to be equated to an outfit, we're striving for a business suit, not shirtless with baggy cargo shorts and sandals.

UNDERWRITING

While a strong project summary will set the stage and get you taken more seriously, whether your application for bank financing is ultimately approved depends in large part on your application's strength. To be considered strong, an application needs to be perceived as an acceptable risk based on the bank's lending criteria.

A thorough understanding of the approval process and insights into the bank's perspective can be gleaned in the Office of the Comptroller of the Currency (OCC) Comptroller's Handbook, "Commercial Real Estate Lending."[8]

This OCC Handbook is a valuable resource because it provides guidance for bank examiners and bankers on commercial real estate lending. It specifically discusses how lenders should assess risk and what criteria they should use in evaluating projects such as your own. Reading the handbook provides a peek behind the curtain.

The process a bank uses to vet the application and make a determination is called "underwriting" and, while specifics for lending can vary from bank to bank, there are some industry standards regarding what criteria are evaluated when underwriting a commercial real estate loan.

At a high level, banks are looking at a borrower's credit worthiness and general project feasibility,

> *"If you would know the value of money, go and try to borrow some."*
> —BENJAMIN FRANKLIN

as well as how that feasibility might change as a result of market factors. Some considerations are specific to the particular type of commercial real estate. A summary overview of underwriting considerations by property type from the OCC Handbook can be found in Appendix C.

In addition to credit worthiness and general project feasibility, underwriters are looking to see whether your project meets bank minimum standards for discrete financial measures. The two most important factors are the debt service coverage ratio (DSCR) and the loan-to-value ratio (LTV).

---

8   The Office of the Comptroller of the Currency (OCC) Comptroller's Handbook, "Commercial Real Estate Lending," August 2013, http://www.occ.gov/publications/publications-by-type/comptrollers-handbook/cre.pdf.

DEBT SERVICE COVERAGE RATIO

As discussed in Chapter 6, the DSCR measures a property's ability to service its debt and is calculated by dividing the NOI by the annual debt service. In general, the higher the DSCR, the more comfortable a lender is with a project. This is because a high DSCR is indicative of a significant cushion with regard to cash available for the borrower to pay their monthly mortgage.

The minimum DSCR can vary depending on the specific bank and nature of the project, but most banks will expect a DSCR of at least 1.20x to 1.25x.

For you to have the strongest application, you should demonstrate a DSCR in excess of 1.25x based on the project's current financials, with a solid plan for increasing the DSCR over time. If you can't hit this threshold under current conditions but have a concrete plan for doing so after closing, you can try to make the strongest case possible. But you may need to start looking at more creative deal structures.

LOAN-TO-VALUE RATIO

The LTV is the ratio of the loan amount to the appraised market value of the property. For the purpose of the loan application, you should usually assume that the market value of an existing income property is equal to the purchase price. If you have access to an existing appraisal (perhaps one provided by the seller) that demonstrates a higher value you can try to use that amount, but the bank is still more likely to default to the purchase price until they issue a commitment letter and have their own appraisal done.

LTV = Loan Amount / Appraised Value

To strengthen your application you should not only demonstrate that the purchase price is supported by the property's current financials, but also present your own proforma showing additional value above and beyond the purchase price.

Each bank sets its own minimum LTV requirement, but for most commercial lenders the maximum LTV is in the 70% to 80% range, and can vary depending on property type. The most common maximum LTV is 75%.

FULFILLING LENDER CONTINGENCIES

If the bank decides it is prepared to move forward with financing your project, you will receive a commitment letter that specifies the terms. The commitment letter is a major step forward in the lending process, and when it's issued, the borrower will often give a huge sigh of relief! At this point, a borrower may begin to feel like things are coming together. However, there is still work to be done.

Within the commitment letter, you can expect a list of contingencies that must be satisfied for final approval. These contingencies can vary depending on the specific lender. As with the initial application, larger national banks tend to have the most expansive requirements.

Some of the common requirements that may need to be fulfilled include the following:

- ▶ **Appraisal:** The bank will usually contract with an approved appraiser to conduct an appraisal on the property. The commitment letter will specify the value at which the appraisal must come in in order for them to lend. If you have provided robust support for your own valuation, it can sometimes help arm an appraiser with what they need in order to provide the most accurate appraisal possible.
- ▶ **Environmental Reports:** There is a wide range of possible levels of environmental assessment that a bank may request, spanning from a simple questionnaire to a basic environmental assessment to detailed environmental reports

such as a Phase I or Phase II. It may depend on the bank's policies and also the nature of the property being acquired. Phase I and Phase II reports can be extensive and costly.

▶ **Property Conditions Assessment (PCA):** Some lenders will hire a third party to conduct a full assessment of the property's physical condition. This is particularly true if the loan being considered is a non-recourse loan. A "non-recourse" loan is a loan where the borrower does not have to give the bank a personal guarantee, leaving the property itself as the only collateral. A non-recourse loan is not easy to secure, and in such cases the bank is highly motivated to ensure that the property is in excellent physical condition. Any deficiencies found will usually need to be addressed.

▶ **Title Insurance:** Since the property you are acquiring is collateral for the loan, the lender will require title insurance to protect themselves. Title insurance protects both your interest and the lender's interest in real property against loss due to such things as liens, title disputes, or other potential claims that might be made against the ownership of a property.

▶ **Tenant Estoppel Agreements:** If there are tenants in place, the bank will usually insist that you secure estoppel agreements with them in order to verify the terms of their lease. If the leases don't already include such language, you may also need to secure a subordination, non-disturbance, and attornment agreement (SNDA). SNDAs are agreements between a tenant and a landlord that define rights of the tenant, the landlord, and the lender under certain circumstances, such as in a foreclosure.

▶ **Insurance Binders:** An insurance binder is a document provided by your insurance company detailing their commitment to provide coverage of the property. The bank will define the minimum coverage and covenants required in order to close, and an insurance broker should be used to help secure the best price for the required coverage.

- **Survey:** The bank will require that an up-to-date survey be provided at closing. There are different levels of surveys and the bank will define what standards will need to be adhered to. In most instances, an older survey will exist for the property. If you can secure a copy of this from the seller, you can sometimes save a significant amount of money by contacting the same surveyor and having them do an update instead of starting from scratch.

- **Borrower Organizational Documents, Resolution, and Certificate of Good Standing:** Most buyers will purchase their property with an LLC. Your attorney will help you select the best legal entity for the acquisition and prepare the appropriate documentation in order to satisfy the bank's requirements.

SELLER FINANCING AND BANKS

The most notable exception to securing debt from banks would be either a full cash purchase, or full owner (seller) financing. As discussed, full owner financing is when the seller acts as a bank and lends the buyer funds to acquire the property, typically with the property itself serving as collateral in case of default. What percentage of the purchase price is lent is entirely negotiable, and in some occasions can be as high as 100%, though that is rare if the seller does not have an established relationship with the buyer.

What is far more common are situations where property is not owned free and clear, in which the seller can still extend financing to the buyer, as long as it is combined with bank financing large enough for them to pay off their debt at closing.

When a seller extends just a small portion of owner financing, the property almost always serves as collateral. But since bank financing is also a piece of this financing puzzle, the owner financing will need to come second to the bank's position. For this reason it is called a "second position," or subordinated debt. In the industry it is also referred to as "mezzanine financing" or "mezzanine debt."

Once again, you are beholden to the whims of the banks, further reinforcing just how important your relationship is with your lender. And not all banks are comfortable with this kind of arrangement.

Assuming the bank is open to the possibility of allowing a second position, there are some things you can do to make the idea more palatable to them. Factors that may improve the attractiveness of owner financing to a bank include the following:

- Demonstrate to the bank that the property's income can easily cover the combined debt from the bank and the seller. The means that you show them the debt service coverage ratio for both the bank's loan and also for the total, combined debt. The higher the DSCR, the more comfortable a lender will be. The DSCR for the combined debt should be higher than the bank's minimum DSCR.
- Reduce the percentage of the deal that the bank is financing. You should never structure a deal where your cash plus the owner financing totals less than 25%, unless you have extraordinarily compelling evidence that there is equity not reflected by the sale price. An example might be a fully executed lease that you have already secured to fill a vacant space with a new tenant after closing. Preferably, you will seek less than 75% LTV from the bank when you're combining bank financing with a private loan.
- Bring another asset to the table as collateral. This is called "cross-collateralization" and the purpose of doing this is to hedge the bank's risk. If you incorporate a second income-producing property (preferably that property's debt is held by the same lender), you can demonstrate that, when combined, the DSCR is higher.
- Establish an excellent track record with the bank over a period of time, and establish trust.

ECONOMIC DEVELOPMENT AGENCIES

Another source of financing that can sometimes be combined with bank financing is a local economic development agency. The availability of such institutions and funds can vary widely depending on where your investment is located. Economic development agencies can often be found at the city, county, or regional levels.

Economic development agencies tend to play a more active role and be better funded in areas that have experienced some level of economic distress. Each agency will have its own mission and unique programs designed to create jobs and economic growth. Oftentimes these programs will include loans that might be suitable for your investment project, particularly if you are attempting to turn around a distressed property.

If and when lending programs are available through a local economic development agency, there are several reasons why they can be advantageous, including the following:

- ▶ Just like owner financing, it can sometimes reduce the amount of cash you need to put into a project. Economic development agencies are often willing to take a second position to a bank.
- ▶ The lending criteria may not be as rigid for a development agency as it is for a bank, but their approval can help position you better with a bank (see next point).
- ▶ You can sometimes use funds from a development agency to reduce the amount you are borrowing from a bank, thereby increasing the bank's level of comfort and improving your likelihood of getting your loan application approved. For example, you might apply for 65% of the purchase price to be provided by a bank, and 20% to come from a local economic development agency.
- ▶ The terms of the debt can sometimes be very attractive. The agencies exist for the purpose of trying to help spur economic development, so they will sometimes offer inter-

est rates or amortization periods that are better than can be found through a bank.

Whatever combination of debt you elect to pursue, whether it includes an owner financing component, an economic development agency, or just conventional bank financing, there are a lot of options out there. Real estate brokers and attorneys see a lot of deals and can be great resources for helping you identify lending programs in your area. It's worth the effort to do your research to figure out exactly what your options are and which one will work best for you and your project.

MORTGAGE BROKERS AND MORTGAGE BANKERS

Some borrowers choose to navigate the lending process with the help of a mortgage broker. The broker can help the borrower determine which bank to seek financing with, and help assemble the application package. Mortgage brokers often bring well-developed relationships with lenders, a thorough understanding of the lending process, and the ability to match your specific needs to the best products available.

Having somebody to help draft the loan package and navigate the waters can sound very appealing, and it is a valuable service. A mortgage broker's assistance does come at a price, however. Mortgage brokers charge a fee for their services, usually somewhere in the range of 1% to 3% of the total loan amount at closing. Brokers may charge up-front fees as well, which are not refundable. Regardless, the brokers' fees increase your costs, and thus your cash outlay.

Also, it is wise to be wary. Ultimately, it is to the mortgage brokers' advantage to generate as many mortgage applications as possible. They are trying to grow their pipeline just like you are. As such, in my experience, some mortgage brokers will overpromise regarding potential mortgage terms or the likelihood of approval.

Another option that offers some advantages is a mortgage

banker. While a mortgage broker is an independent entity that forwards your loan application on to the lender for processing and ultimate approval, a mortgage banker is actually granted authority by the lender to process loans on their behalf. Basically, mortgage bankers offer a convenient way for life insurance companies and financial institutions to lend money without having to process loan applications in-house.

Dealing directly with a mortgage banker has the advantage of streamlining and expediting things for the borrower. Also, because a mortgage banker does not typically collect any fees unless the loan closes, they are apt to be more diligent in vetting borrowers up front and not wasting your time.

None of these conveniences come cheap. Given the cost of a mortgage broker or a mortgage banker, it can be beneficial to work directly with banks as much as possible. But an honest and reliable mortgage broker can be a great resource and match you up with the ideal lender. And a good mortgage banker can help craft a financing package that will work best for you and efficiently process your loan application.

As with any vendor or partner, you are advised to seek referrals and check references. Even with the assistance of a professional, the loan application process is too time-consuming and cumbersome to justify taking chances on an unknown.

THE SOLAR BUILDING PROJECT: PART IV

 Mixed with the jumble of other emotions that followed the Solar Building closing were feelings of gratitude and relief. Most people would never know, but we had managed to finance the purchase with a traditional bank loan, even though it was a foreclosure auction, which required us to close within 30 days of our winning bid or lose our deposit.

In my experience, this kind of speed and service from the bank and attorneys involved were truly extraordinary. Because of the 30-

day closing requirement, foreclosures usually need to be paid for with all cash, or some alternative source of expensive short-term money. The attorneys and local bank that we had been working with for years had really stepped up and come through for us.

We had reached out to the bank several weeks before the auction took place to get started and they agreed to work with us without even knowing if we would be the winning bidder. Once we won the auction, everything was lined up. They proceeded to expedite all of their internal processes and leveraged their relationships with third parties to get it done. Working with me to meet the deadline was an exceptional demonstration of partnership and commitment by everyone involved. I was both impressed and appreciative.

Pulling off the closing must have depleted all my luck though, because bad things started to happen right away. Shortly after passing around the pepper spray, we received our first call from a tenant. My property manager informed me that it was a complaint—somebody was standing at the top floor atrium railing and urinating on the roof of the exposed elevator.

Unfortunately for everyone involved, there was an open grate on the elevator ceiling for ventilation, and the people inside the elevator (quite understandably) didn't appreciate the unexpected shower. We quickly huddled to discuss proper protocol for handling such a situation.

We came up blank. Oh my God. What had I gotten us into? Was this the diamond in the rough I had imagined? Or had I gone too far this time? It couldn't get any worse... could it? We cleaned the elevator and committed to accelerating our timetable for the installation of security cameras.

The following morning, I did my first walk-through as the new owner. While touring a vacant unit on the second floor, the quiet stillness of Tuesday morning was shattered by a woman's terror-stricken screams for help from upstairs. It was bloodcurdling. I asked my property manager to call 911 and ran up the stairs, petrified at what scene might await me. An apartment door was wide open at the top of the stairs and the screams emanating from within came to an abrupt halt just as I arrived.

I burst through the open doorway and was confronted by a wiry, shirtless man whose most striking feature was a wide grin that revealed rows of broken, jagged, and yellow teeth. I took in everything at once—the foul odors and completely trashed apartment, his sideways baseball cap and filthy, drooping pants. The baseball bat in his hand.

In barely decipherable words, he strung together a series of expletives asking who the hell I was, what the hell I was doing in his apartment, and telling me to get the f@#% out. His assurances that everything was fine did little to ease my concern. I backed up but stayed in the doorway, shifting uncomfortably and trying to ignore the nasty threats being lobbed my way. The standoff lasted about five minutes until the police arrived, and I walked away badly shaken.

The police came downstairs about 10 minutes later and informed me that this skinny man's obese girlfriend claimed to have fallen in the shower and was stuck in the tub. Unable to extricate herself, she grew increasingly panicked and began screaming for help.

Wow. Not what I expected. I was glad the skinny guy had stopped me from rushing all the way in.

This was the beginning of an ugly war with one of the property's worst tenants. At wits end and concerned about the safety of other tenants and my staff, I eventually decided to use a technique landlords refer to as "cash for keys." I bribed them to move out peacefully with a fat wad of cash, and screwed the door shut behind them so they wouldn't decide to sneak back in. "Cash for keys" is an approach I've rarely resorted to, but I felt it was the right thing to do in this instance.

Later that same day, I questioned why an apartment door was smashed in. Apparently there had been a major drug raid, and the tenants had been hauled away. Looking through the abandoned apartment, I wondered about things that hadn't occurred to me before.

How long is a landlord obligated to hold a vacant apartment for tenants who had been arrested? What should we do with the crack pipe and needles left behind—aren't those evidence or something?

Do we have to store them because they are the tenant's property? The questions later proved pointless as neither the tenant nor the police ever returned to the unit.

I wondered if the bank found out about all this stuff whether they would ever lend to me again. I decided if the answer was no, I wouldn't blame them. To be continued…

KEY POINTS

- ▶ Investors should work hard to cultivate positive relationships with banks. It's not easy to borrow money and a good lender is one of the most valuable business partners you can have.
- ▶ Securing a mortgage from a bank can be an onerous process. There is significant documentation required and approvals often come with many contingencies.
- ▶ In addition to credit worthiness and general project feasibility, underwriters confirm that a project's debt service coverage ratio (DSCR) and the loan-to-value ratio (LTV) are within their established lending criteria.
- ▶ Mortgage brokers and mortgage bankers can help a borrower assemble a loan package and professionally navigate the lending process. This valuable service comes at a price, so investors should carefully weigh the pros and cons before taking this route.

POST-ACQUISITION

CHAPTER 9

RUN YOUR REAL ESTATE AS A BUSINESS

"Sometimes if you want to see a change for the better,
you have to take things into your own hands."
—CLINT EASTWOOD

"The most effective way to do it is to do it."
—AMELIA EARHART

■

WHEN YOU CLOSE ON a commercial property, it can and should feel like a tremendous accomplishment. It can take an extraordinary amount of work and determination to get through the acquisition process and come out on the other end with a solid investment property that's a good fit for you.

Successfully reaching this point sets you apart from the vast majority of prospective investors. You're now a doer, not a dreamer, which bodes well for the future. But the reality is that there isn't a lot of extra time to stand around patting yourself on the back. Because now you're open for business. You have a product. You have customers. You have bills to pay. You've got work to do.

Such a call to action goes counter to the mainstream view of real estate as a passive investment. Truly passive investments—like stocks or bonds— require little or no work. You buy them and then sit back in your recliner and collect your checks. You let others do the work. You're on the sidelines and don't have any influence on the outcome.

This image of real estate is likely rooted in the evolution of the industry. For centuries, the ultra-rich owned large quantities of real estate and paid other people to oversee their assets. That perpetuated the view that still exists today—that real estate can generate wealth without getting your hands dirty. This is a view that has been hammered home by decades of get-rich-quick schemes and seminars appealing to that illusive dream of easy wealth.

As a result, real estate is more commonly viewed as an "asset class" than an actual business. It's been shoehorned and packaged as a passive investment, even for assets such as apartment complexes, which are management intensive. Owners are called "investors" instead of entrepreneurs or small business owners.

Now, I'm not going to pretend there aren't passive investment opportunities in the real estate world, because there are. Legal instruments are structured specifically for the purpose of facilitating such arrangements. You might hold a land lease, or a building that you rent to Family Dollar with a true NNN lease. Land leases and NNN leases are types of commercial real estate investments that shift all of the financial burden and the management responsibilities to the tenant, leaving the investor with little to do but cash the rent checks.

These types of investments are a good fit for some investors. Workload is low, risks are low, and... *returns are low*. But if you're motivated to build an empire and accomplish something truly extraordinary, you have to go into it with the correct frame of mind.

Small investors who want to get the maximum value out of their investment can't get their desired outcome by being passive. They need to run their real estate like a business.

If you're able to take it on, a willingness to be actively involved in managing your properties can be one of the largest competitive advantages at your disposal.

PROPERTY MANAGEMENT

One of the first decisions you'll face as an investment property owner is whether to outsource property management or do it yourself. Yes, a business is an investment. And yes, any business can generate passive income by outsourcing management. But is that the wise thing to do when you're first getting started?

Based on my experience I'd say no. Part of my own success is unequivocally rooted in the fact that I've run my real estate business with the same level of attentiveness I'd have given to a barbershop, a dry cleaner, or any other entrepreneurial venture.

Those first few properties are absolutely critical to your success, and if you self-manage, you're putting yourself in a better position to determine your own fate. How motivated and determined are you? If you

> *"Some people want it to happen, some wish it would happen, others make it happen."*
> —MICHAEL JORDAN

are truly driven to succeed and refuse to fail or settle, you will set standards that a third-party management firm just cannot achieve.

Excellent property management companies are rare, and even the best of them will never care about the property as much as an owner. Self-managing also frees up considerable cash flow that can be reinvested to improve your odds of success.

Management Fees

If the lack of attentiveness alone isn't enough to convince you not to outsource your property management, then certainly the management fees should give you pause. Avoiding the typical fees paid out to a management firm by keeping things in-house can dramatically improve your cash-on-cash returns.

Your typical management firm charges anywhere from 3% to 7% of the gross income depending on the property and the market, with larger properties falling on the lower end of that range. That's not a slow-drip leak of cash; it's a steady stream! As we learned in Chapter 1, there is a significant long-term cost associated with this lost cash.

Can you negotiate the management fee down, or find somebody to do it for less? Sometimes. I've seen management fees as low as 1.5%, but it doesn't provide much incentive for the management company to give the asset adequate attention, so you'll likely wind up paying for it in other ways. The lower the fee, the less aligned your interests are with those of the management company.

Lessons from Franchisors

What are the primary factors that determine whether a business succeeds or fails? One place we can look for answers is in the franchise industry. Based on their experiences with thousands of business owners, franchisors know what to look for in their prospective franchisees. They establish criteria for who they will allow to open a business in their network.

One of the most common requirements for franchisees is that the owner be present. Franchisors hate absentee ownership and in most cases it is prohibited. Why? Because statistics show that there is a significantly higher failure rate among businesses with absentee owners. The same is true in real estate, where an involved owner can make a substantial difference in the business performance.

Taking Control of Your Destiny

The opportunity to take control of your own destiny is part of what makes real estate appealing to many prospective investors and should be weighed when considering how to manage your investments. I'm not a big fan of luck. I prefer to take fate by the horns and turn it in my favor through brute force of determination. This approach can help you be successful in real estate and in life.

> *"Either I will find a way, or I will make one."*
> —PHILIP SIDNEY

The benefits of self-management can be lasting even if you don't take it on for the long term. Once an investor has established a large portfolio and is seasoned in the art of property management, they are in a much better position to navigate the selection and oversight of a good management firm. But for some investors, self-management is just not a viable option. In this case, you take on the role of an asset manager, which we will discuss later in the chapter.

THE BUSINESS STRATEGY

Looking at things from a more technical viewpoint, there is a fairly interesting strategy underlying self-management. When you deconstruct the traditional commercial real estate model, you'll realize that the "value chain" has multiple links to it—in other words, it's layered with people taking their cut and making money.

You've often got portfolio and/or asset managers who are overseeing property management, and then property managers who are overseeing a stable of contractors, each of which is eating into the revenue that the investment property generates. That rent is feeding a lot of people.

When small investors jump in and manage their own property or do other work themselves, they are effectively collapsing the value chain, allowing them to not only operate more nimbly and efficiently, but also to keep all the fees and costs that would have been portioned out by each party along the chain.

In business strategy terms, this is called "disintermediation," which is just a fancy way of saying you are cutting out the middlemen.

More important than what you call it is the oodles of cash you save. When these savings are in turn reinvested back into the business, whether it be through property improvements or additional acquisitions, it helps create more equity and accelerate your business's growth.

The same rationale can be applied across all areas of your real estate business. For example, you might evaluate the feasibility of doing your own marketing and leasing, or landscaping and snow removal. Or even brokering your own deals, writing and reviewing your own leases, and managing small construction projects.

DO YOUR HOMEWORK AND KNOW WHEN TO CALL IN A PROFESSIONAL

Doing any or all of the work associated with your property can help you manage your own destiny and save you money when you're just starting out. My advice is to be open to as many things as possible. Don't be afraid to try, but do your homework—research whatever you're doing and talk to people with experience.

 The knowledge you gain and your experience doing various tasks will also serve you well later as your business grows and your personal role evolves to focus more on leadership and management. You're at a distinct advantage managing staff or contactors if you've actually done the work yourself. You'll understand the nuances and get a lot more respect.

Will you make mistakes? Absolutely! Lots of them! But that is how you learn. You either get things right the first time, or you chalk it up to a learning experience. That's how you need to look at it. Don't be paralyzed by fear or nothing will ever get done.

> *"The only people who never tumble are those who never mount the high wire. This is your moment. Own it."*
> —OPRAH WINFREY

Now does this mean you should do *everything* yourself? Absolutely not. A successful business owner knows what they *can* do and what they *can't* do. You need a team. This doesn't mean that you necessarily need *employees*. It means you need to have a network of professionals in place that you can turn to for assistance when something comes up that requires their expertise.

It's extremely important not to overstep your bounds and do something that should be handled by a professional. Admittedly, determining what to do yourself and what to outsource can sometimes be difficult. It often requires a level of objectivity and self-awareness that is beyond what many entrepreneurs possess.

When considering whether to do something yourself, some questions to ask yourself include:

▶ What skill set is required to get the job done? Is it a skill set I possess or can learn?

▶ Can I carve out the time necessary to do the work? Can I complete it in the timeframe required? Will it mean that other more important responsibilities won't be fulfilled?

▶ What are the potential consequences if the work is done poorly? Is it something I can live with? What costs might be incurred and how do those costs compare to the savings of doing it myself?

For example, based on these questions, when I acquired my first property I felt pretty confident that I was capable of walking the property each morning and picking up trash before I went off to do my day job. I knew I could get up a little earlier and fit it into my mornings, and I knew I'd do it with a level of attention to detail that I wasn't likely to find in a contractor or employee. In fact, I could do most of the general maintenance duties on the property—squeezing them into my lunch hour, or doing them later in the day or on weekends.

But I was also keenly aware of my limitations and I knew, for example, that I had to call in professionals to do things like service the steam boiler or to do plumbing and electrical work. What are the potential consequences of doing electrical work if you're not qualified? Well, death is a pretty big one that comes to mind. Extra crispy. No thank you.

Other tasks might be regulated or just too unpleasant for most people to handle. Recently I got upset when I saw a $5,500 cleaning charge from one of our contractors. As our manager explained it to me, "That was for the two units last month where the residents passed away. Unfortunately, the bodies were not discovered until several days after they died. Due to the condition and circumstance, we needed to have the units professionally handled to deal with the bodily fluid issues."

Hmm… yeah, um, OK. That's one of the few tasks I'm not prepared to tackle myself. And if I wouldn't do it myself, I'd never ask my staff to do it either. Let's leave that one to the professionals as well.

We'd been fortunate to have had only one tenant die in his apartment in the last five years. Then suddenly there were two in one month, neither of which were found right away. That's bad luck for us. But admittedly far worse for the two tenants—and the people who found them.

BUILD A TEAM

Most tasks that need to be completed when managing a property are much more mundane than cleaning up dead bodies. Whether it's contractors or employees, it can be tempting for entrepreneurs to hire help before they really need it. Don't fall into that trap. You need to be particularly cautious when considering bringing on an employee.

The maxim I've tried to follow is "slow to hire, and quick to fire." My experience in business and real estate strongly supports this as the right approach. Remember that extending an offer of employment is easy, while firing is difficult. But getting the timing wrong on a hiring decision can be extremely damaging. Likewise, hiring the wrong person can be a devastating blow to a startup. And keeping that wrong person on too long can be fatal. Once you realize that someone isn't going to work out, it's best to tear that Band-Aid off.

Understand that being "slow to hire" doesn't mean doing everything alone. The best approach is to build a strong team. To surround yourself with the people you need to help guide you and that you can call on when needed.

The team is likely to consist initially of advisers you can bounce ideas off of, and also contractors, consultants, and professionals that can work for you on a contract or hourly basis. Once your business grows, it will eventually include employees.

Always be an active, hands-on manager, even when you outsource work or parts of your operation. This means going the extra mile in a way that most property management firms would not. You do your research to find the best contractors. You get multiple bids and walk through each of them with the bidders. You check references. And you inspect the work as it's completed and ensure high quality. You stop by when you can to stay on top of things—being caring and attentive in a way that only an owner can be.

Almost every activity associated with managing a property can be outsourced. For the sake of preserving cash, you're encouraged to do as much of these activities as you can yourself. But, as discussed, you need to use good judgment and know when to call in a professional. Good contractors are extremely valuable to a real estate investor, so finding them and establishing solid relationships should be a high priority.

You will find a fairly comprehensive list of the kinds of key contractors and other partners you might need, together with explanations, in Appendix B. Please take the time to familiarize yourself with this list. It's fairly long, but depending on the nature of your property, what kinds of projects you might be undertaking, and what you're doing yourself, the actual list of contractors that ends up on your speed dial is likely to be much shorter.

The process of hiring and managing contractors is not something that comes easily for most people and is one best learned through experience. Finding the good contractors can be difficult, and it's a road often fraught with difficult lessons learned. But set high standards and don't be deterred. The best of us will make mistakes when hiring contractors or other service providers. The key is to recognize when things aren't going well, then promptly fix it, learn from it, and move on.

Outsourcing work to contractors is also important because it allows you to slow and limit the need to hire employees. Contractors will remain necessary even as you begin to grow. Commercial real estate will typically create an irregular demand for specialized services, and it doesn't usually make sense to bring staff on board when there isn't enough work to keep them steadily productive.

Only when a need can be consistently sustained over time is it worth considering hiring an employee. Even then, it can sometimes be better to outsource. This is particularly true if bringing an activity in-house might require a substantial investment in equipment or distract you from your core focus on taking care of your tenants.

For example, on paper my company could easily rationalize hiring an employee and bringing our contracted daily office cleaning in-house. A simple calculation would say that it could save us money. But we have to weigh all the other considerations.

The cleaning company has other staff to cover when an employee calls in sick or quits without notice. If we did it ourselves, how would we get cleaning done if our staff person quits? We'd have to go through the potential lengthy process of advertising a vacancy, scheduling and conducting interviews, extending offers, waiting for the new hire to become available, then training them. Am I prepared to work extra eight-hour shifts cleaning every night in the meantime?

And what if, after a few days, we realized that our new employee wasn't going to work out and we had to replace them and start all over again?

The cleaning company has a core competency at cleaning. All of their new hires are provided with training on the proper methods to clean, products to use, etc. They have them watch videos and shadow other more experienced people. They spot-check the employees and do cleaning the right way. We have exacting office tenants so this level of quality control is important to us.

Are we prepared to take on that level of responsibility? It would be a distraction, and we'd be unlikely to perform as well because we're not in the cleaning business.

These are the kinds of considerations you need to give before hiring an employee. It's worth the effort to be deliberative. Remember it's easy to hire. But it's disruptive and stressful to fire.

THE TIPPING POINT

As your business grows, your role will need to evolve. While it's quite feasible (depending on the size) for one person to self-manage one or two properties, and even do much of the hands-on work, this becomes less realistic as you grow.

> *"Even if you're on the right track, you'll get run over if you just sit there."*
> —WILL ROGERS

If you've been agonizing over the decision of whether or not to hire an employee, it's going to get worse as your workload continues to expand. The debate over whether to hire at some point is likely to elevate from painful to downright excruciating. That is a good sign that it's time to take action! This is probably a tipping point and what you decide to do can be pivotal for your business.

Again, consider all of your options. You may in fact elect to move forward and hire an employee, but you could also elect to rely even more heavily on contractors. Or you can take a step back and completely outsource property management. As discussed, there is a trade-off here that needs to be carefully weighed.

Also think about whether you really need somebody full-time. Can you start with somebody part-time? Maybe consider hiring through a temp agency so you can try a person out, and have a window of time to see if you really need them. A trial period can be a good idea, whether you're hiring through a staffing agency or hiring directly.

If you elect to hire, be prepared for your role to shift because managing employees carries a broad spectrum of implications. You will become a coach, a cheerleader, a mentor, a supervisor, and a leader. While you may have started out managing contractors, this is different. Contractors work relatively independently, while employees are going to expect, and in most cases require, some closer direction.

In a life that's already busy, where will you get the time to fulfill all of these new roles? With each added responsibility, you'll have to hand something off to make room. This might mean that you eliminate some of the more tactical and menial tasks from your daily routine and entrust those to others. Time previously spent raking leaves or painting, for example, might now be spent dealing with human resource issues.

As your staff grows, your responsibilities should continue to evolve until you're a full-blown CEO. It becomes your responsibility to set direction, make the most important decisions, and cultivate the most valuable relationships with lenders, brokers, and other critical partners. You'll be the rudder steering the ship.

Recognize that your own behavior will set the tone going forward—you will be the one others take their cues from. If you started out on your own, you'll command more respect. You'll have a better understanding and appreciation for everyone's job, because you've done them all yourself.

This can make you a great boss, or it can make you a poor one. While your experience can help you coach and empathize, you're going to have to learn to let go and delegate. This is not easy. But when there is too much else to do, you're left with no real choice.

If you're not CEO material or don't enjoy the trials and tribulations of managing other people, you can hire somebody to fill that role, you can sell your portfolio, or you can outsource the management.

ASSET MANAGEMENT

There is a wide range of very good personal and professional reasons that, despite the drawbacks, an investor may need to rely on a property management firm. There are also quality-of-life considerations. The potential superior returns of self-management might not be worth the price it could exact in other areas of your life, and it may not mesh well with your personal goals or priorities.

These and other valid reasons can compel investors to outsource property management, knowing that they're making a trade-off.

This is a less desirable position for all the reasons already touched on, but thousands of investors rely on property management firms and make it work. And if they are fortunate enough to connect with one of the better management companies, it can alleviate stress and work very well.

Another option is to do your own property management initially, and then outsource more down the road. If you elect to outsource management, whether it's to start out or after growing your business to a certain size, you should at least commit to being an active asset manager. As an asset manager, I'm referring to your role as the manager of the property manager.

In such a situation, you are well served to be selective in choosing a property management firm and stay on top of them. Ideally you would still try to visit the property as often as possible (even daily if feasible), and review all reports in detail. I recommend insisting on a monthly report showing all journal entries (every individual expense and income transaction), and I'd review every single one, keeping an open line of communication with the manager.

Consider scheduling a standing weekly one-hour meeting with the property manager for full updates. Ideally you'd hold that meeting in person, because there is so much at stake. Think of your property like a vulnerable loved one entrusted to someone else's care. Best to make sure she's attentively looked after!

If you're not able to commit to this basic level of involvement, you may need to reconsider whether real estate is the right path for you. It is possible to make money as a passive investor (and many people do), but you need to accept that the upside potential for a passive real estate investment is substantially lower, and that it will remain, for the most part, outside of your control. Such concessions might be worth it depending on your goals. Just go into a passive real investment opportunity with your eyes wide open and accept the risks.

If you're ready to take the plunge and manage your real estate like a business, roll up your sleeves and get to work! Set high standards. *Make yourself successful.*

KEY POINTS

- ▶ Investors should not think of apartments and other commercial real estate as passive investments. Real estate is a business like any other, and running real estate like a business is the surest way to grow an empire.
- ▶ Investors who are willing to do as much of the work as they can themselves can cut out the middleman and dramatically boost returns.
- ▶ Know your own limitations and don't take unnecessary risks. Develop a network of professionals who are at the ready, and always hand things off to them that you're not qualified to do yourself.
- ▶ As your business grows, you will reach a tipping point and your role will need to evolve. Doing everything yourself will no longer be feasible.
- ▶ There is a wide range of reasons that an investor may need to rely on a property management firm. These investors should be active asset managers. If even that is too much, they should reconsider whether real estate is the right path.

CHAPTER 10

ADD VALUE, ADD VALUE, ADD VALUE

"All intelligent investing is value investing—
acquiring more than you are paying for."
—CHARLIE MUNGER

"The wisest landlords know that repairs and improvements
are an NOI financial game. They know that it is not always wise
to minimize operating costs at the expense of income and equity
gains. They understand that these operating costs are
in fact another form of investing."
—GARY KELLER

■

ONE OF THE BEAUTIES of commercial real estate is that property values are more easily measured and controlled than in residential real estate. For income properties, the value is directly correlated to net operating income (NOI), which is the difference between the gross income and expenses.

Average cap rates may cycle up and down for different types of assets across the industry, but they are directly applied to NOI in order to determine a property's value. This is in stark contrast to residential real estate, where the use of comparable properties for valuation is more prevalent.

The implications of this are extremely important. It means that by taking steps to boost income or cut expenses, you can directly impact a property's value. *This is hands-down one of the greatest things about commercial real estate. It is within your power to change*

NOI and thereby directly influence the value of your property.

As a prospective commercial real estate investor, it behooves you to develop a thorough familiarity with net operating income and its role in wealth creation—because boosting NOI creates value. Within the industry, the projects that accomplish this kind of forced appreciation are called "value-add."

The ability to add value is one aspect of commercial real estate that appealed most to me right from the beginning. This was a refreshing difference from other types of investments that are more passive, like stocks or bonds. Individual investors in publicly traded stock, for example, cannot usually do anything to affect the stock price.

When I started my commercial real estate business, it was very satisfying and motivating to realize that improvements I made in a property were creating a very real value—additional equity that could be calculated. And there were a variety of ways to accomplish this, many of which could be identified prior to making an acquisition. In other words, you could get more than you paid for.

THE NUTS AND BOLTS OF VALUE-ADD

Remember that NOI reflects both the income and expenses. Boosting income or reducing expenses (or both) will increase your NOI and proportionally drive up the value of your property. For reasons we will cover later, it's best to focus on boosting NOI over the long term and be less concerned about the shorter-term effects of your decisions on NOI. Make the decisions that will improve NOI five years into the future.

For example, let's assume you purchase a 12-unit apartment building and one of the units is badly damaged and not rentable. You figure out that it will cost you $10K to renovate this unit and bring it up to a level you are comfortable with. You estimate that it will rent out for $500 per month, without any significant increase in your monthly expenses. Is it worth it? Let's figure it out.

First we look at the increase in income that will result from leasing the unit.

$$\text{\$500/month} \times \text{12 months} = \text{\$6,000 per year}$$

Now, let's look at the cash-on-cash return for our investment in the renovation.

$$\text{\$6,000/\$10,000} = 60\%$$

Well, that certainly beats the stock market!

Now we can look at the equity created by the improvement, which is the resulting increase in the property's value. Let's conservatively assume the prevailing cap rate for apartments in your market is 9%. The value added by renovating the unit can now be calculated as follows:

$$
\begin{aligned}
\text{Value Added} \quad &= \text{Incremental NOI / Cap Rate} \\
&= \text{\$6,000 / 0.09} \\
&= \text{\$66,667}
\end{aligned}
$$

So for a $10K investment in renovating a unit, you can create more than $66K in measurable equity in your property. This additional NOI would contribute directly to the property valuation in an appraisal. The renovation is a slam dunk. Yes! Get to it!

When you can identify value-add opportunities like this prior to acquisition, you're lining yourself up to create incremental value in your portfolio. In effect, you're also changing an acquisition's risk profile, making it more attractive. This approach can accelerate your business's growth through one of two ways:

▶ Increased equity, which can be partially leveraged to provide an infusion of cash for growing your portfolio.
▶ Improved cash flow, which can be siphoned off over time to do additional value-add projects or accumulated for future acquisitions.

So when you're evaluating properties, it's worth investing some effort to identify where such opportunities might lie. This requires careful due diligence and no small amount of creativity. Pay close attention to any ways you might improve the NOI, either through reduced expenses or boosting revenue.

Here are some examples of ways that you might be able to add value to a property:

1. **Changing its use.** Often a property can be repurposed, in part or in all. An example might be converting any underutilized common space into leasable space. Storage space can be upgraded to office space. A three-bedroom apartment might be converted to two one-bedroom apartments. Once you're established you can consider undertaking larger change-in-use projects. Last year we successfully converted a distressed hotel into studio apartments.

2. **Improving utility efficiencies**, including water, gas, electric, etc. Investments that can reduce utility consumption over the long term can lead to significant drops in expenses and boosts in NOI. Examples might include installing water reducers in faucets and showers, insulating hot water piping, putting lights on motion sensors, installing new LED lighting, etc. Often such improvements can qualify for incentives through utility programs. In some cases, the upgrades can even be completed for free.

3. **Improving a property's quality and image** to command higher rents. Sometimes even small improvements such as fresh paint and landscaping can make a dramatic difference, particularly when coupled with improved customer service and responsiveness.

4. **Creating new sources of revenue.** Examples might include signing up for a cable company revenue-share program, installing an ATM or vending machines, or renting out storage space or excess parking capacity.

5. **Marketing a property.** Sounds too easy, but many commercial properties are not marketed at all. A little signage and advertising (even limited to free advertising such as on Craigslist) can be enough to boost occupancy levels.

6. **Raising or lowering rents.** When a property is not closely managed or is not locally owned, rents are often not adjusted to reflect a shift in market conditions. If rents are too high, it can result in low occupancy levels. In this case, implementing more competitive rates can fill a building up. When rents are too low, existing rents can be slowly raised, either through annual bumps or by charging full market rates when units are vacated.

7. **Changing staff or vendors.** Sometimes a property will carry unproductive or even destructive staff that can be replaced or eliminated. Or vendors and service providers might be in place that are overcharging. Seeking out competitive bids and thoroughly investigating all options for getting work done can yield some nice dividends. Likewise things that have previously been outsourced might be done in-house, or vice versa—the most sensible approach depends on the specifics of the situation.

8. **Better property management.** Lucky for us value-add investors, a shockingly high number of commercial properties suffer from neglect or are poorly managed. Poor property management can manifest itself in innumerable ways, including bloated expenses. Improvements in property management can yield perhaps the biggest returns of all, driving down expenses and boosting income. Taking over a property that has been poorly managed is like opening a treasure chest of value-creation opportunities—you never know what you're going to find to add value!

The above list is in no way intended to be comprehensive. In fact, it's nothing more than a small sample. Opportunities to add value to a property are only limited by your own creativity and determination. The more you do it, the more you'll learn and the better you'll get at it. Value-add is also a mindset and should be viewed as an ongoing process.

MANAGE NET OPERATING INCOME

Many of the value-add projects you implement will be investments in capital improvements, such as the apartment renovation example earlier in the chapter. What is less obvious is that it's just as important to create value slowly over time, through much smaller investments made routinely over months and years. Intentionally directing small expenses for the purpose of boosting long-term NOI is called "managing your net operating income," and it's an important extension of the value-add concept.

The single most important step to effectively managing NOI is to constantly consider how your decisions, large and small, will affect NOI *over the long term*. And while it might seem counterintuitive, you should note that in most cases, maximizing NOI over the long term means accepting a *lower* NOI over the short term. This is because from an accounting standpoint, many value-creating improvements will be captured as expenses. Larger improvements will be capitalized and depreciated over their expected life.

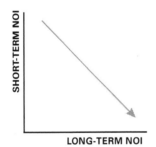

Let's examine this in the context of some of the value-add scenarios provided in the prior chapter. For example, say that you decide to paint the main lobby of your apartment building, do some new landscaping, or update some lighting fixtures. The immediate short-term effect is that your expenses go up and your NOI will be lower. But enhancements such as these tend to improve a property's image, and little by little, they add up to make the property more appealing. A more attractive property retains tenants, attracts new ones, and may also allow you to command higher rents.

Long term, the higher occupancy and higher rental income translates to higher NOI and therefore a higher valuation.

One of my favorite types of projects is the water and/or energy conservation upgrades mentioned earlier, many of which are eligible for utility company incentives. Such projects have quick paybacks and gaudy returns, particularly in older properties. They are also a gift that keeps on giving, both through reduced expenses, and the higher equity resulting from the long-term boost in NOI.

Savvy investors are always looking for the best ways to trade NOI today for the strongest future cash flows and value creation. I purposefully try to keep these kinds of "improvement expenses" high. That's right—even though cash is king, I boost my expenses intentionally.

Why would I try to keep expenses high? I do it because if I'm strategic about what I spend my money on, those investments can boost my overall return. I do it for the long-term value creation and higher future cash flows. Or if the market heads south, I can keep rents steady and offer tenants greater value, which puts me in a better position to weather the storm.

Boosting expenses in this manner is not wasteful. It is the strategic and purposeful reinvestment of a property's income into small projects that can yield a high return. Employed properly, the strategy adds value and maintains a company's growth.

Managing Income Taxes

In addition to creating long-term value, there are also significant tax advantages associated with managing short-term NOI. This is because the associated expenses reduce your short-term profits. At the end of the year, investors will need to pay income taxes on any profits generated in the business. I highly recommend that you find a good tax accountant with real estate experience to help guide you through this process and answer any questions that might arise. For investors just starting out, and particularly for value-add investors,

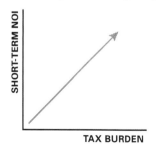

profits are typically nominal, and a significant portion of otherwise taxable income can frequently be offset through depreciation.

As your business grows, reinvesting cash flow into carefully chosen expenses (those associated with improving a property's performance) can play a larger role in reducing your near-term tax burden while yielding a higher long-term return on investment. In some cases, income taxes can be dramatically reduced or even eliminated through the higher expenses, particularly when combined with the additional depreciation associated with capital improvements.

> "I am proud to be paying taxes in the United States. The only thing is I could be just as proud for half of the money."
> —ARTHUR GODFREY

This strategy can keep money in your business and working hard for you—money that would have otherwise gone to the IRS. It keeps rocket fuel in the business instead of giving it to the government.

And perhaps more importantly, it also commits you to the steady improvement of your properties, which makes your tenants happy, improves your competitive position in the marketplace, lowers your risk, and will eventually yield a higher cash flow.

As a value-add investor the reinvestment process can continue indefinitely, though it's likely that the returns associated with upgrades will diminish over time. Not all improvements yield equally large returns, and at some point you'll work through the most attractive ones. Once returns start to decline, you should be able to gradually scale back on improvements while still maintaining a high standard. This is the point where you are likely to see your greatest jumps in cash flow and NOI, which positions you well for refinancing.

Unfortunately the higher NOI will result in higher income taxes. But if you refinance and pull out some cash, the higher interest payments can offset some of the income and mitigate the tax burden.

An Uncommon Practice

A commitment to adding value by managing NOI can be highly effective, but it's also extremely rare. Why doesn't everyone take this approach? Simple. Too many investors are distanced from their properties and focused on the short term. The overwhelming majority of apartment and commercial real estate investors are pulling as much money out of their investments as they can justify.

As discussed in an earlier chapter, many commercial investors have syndicated their acquisitions or have obliga-

> *"Strategy is about making choices; it's about deliberately choosing to be different."*
> —MICHAEL PORTER

tions to return cash flow to investors, so they don't have a choice. Others are trying to jack up short-term NOI to position a property for a sale. But to achieve maximum success over the long term, I believe that it is very important for any business to reinvest in itself. And real estate *is* a business.

If your goal is to maximize wealth creation over the long term and you're in a position to be patient, managing NOI can be a powerful strategy. In my own investing, it didn't take me long to realize that the projects where I was able to add the most value were consistently my biggest success stories. I became focused on identifying properties where there was a clear path to upside potential—ways to create that added value.

The more poorly the property was being managed when I acquired it, the more excited I was. This is because such situations offered the most potential to add value just by stepping in and turning them around. And it was even better when I could avoid debt by funding improvements with the property's own cash flow.

This was the case with my first investment property, the office building where, similar to Harry Potter, I worked from the cubby under the stairs.

THAT FIRST PROPERTY

My first investment property had already been on the market for a couple of years by the time I set eyes on it, and a long line of people tried to talk me out of buying it. Nobody wanted to own this building, primarily because it was losing about $40K per year, but also because the absentee landlord had completely let things go.

Breaking down the financials revealed problems on both sides of the balance sheet—income was hindered by a high vacancy rate, and expenses were out of control. Sounds like a great property, doesn't it? I saw lots of potential. And as I peeled back the onion, I kept seeing more of it.

Digging deeper into the numbers, three expenses stood out above the rest: utilities, taxes, and salaries. Now, other than reading stacks of books on the subject, I had limited knowledge of operating an office building. In fact, I remember when I walked into the boiler room for the first time. It pretty much looked like the interior of a space shuttle to me.

But I took the time to do my due diligence and dug deeper into each area of concern as best as I could manage. My research regarding the income and expense situation revealed four areas where I could add value:

▶ **Utilities**: Over the course of the six months I had the property under contract, I noticed that the tenants were using the only method available to them for adjusting the temperature— opening the windows! In the summer, the air-conditioning system was set to run continuously on full blast. Since all that AC made it uncomfortably cold, the tenants would open their windows to let some warm air in.

In the fall, the AC was turned off and the boiler was turned on. That was also set to run continuously at full blast! Of course this meant that the building was now uncomfortably hot in the winter, so windows were opened to let cold air in. I didn't know much about heating and air-conditioning systems, but I was pretty confident this wasn't the way it was supposed to work!

▶ **Taxes**: A review of the tax record showed that the property was assessed at nearly double what I was going to pay. A visit to the assessor's office confirmed that the assessment had already been challenged by the seller and was set to be reduced the following year.

- ▶ **Salary:** There was one full-time employee—a superintendent who took care of the property maintenance. He was frustrated by the long-distance owner's unwillingness to spend money and, not surprisingly, that seemed to have left him devoid of motivation. During one of the inspections, I discovered that the superintendent had set up a large woodshop on the property to refinish furniture during his "spare time." The woodshop was tastefully decorated with pornographic pinups.

- ▶ **Rental Income:** Area brokers shared with me that the sellers were overly stingy and had a reputation for not paying commissions. For this reason, most brokers refused to show the building to prospective tenants. In addition, the property was clearly not well maintained—trash littered the property, landscaping was overgrown and unsightly, and the existing tenants were quick to express their frustration with management's unresponsiveness and lack of upkeep.

This assessment of the utilities, taxes, salary, and rental income situation was promising because I thought they could all be addressed. But I knew I was going to have to find a way to turn things around without spending much money.

Even though I had assumed the seller's mortgage to acquire the property, I used most of my personal financial resources to cover the rest of the purchase price and closing costs. Most of the savings I had accumulated over the preceding years was now gone. In fact, not only did I invest all of my savings into my real estate business, but I also drained my retirement account. I was also carrying a lot of personal debt, including student loans, a mortgage, and a car loan. In hindsight, I can see that extending myself the way I did could be considered reckless, and I certainly do *not* recommend it.

So that was the situation I found myself in. I had very little in the way of cash reserves, but I was determined not to fail. I was convinced I could make this work.

Let's fast-forward to six months after closing to see how each of these items was addressed.

- **Utilities, Value Added:** The first day I owned the building I asked the superintendent how to adjust the thermostat. He didn't know. He said it was locked and he didn't have a key. I called the customer assistance number for the thermostat manufacturer and they walked me through how to unlock it and program it.

  I changed the settings so that it didn't just run on high, but actually fluctuated according to the temperature. I also set it to turn down at night and on weekends. I had an energy audit completed free of charge by the local utility and implemented a wide range of low-cost improvements, including things as small as weather stripping or putting the bathroom lights on motion sensors. The gas and electric bills dropped by 50% in my first year of ownership.

- **Taxes, Value Added:** After the sale, I followed up with the tax assessor and provided information regarding the transaction and the property's historical financials. In the first year after the sale, the assessment was dropped close to the price I paid for the property, cutting the tax burden nearly in half.

- **Salary, Value Added:** I fired the superintendent before the end of my first day as owner. And I replaced him with... *me!* I had very little relevant experience, but enough to get by. I can sweep, shovel snow, and change lightbulbs just as well as the next guy. I can even do a passable job with painting and planting flowers. And for stuff that was too technical, I knew I could use contractors as necessary until I reached a point that I could afford to hire a good maintenance technician.

- **Rental Income, Value Added:** I had numerous face-to-face meetings and lunches to establish relationships with the local commercial brokers. I agreed to always look out for their interests and pay their commissions if they secured an agreement with a new tenant. I had sit-downs with every tenant. I took copious notes and followed up on every suggestion and idea I could. I couldn't afford major improvements, but the most common complaints weren't expensive to fix—they were things like keeping the grounds clean or planting some flowers.

My first investment property

So I scoured the property daily for litter and tended the landscaping. Through a combination of broker leads and word of mouth, leasing activity picked up, and the building started to fill.

Results

Addressing these four items turned the property around and made it cash flow positive, literally from day one. There were plenty of mistakes and setbacks along the way, but the net operating income continued to steadily climb over the first two years of ownership, eventually creating an opportunity to refinance and pull some money out to grow my portfolio. I was learning how to manage NOI, even though I didn't realize it.

Transforming this investment property was like rolling a big boulder up a bumpy mountain. Lots of slipping, stumbling, bumps, and bruises, but all the while pushing higher. It was a rewarding experience though, if sometimes painful. It was also very educational, and the lessons I learned proved valuable moving forward.

KEY POINTS

- ► One of the greatest things about commercial real estate is that values are directly correlated to NOI. Boosting income and/or reducing expenses will directly drive up the value of your property, and projects that accomplish this are called "value-add."
- ► Investors should try to identify value-add opportunities prior to acquisition. This approach creates incremental value and accelerates business growth through increased equity and improved cash flow.
- ► Savvy investors find ways to trade NOI today for the strongest future cash flows and value creation, combined with significant tax advantages. This might involve purposefully keeping "improvement expenses" high or "managing NOI."
- ► A value-add mindset over the long term also commits you to the steady improvement of your properties, which makes your tenants happy, improves your competitive position in the marketplace, and lowers your risk.

CHAPTER 11

LOWER RENTS AND LEASE IT UP

"I like to think of sales as the ability to gracefully persuade, not manipulate, a person or persons into a win-win situation."
—BO BENNETT

"Stop selling. Start helping."
—ZIG ZIGLAR

∎

'M ALWAYS SURPRISED BY some landlords' willingness to sit on vacant space for long periods of time, holding out for the highest possible rent and the best possible tenants—tenants that all too often never materialize.

It's natural for a landlord to want to maximize his rental income, but that doesn't mean charging the highest rent. There are multiple factors that influence rental income. The tendency is for landlords to focus on how much they are charging per square foot (SF) of space and to try hard to maximize this number.

Charging the highest rent you can command per square foot is a risky game, however. This is because it's difficult to gauge exactly how high you can go, and there are consequences for overcharging, even if you can find some poor sucker to pay it.

You're much better off focusing on providing tenants with a good value. Tenants gauge "value" by weighing what they're paying versus what they're receiving. You want to make sure that your tenants feel good about that equation. The benefits of providing superior value far outweigh any shortsighted attempts to grab high rents.

Here is what happens when your rents are at or above the market rent:

- You are more likely to sit on vacant space for longer periods of time.
- Assuming you confirm a tenant's ability to pay, it reduces your pool of potential renters.
- Your tenants are more likely to leave for cheaper space when their lease expires, which increases turnover and downtime.
- For commercial tenants, the rent burden can make it harder for their businesses to be profitable and survive.
- For residential tenants, it's harder to maintain a budget and stay current on rents due.
- Tenant expectations are understandably higher when they pay more.

OK, now let's compare that to charging slightly below market rents and providing superior value:

- You're more likely to sustain high-occupancy levels, keeping your overall property income higher.
- Tenants are less likely to leave, reducing turnover costs, marketing costs, and the cost of carrying vacant space.
- Commercial tenants are more likely to survive and be successful. They will view you as a partner in that.
- When you set your rates a little lower, you increase the pool of prospective tenants, including tenants that could afford to pay much more but are attracted to the value of what you're offering. Don't assume that higher rents are going to filter out the bad tenants and assure good ones. That's definitely not always the case.

Sitting on vacant space for extended periods of time can be very costly, as can high turnover. You lose time and money every time you need to prep apartments for new renters or commercial space for a new business.

To help illustrate, let's return to our two investors, Winston Carter and Judy Smith. Each is the proud owner of identical small 5,000SF retail plazas with five storefronts. Both have recently become completely vacant and ready for lease-up.

Investor A is Winston Carter. Winston tells his property manager that he wants to charge $25 per square foot for space in his plaza. The property manager tells him that seems a little high. Similar properties are typically getting $22 to $24 per square foot. Winston insists on the high price, because he has calculated that at $25 per square foot, a full plaza will bring in $125K per year, and that's the target number on his spreadsheet.

So what happens? The property manager spends a lot of money on advertising and manages to lease up three of the spaces, though it takes two years to secure the tenants and he has to take whoever is willing to pay. He ends up with an odd mix of tenants—a physician on one end of the plaza and a vapor shop on the other.

Even at its peak, the property is earning:

$25/SF/YR × 3,000SF = $75,000/YR

But in truth, Winston is not earning this much. Why? Because he spent a lot more than Judy on marketing and sat on vacant space for so long. He collected almost no rent during the first year. Depending on who he leased to and the terms of the leases, he might eventually lose a tenant or two. He got greedy. He is swimming upstream and going nowhere fast.

Investor B is Judy Smith. Judy has her finger on the pulse of the market, and prices space in her plaza at an attractive $20 per square foot, which is below market. She gets a lot of interest in her storefronts and is able to be selective when choosing her tenants. It's full within six months. Annual income is now at:

$$\text{\$20/SF/YR} \times \text{5,000SF} = \text{\$100,000/YR}$$

Judy is now in a good place. Here current income is a third higher than Winston's after the two-year period, and she brought in substantially more rent over that same two-year period.

Tenants are getting a good value and want to stay, so it's a win-win situation for all parties. Judy can still gradually raise rents in the future, or experiment with slightly higher rents if a space opens up. But she might not want to. She has put a small cushion in place to protect herself from downturns in the rental market. She has managed her risk and done a good job of maximizing her income over the long term, thereby improving the value of the property.

THE RIGHT TENANT MIX

It's also important to screen tenants thoroughly and get the right tenant mix. As you place tenants into a property, it's like selecting the proper ingredients to bake a cake. If you get it right, the results can be fantastic. If you mess it up, the results can be wretched.

This same philosophy holds true for both apartments and commercial space. If you have apartments, think about who your target demographic might be. For example, if you have a lot of quiet senior citizens, it might not be the best idea to market to college students. Or maybe you have a building full of young singles, in which case it might not be a great idea to promote the property as family friendly. It really all depends on the specific situation and nature of the property. But the goal is to create an environment where tenants are living in harmony and can create a long-term home for themselves.

"What helps people helps business."
—LEO BURNETT

In commercial properties, getting the right tenant mix is just as critical, if not more so. Tenant compatibility can play a significant role in the success or failure of a business, and since commercial leases are often for longer terms than residential, it can be more difficult to correct mistakes in a timely manner. In addition, commercial tenants often place a very high value in a property's image and reputation. Medical practitioners, for example, tend to want to be in a property with other health-care providers.

Multitenanted commercial properties can best be described as a business ecosystem. Preferably, each tenant helps contribute to the success of the other tenants. Customers of one tenant will frequent neighboring tenants. So you are well advised to consider in advance what kinds of businesses fit well with others and which ones might clash. If you don't know, you can always ask your existing tenants. But for the most part, it's common sense.

You don't want to put a marijuana dispensary next door to a children's store, for example. But putting the dispensary next to a pawnshop, liquor store, or tattoo parlor is probably fine. You also don't want to put a nail salon right next door to a competing nail salon, unless you want an all-out war on your hands.

Just try to put yourself in the shoes of the business owners—who would you want as your neighbor? If it doesn't feel right, you should probably go with your gut instinct. If you get it right, the tenants will help each other thrive. But if you get it wrong, things can break down quickly. Tenants can turn on you, and on each other, and it won't end until somebody leaves. Though even then, resentment and hard feelings can linger.

Sometimes mistakes happen even though you make your best efforts. We placed a medical practitioner next door to a higher-end restaurant and didn't foresee any issues. But when the restaurant eventually changed ownership, the new proprietor started staying open later and marketing drink specials. The restaurant eventually evolved into a popular nightclub.

Next thing we knew, there were nightly arrests for disorderly conduct, Facebook videos of lewd dancing at the club, and the property was getting trashed. Who could blame the doctor for being upset when he found the common areas littered with empty beer cups, bottles, cigarette butts, etc. The situation reached a head when the doctor's staff arrived one morning to find that one of the bar patrons had vomited in front of their entry door.

How do you avoid this kind of situation from happening? A competent attorney will ensure your lease defines specifically what business purposes the space is to be used for, so that the tenant who is a good fit doesn't change into one that is a poor fit. And make sure you include a list of building rules, or at least the right to implement them.

When you get it right, business can blossom for all of the tenants, making your investment a strong and stable property. I spoke with a spa owner recently who attributed the health of her thriving business to the referrals she got from neighboring tenants in her plaza.

In addition to her spa, this particular plaza includes a Subway restaurant, an insurance office, a chiropractor, a physical therapist, a vet, and a hair salon. This is nearly an ideal tenant mix as there is significant overlap in the business's target customers and yet no direct competition. All of the tenants gladly refer their customers to one another, boosting each other's business significantly and reducing the need to spend money on marketing. It functions as a healthy ecosystem and everyone benefits. That's how it's supposed to work.

SCREENING TENANTS

Even if a tenant fits perfectly with the desired tenant mix, you should still do a background check on them. This is particularly true of residential tenants and smaller local commercial tenants.

You'll be doing yourself a favor by implementing a thorough screening process. This is simply not an area where you should cut corners. There are a variety of reasonably priced tenant-screening services available online that will check a prospective tenant's credit score, collections, and criminal record. Do this to avoid headaches and to protect your property, but also to ensure the safety of your existing tenants.

You should also have prospective tenants complete a simple application, and take the time to collect and check references. For residential tenants, you should always speak with prior landlords and verify their income levels.

For commercial tenants, this can be a little tricky. If they have a current location, they are often less willing than residential tenants to grant you permission to speak with their landlord. If they're a new business, that is always a risky proposition, and it may come down to using your best judgment and a self-assessment of whether you're willing to take the risk.

 New business failure rates are very high. But depending on the supply and demand in your location, you might decide it's a worthwhile risk. Personally, I like helping entrepreneurs get started. But a lot of them fail. I try to sit down ahead of time and have an open conversation where I share my concerns and assess what level of planning they have done, how they're going to be funding the startup, their experience, and so forth to get some level of comfort.

You're taking a big chance when you lease to a startup. While you might not have as much on the line as they do, you're betting on their future. Being their landlord is almost like being an angel investor. Portions of your fates are now intertwined to an extent. It would not be out of line to ask for a copy of their business plan.

For locally owned businesses, your attorney should include a personal guarantee in the lease, even though the likelihood of actually collecting anything is low if they fail. This is a guarantee that binds the business owner personally to the obligations of the lease, in addition to their business entity. If nothing else, including such a guarantee reinforces that this is a serious commitment on their part.

Your attorney should also ensure that there is a provision in the lease prohibiting subleasing of the tenant space without landlord approval. Subleasing without permission can be dangerous because it fills your space with a tenant who skirts the screening process. Once somebody takes up residence in your property, it affords him or her certain rights even if they aren't the ones on the lease agreement.

We had a student who left the area during his summer recess and sublet his apartment to a drug dealer. He did his own advertisement on Craigslist and just rented it to the first person he could find, even though subleasing was prohibited in the lease. By the time we discovered what was going on, the drug dealer was already ensconced in the apartment. Now we had to go through two evictions—one for the tenant we leased to originally, and one for the sketchy person he sublet to. While it might not seem so at first, having the appropriate lease language in this instance was critical. It didn't prevent what happened, but it gave us grounds to promptly rectify the situation.

In another instance, one of our commercial tenants decided to sublease her retail storefront to a business that was a direct competitor of our tenant leasing the adjacent space. In this case we had inherited her lease from the prior building owner and it didn't have the proper language to protect against such a situation. We eventually worked the problem out, but it was messy, and we were not able to deal with the offending tenant from a position of strength. The experience really reinforced the importance of having a sound lease.

RAISING RENTS

Your operating costs are likely to rise over time due to cost-of-living increases, and you may need to raise rents to maintain your margins. But when you do raise rents, it should be done with care, and in a way that won't traumatize tenants. You're walking a fine line. If the rent places a high degree of business or emotional stress on a tenant, they will feel forced to investigate other options.

New property owners are often the guiltiest parties when it comes to raising rents. When you acquire a property where you know the rents are below market, it can be tempting to jump in and raise rents immediately. Ratcheting up rents like this is not usually the right approach.

As a new property owner, cash flow should be looked at as the top priority in the near term. Are you better off collecting below market rents, or collecting no rent at all? Have patience and don't be greedy! As long as you accurately analyzed the property before acquiring it, you should have ample NOI to pay the bills. If you have good tenants in place, it's generally best for everyone if rents are raised more gradually.

In addition to the business argument, there are moral considerations as well. For example, you may buy an apartment complex with elderly tenants living on fixed incomes. Even if you could replace them, is jacking their rent up really the right thing to do? I would argue that it is not.

When your property is mostly full and you have a unit open up, that would be a good time to raise the rent. Make sure that the recently vacated space is up to your standards when you advertise it, then raise the asking rent on that space up to market levels, or slightly below.

Again, give the highest priority to filling a property, and then look to increase rents over time. This mitigates your risk (especially for multitenanted properties) and the rent increases are better tolerated when the tenants see value being added over time.

Another thing to consider is that, regardless of what your plans are after a closing, a change in ownership of apartments or other commercial property often creates fear in the tenants. Rumors often run rampant. In some instances these fears have prompted tenants to leave our properties even though we had the best of intentions. As a result, we've learned how critical it is to have an open line of communication and reassure tenants. This means meeting with them immediately after closing to introduce yourself and clarify your intentions, or preferably prior to closing as long as the seller is agreeable.

RENEWALS

Another common mistake that landlords make is focusing too much effort on marketing and undervaluing existing tenants. It almost always costs a lot more to secure a new tenant than it does to retain an existing one.

In addition to the up-front costs of securing a new tenant, you are taking on the risk of an unknown commodity. Are they going to be a problem? Who knows? You can screen all you want—believe me, you will still get bad tenants. For residential tenants, they could be criminals, drug dealers, not pay their rent, or be flat-out crazy.

Seemingly great prospective tenants can quickly turn into a huge pain in the butt, or even turn out to be downright scary. One of our new apartment tenants was a surgeon, for example. He would pass anyone's screening. But when a neighbor complained of rodents coming from the surgeon's apartment and we notified him we needed to do an inspection, he freaked out and threatened to sue us if we entered.

Sometime over the next couple of days, he moved out in the middle of the night without telling us. When we figured out he had left and entered the apartment, our staff found blood stains on the floors, an empty organ transfer cooler, blood streaks on the white refrigerator, and blood in the freezer. Huh?!

We called the police, who tested the blood and later notified us that it was not human... Try as we might, we had a lot of trouble coming up with a plausible explanation for these findings that wasn't disturbing.

We've had tenants who turned out to be *all kinds* of bad news. More than one who walked around outside naked, trash hoarders, sexual predators, and a "nice" little old lady who tormented her neighbors incessantly and claimed we were poisoning her through her electrical outlets. One tenant tore out all the plumbing, electrical, and heating fixtures, and covered every surface of their apartment in scripture. Biblical verses were even carved into the hardwood floors. Chains were bolted into the walls.

While the vast majority of these nightmare tenants were inherited when we purchased distressed properties, sometimes a horrible tenant can slip through your screening process, like our surgeon. Another one of our tenants was a perfectly nice and well-qualified older lady. How were we to know that she had a 30-something mentally disturbed son who would sleep over on her couch most nights? That he was violent and would harass the neighboring tenants?

How would you figure that situation out ahead of time if the

tenant isn't forthcoming and doesn't list him as a co-occupant on her application? The answer is simple—you can't. It's just one example from a million different real situations you could encounter, and it's a very tricky business. Commercial tenants can be all kinds of dreadful as well. Just because somebody is a business owner doesn't make them any less likely to be disturbed.

As your portfolio grows and you deal with more and more tenants, you're going to encounter horrible situations on occasion despite your best efforts to avoid them. There is little you can do other than carefully screen tenants, keep a close eye on things, and be aggressive in dealing with problems early on before they spin out of control. Insurance can help limit your exposure to major costs. Requiring tenants to carry their own renter's insurance can also help cover the costs incurred by certain situations.

The point is not to scare you, but to reinforce that every new tenant is an unknown and a risk. Meanwhile, somebody who has already been a tenant and demonstrated that they are stable and reliable is really worth something. Something extra. Good tenants are valuable and should be treated as such.

This means that you should dedicate a substantial amount of effort toward ensuring that good tenants are well taken care of and make sure they renew their leases. For many investors, renewals are often forgotten until it's too late—you might not hear from a tenant whose lease is coming up for a renewal until they've already signed a lease at somebody else's property. I know this for a fact, because I have lured good tenants from inattentive landlords numerous times!

MARKETING

There is a wide range of ways to market properties and attract tenants. The methods we have generally found to yield the best return on investment are the following:

- ▶ Signs, both temporary and permanent
- ▶ Word of mouth
- ▶ Referrals from existing tenants
- ▶ Brokers
- ▶ Online classifieds
- ▶ Facebook
- ▶ Press releases and PR

In terms of biggest bang for the buck, we have had the most luck with signs, free online classifieds such as Craigslist, and broker referrals. For apartments and apartment open houses, Facebook advertising has also been effective.

The appropriate marketing channels can also depend on the target demographic. While we have had limited success with newspaper advertising, for example, it can sometimes be more effective with an older demographic.

In addition to the above avenues, we will occasionally approach an ideal tenant directly, particularly when trying to market a vacant commercial space. Any tenant that you think might be a good fit (who doesn't currently own their own space) should be considered a prospect.

LEASES

Many people new to commercial real estate are intimidated by the idea of leases—primarily due to a lack of knowledge. The truth is that leases are not particularly complicated. Most of the language in a lease is fairly easy to understand, legalese notwithstanding. Writing a lease or even knowing what to include is another matter altogether.

If the idea of writing a lease sounds daunting, you're right. It would be quite a monumental chore to sit down and write one from scratch. Fortunately, you'll never have to do that unless you're a real estate lawyer. Remember, you're purchasing an investment property with tenants in place, and with those tenants will most likely come existing leases that you'll review during your due diligence and then inherit at closing. It might be a good lease and it might not be, but it's yours going forward.

When you secure a new tenant, you'll need to prepare a lease. You have several options here. Some investors elect to recycle the lease template they inherited with the property. They just change out anything that's different such as the tenant name, dates, term, rent, etc. I don't recommend this approach unless you have a qualified attorney review it first and make any necessary edits.

If you are going to prepare leases on your own, the best option is to have an experienced real estate attorney create a lease template for you to use that includes all the safeguards and provisions necessary to protect your interests as the landlord. Don't try to write it yourself, use one your cousin emails you, or pull something off the Internet. You won't have any way to know whether somebody qualified created it. Also, be aware that a landlord's legal rights and the associated lease provisions can vary by state and the specific type of real estate.

Here is some of the basic information you should expect to include in a lease:

- ▶ **Parties**: The landlord and tenants are defined using the full legal names of the business entities.
- ▶ **Premises**: The specific location of the space the tenant will be occupying, including a street address and, when appropriate, a suite number. It may also reference common areas that are shared with other tenants.
- ▶ **Use**: How the space is to be used by the tenant. For a commercial lease this will usually be for a specific type of business operation.
- ▶ **Term**: Defines the start and end dates of the lease. There may also be renewal options included for the prospective extension of the term.
- ▶ **Rent**: The monthly rent obligation is defined, including the dates and amounts of rental increases.
- ▶ **Improvements**: When the premises are to be altered in any way, the scope and responsibilities should be defined.
- ▶ **Maintenance, Utilities, Taxes, and Insurance**: The lease should define responsibilities for maintenance, utilities, property taxes, and insurance. Maintenance responsibilities may be different for the premises and the common areas.
- ▶ **Deposit**: The amount of the security deposit is defined, together with the conditions under which it is to be retained or returned.

These are the main clauses, though this is certainly not intended to be a comprehensive list. Your attorney will help ensure everything that you need is included, and once you have a strong template it can be fairly easy to use.

This is particularly true for apartments and self-storage because there is so little variation from tenant to tenant. You may only need to change the names, dates, and unit number each time. Commercial leases on the other hand can be substantially more complicated, and when in doubt, get help from an attorney. You can use an existing lease as a starting point, but remember that almost everything is negotiable in a commercial lease.

I use lease templates for all residential tenants and also for small commercial tenants. I do this to save money, and I accept the risks involved. Resources I have turned to for reference include the books *Negotiating Commercial Real Estate Leases* by Martin Zankel and *How to Succeed in Commercial Real Estate* by John Bowman. But I always engage the services of my attorney when there is a lot at stake. This is particularly the case when dealing with a national tenant. For me, determining when to seek counsel is a judgment call and another occasion where I'm weighing the cost of an attorney versus the risk of doing it myself and making a mistake.

There is no need to let leases or the potential need to use an attorney cause you anxiety. It's just part of doing business and there is nothing scary about it. People hire attorneys to assist with the legalities of buying a home all the time. A good attorney can help you. In fact, if you're really uncomfortable with leases, you can abandon the idea of templates and have an attorney do all of your leases. Many commercial investors elect to take this approach, though it is less common with apartments since the leases tend to be more uniform. You need to do what's right for you and only take on as much risk as you're comfortable with.

THE LIMITATIONS OF A LEASE

In my experience, the average person overestimates the power and enforceability of a lease. That's not to say they aren't important, because they are. But even the best lease can be difficult to enforce and can sometimes leave you with limited recourse. This is particularly true when dealing with apartment tenants or smaller local commercial tenants, compared to regional or national commercial tenants.

A lease, while binding, is primarily intended to make sure that all the expectations for both parties are clearly understood and documented. In theory, both parties are happy with the situation. It's a symbiotic relationship, for better or for worse. But when one party or the other becomes deeply determined to part ways, the situation can get ugly and the lease becomes tenuous.

A lease isn't some divine document that's going to save you, no matter how well written or thorough it is. For one thing, regardless of what terms are in a lease, both a tenant and/or a landlord are capable of making life positively miserable for the other if things fall apart. Either party can hang their hat on some lease "violation" whether actual or fabricated.

We had a national office tenant whose local manager desired to relocate across town for personal reasons. So he rallied his employees and made our life hell. They complained every day to their corporate headquarters facility manager about everything you could imagine. The temperature was too high or too low. It was high in one area and low in another. They would hide clumps of dirt and complain if the cleaning crew didn't find them. They claimed there was mold and made their corporate facilities department hire a company to test the air (no mold was found). Every day we received strings of emails and angry phone calls, claiming we were not fulfilling our obligations under the lease.

When they finally pulled up stakes and left, we were relieved. In what could only be described as karma, their newly relocated office was soon shut down by corporate. And that office manager who spearheaded the campaign against us? He submitted his résumé to our property manager in search of a job. He let us know how impressed he was with our level of professionalism and responsiveness. Would we have a position for him in our company? Um, no.

When a tenant defaults on a lease, whether it's failure to pay or leaving early, you have some hard decisions to make. The terms of the lease may provide you with the ammunition to seek recourse on a default situation, but other factors come into play. How much will the legal bills add up to if you take legal action? Are you prepared to fight an 800-pound gorilla? And for the smaller tenant who defaults, does the person you're preparing to go after have the resources to pay up, even if ordered by a judge to do so?

> *"Discourage litigation. Persuade your neighbors to compromise whenever you can. Point out to them how the nominal winner is often a real loser—in fees, expenses, and waste of time."*
> —ABRAHAM LINCOLN

The most common way that a residential or commercial tenant breaks their lease is a failure to pay rent. Or they move out early. And 90% of the time a tenant leaves or doesn't pay it's because they don't have the money. If it's a business, they are probably circling the drain. If it's a residential tenant, then maybe they lost their job, or maybe they have an addiction, or maybe they took on too much debt. There are a thousand potential reasons, good and bad. The point is you can't squeeze blood from a stone. Yes, the lease binds them to pay. But if they leave and you take them to court, how do you expect to collect? You have to look at each situation individually, but the practical reality is that it's often difficult to recover enough to offset the legal bills you'll incur going after somebody.

For an apartment tenant who owes money when they vacate, we have found it to be more economical to hand the matter off to a collections agency, who will pursue the tenant on a commission basis. A collections agency can sometimes have more leverage because a failure to pay can now affect a tenant's credit score. While it might cost you half of what's owed, what do you really have to lose? And it avoids having to front legal costs that may very well never be recouped.

If the tenant owes back rent but stays in place, there is other recourse. The laws governing eviction vary by state, but most allow for a three-day notice to "pay or quit," which compels a tenant to pay all the rent due within three days or move out.

While we started off using an attorney for all evictions and terminations, we eventually learned the process, and now we do most of these ourselves for apartment tenants, though we still rely on attorneys if there are any out-of-the-ordinary circumstances. We also rely on attorneys for any legal actions that we elect to take against commercial tenants.

Some landlords feel compelled to aggressively go after anyone who defaults, to set a precedent and let everyone know not to trifle with them. Others turn to lawyers based on their emotions running high. If possible, should you find yourself in such a situation, try to look at it in a pragmatic way. Make the best business decision you can.

On different occasions, I've weighed the situation and fallen on either side of the fence. In those cases when we've elected to go after commercial tenants who've broken their lease and left early, our success rate in recouping damages above and beyond our legal fees is about 50%.

THE SOLAR BUILDING PROJECT: PART V

 In the midst of all the chaos and excitement at the Solar Building, our property manager was reviewing the lease situation to see what kind of recourse we might have for some of the more appalling activity that was going on. What we found wasn't particularly encouraging. The old property management firm had left rudimentary one-page leases for about two-thirds of the tenants, and the rest of the tenants' leases were either missing or nonexistent.

We consulted with our attorney and realized that we were actually in a better position than we had feared. Because the existing leases were month to month, he explained, it would actually be easier for us to get rid of a problem tenant when compared to longer-term leases. Basically, he explained, the month-to-month term worked in both directions. Just like the tenant could terminate at any time, so could the landlord. We just needed to give one month's notice and we could avoid going through a protracted eviction process. A month seemed like an eternity to me given some of the things we were dealing with, but it gave us something to work with. In fact, we later decided to use strictly month-to-month leases until the property was turned around.

Armed with this new information, we decided it was important to get into each apartment to see exactly what we were dealing with. And the tenants weren't the only ones that were completely out of control here—so were the cockroaches. They were *everywhere*, and we needed to find the source. So we decided to kill two birds with one stone, and promptly scheduled a pest control company to inspect and treat the entire building. We gave every tenant the required notice to enter in advance, explaining the importance of addressing the pest issue. We then sent two of our staff around with the pest control technician to ensure his safety, while also using it as an opportunity to view the apartment units and take notes.

They didn't make it past the first floor of apartments before they encountered a problem. I got a phone call. "Hey, Brian. I know the plan was for us to take notes, but you're going to want to see this one. You're not going to believe it."

Hmm... I told them I'd be right there. This couldn't be good. We were due for our luck to change though. Maybe, I thought desperately, they are in shock about how *nice* this unit is and want to share the good news. Maybe the tenant had fixed it up and it's gorgeous! But as quickly as this thought materialized, I knew it wasn't plausible. It was more likely they encountered another tenant stuck in the bathtub. I braced myself for the worst.

When I stepped through the apartment door into its dark front hallway, the foul, acrid odor hit me like a physical blow and stopped me in my tracks. My first thought was, how could somebody live here? I looked around with wide eyes. The entry hallway felt uncomfortably cramped because along the walls were stacks and stacks of old trash, going all the way up to the ceiling in some places. What was left was a narrow path, winding down the middle. It felt oppressive. I covered my mouth and nose, and took a few steps forward toward a lit opening on the left.

As I peered through the opening I could see a stove and refrigerator and realized I was looking into the kitchen. The refrigerator was practically buried in mounds of garbage, and it reached the ceiling in places, just like in the hallway. There was a harsh yellow light on the ceiling, and as I studied the trash, my eyes were having trouble focusing for some reason. I felt momentarily disoriented. I leaned forward a little, put a hand up to shield my eyes from the glare, and took a closer look at the heaps of refuse. It's at this point that I heard a soft rustling sound, like from a pile of dry leaves. That's when I realized that *the trash piles were moving.* Then everything crystalized and I knew exactly what I was looking at. I stared with revulsion and amazement. The mounds of garbage were absolutely *swarming* with cockroaches. UGHAAAH! I guess we found the source of our infestation.

The tenant who lived there turned out to be a nice person, though clearly unwell. He was meek and scared, and extremely uncomfortable with anyone being in his apartment (cockroaches excluded, apparently). Our staff tried to help him, but he insisted we leave. He did agree to start cleaning up if we brought him supplies, which we gladly dropped off for him later. We were concerned for this tenant's well-being and called around to various social agencies in the area trying to find assistance, but a couple of days later he left without telling us, and we never saw or heard from him again.

The rest of the apartment visits were eye-opening as well, if not so dramatic. Our staff members were yelled at by some tenants, but were warmly welcomed by others. Between the apartment inspections and some online searching, we were able to get a much better overall picture of the tenant base. In addition to the trash hoarder, the rent roll at the time included an assortment of criminals, people living in various states of squalor, and lots of tenants with random, weird, and/or disturbing possessions or behaviors that made us frown, scratch our heads, and wonder.

It was nice that we were starting to get to know some of the Solar Building tenants. I wasn't going to add any of them to my Christmas list, but at least we had a better handle on who and what we were dealing with. So the question now was what to do next? This was supposed to be a real estate investment, but it was starting to feel more like we were on a reality TV show. I was trying to turn a property around. Add value. Not risk lives or go to war. What would happen next? Who the hell knew? To be continued...

KEY POINTS

▶ Setting rents slightly below market can help mitigate risk and maximize value by reducing turnover and keeping occupancy levels high, ultimately creating a higher, more sustainable NOI.

▶ It's important to screen tenants, maintain the right tenant mix, raise rents slowly, and place a high priority on retaining your best tenants.

▶ Focus your marketing efforts on channels that provide the greatest return on your investment. This may include signs, free online classifieds such as Craigslist, broker referrals, and Facebook.

▶ Leases are important legal documents and are mostly enforceable, but investors should recognize that they have their limitations.

CHAPTER 12

DOING THE RIGHT THING

"Do the best you can do. Never tell a lie.
If you say you're going to do it, get it done."
—CHARLIE MUNGER

"Many novice real estate investors soon quit the profession and
invest in a well-diversified portfolio of bonds. That's because, when
you invest in real estate, you often see a side of humanity that
stocks, bonds, mutual funds, and saving money shelter you from."
—ROBERT KIYOSAKI

■

ONE THING I REALIZED pretty quickly is that a commitment to operating with the highest level of integrity would be a key competitive advantage and imperative for long-term success. Why? Well, first off, it's just the right thing to do. We all need to be able to look at ourselves in the mirror and sleep at night.

To be successful as an entrepreneur you need to sustain a high level of motivation. If you feel good about your work, it can help fuel the passion necessary to be successful in both yourself and your employees. In fact, good feelings and positive energy are contagious, and they can extend beyond your company walls to motivate third parties to work harder on your behalf. People want to help other people who are doing the right thing!

The reverse is just as true. Do things the wrong way and nobody wants anything to do with you. Cutting corners and conducting yourself unethically is shortsighted and will always come back to haunt you in the end. When people have a bad experience, it can also blow up and spread like a highly infectious disease.

Lashing out at somebody might make you feel better or even benefit you in the very short term. But remember you can't take it back and those types of incidents don't stay private for long—especially in today's social media world. Next thing you know the story is told, shared, and it's further exaggerated as it spreads. Until you are Satan. It's extremely difficult, if not impossible, to put that toothpaste back in the tube.

INTEGRITY AS A COMPETITIVE ADVANTAGE

Doing things the right way has the added benefit of setting you apart from the competition. In my experience, there are some wonderful people in the real estate industry. I admire how they conduct themselves and I've made some good friends. But the industry is also a shark tank with a surprising number of people who are unethical, ruthless, pompous, corrupt, and/or overly aggressive jerks.

This assessment isn't intended to be pessimistic and you shouldn't let it deter you. While on the surface the pervasiveness of poor behavior in real estate might seem intimidating or even

> *"It is our choices that show what we truly are, far more than our abilities."*
> —J. K ROWLING

depressing, it's actually great news for you! Why? Because it means that an honest, hardworking landlord can be a breath of fresh air!

If a small investor establishes a reputation for integrity, excellence, and professionalism, it can be a powerful competitive advantage—particularly in smaller cities and towns where word of mouth spreads so quickly. Acts of kindness and doing what's right will consistently reap rewards over the long term. So don't be a jerk.

This means you conduct yourself in a way that earns the respect and appreciation of others. It means that people want to do business with you. They want to work for you. You honor your word as though it were a legally binding document, even if it means a significant financial setback. You always look at things from the perspective of others and show consideration. You always pay contractors, lenders, and vendors on time.

Perhaps most importantly, you also treat your tenants the right way. You make excellent customer service a cornerstone of your business.

KINGS AND QUEENS OF THE KINGDOM

 How important should a tenant be to you? They aren't really tenants, they are *customers*, and thus are entitled to great service. They are your source of cash, and cash is king. So that means tenants are the kings and queens of the kingdom. They are your livelihood, and you need to do right by them.

The truth is that tenants *are* your business so they should be just as important to you as your business's survival. Be a partner with your tenant. When you sign a lease, you've essentially gone into business with someone. Like it or not, your fates have become intertwined. Think of things you can do to make their lives better or their businesses more successful. And respond to tenant calls and requests as you would want to be taken care of if you were a renter... or better!

> *"There is only one boss: the customer. And he can fire everybody in the company from the chairman on down, simply by spending his money somewhere else."*
> —SAM WALTON

In his tome *Competitive Strategy*, Michael E. Porter observed that smaller firms are well positioned to gain a competitive advantage in circumstances where attentiveness and personal service are keys to success. What does this mean? Your excellent customer service can be another key strategy for outcompeting larger investors.

The Case of the Stolen Diapers

Recently, I walked into the office partway through an agitated conversation between two of our staff members. They filled me in on what was going on. They were at wit's end trying to deal with an apartment tenant. The woman was distraught because she had left a pile of cloth diapers in the common laundry room and returned later to find them missing.

Unfortunately, our security camera didn't have the right angle to see what had happened, and based on that, she decided that it was our fault. She posted her complaints to Facebook and shared her woes with the world. We asked to talk with her and she sent us an email stating that she was just too traumatized to speak with us. Her estimated dollar value associated with the stolen diapers crept upward like a thermometer on a hot day, and now sat at an impressive $300.

To me the solution was simple. I walked into my office and placed an order on Amazon for 20 new cloth diapers—more than she had lost. The total cost, including overnight shipping, was $33.58. I asked our staff member to stop by the next day and present her with the diapers. The woman was moved to tears by our gesture. She told everyone she knew. With a simple and inexpensive act of kindness, we converted her into an outspoken advocate for our company.

Was it our fault the diapers were taken? No way. But it wasn't really about who was right and who was wrong. Or at least it shouldn't have been. It was about the fact that we had a tenant who was very upset. She took what happened personally and felt violated. We're not a charity, but I think replacing the diapers was the right thing to do, both from a moral standpoint, and also for the business.

I've found that all too often emotions get in the way of good business decisions. It's important to remember that you're not just dealing with *tenants*; you're dealing with *people*. You need to really listen to them. Be thoughtful, and try not to take things personally.

And whenever possible, be proactive and look at things from your tenants' perspective in order to avoid complaints before they ever happen. If you lived there, what would you be looking for? What would your expectations be?

The Opera Singer

One of my managers returned from showing a commercial space located on the ground floor of one of our mixed-use apartment buildings. "An opera singer was interested in leasing the space as a place to give opera singing lessons to her students," the manager said. "I think they would be a great tenant, but I was concerned about whether or not the singing would disturb any of our other tenants."

"So what did you do?" I asked.

"I got permission to enter each of the neighboring units," she replied. "Then I asked the opera singer to sing while I listened on the other side. Wow, could she sing! What a voice! But there is no way we can lease to her unless we construct a sound barrier."

Hearing this story made me proud. I just loved the fact that my manager was thinking about keeping our tenants happy. She was thinking about what it would be like to live there and have to listen to an opera student futilely but determinedly try to belt out an aria. She was thinking about *avoiding* complaints altogether instead of just leasing mindlessly and then trying to react to complaints later.

On top of that, the manager was showing initiative and problem-solving. Instead of just saying no to the opera singer, she came up with a potential solution—soundproofing—that might allow us to accommodate the opera singer while still preventing potential noise complaints.

"Profit in business comes from repeat customers, customers that boast about your project or service, and that bring friends with them."
—W. EDWARDS DEMING

The manager approached the entire situation in a responsible way. Consistently doing things the right way will allow you to set yourself apart and come out ahead in the long run.

Unfortunately, no matter how proactive you are, there will always be complaints that need to be handled. How you deal with those is just as important as being proactive. When it comes to customer service, remember that there are also positive sides to having a tenant who is upset. First, tenants generally only complain when they still care. If something bad happens and they don't complain, they've probably already given up on you and are looking for their next place to call home.

Another thing to remember is that even if you completely disagree with what a tenant is saying, there is almost always at least a small grain of truth or something to be learned from what they are saying. The challenge is to set any defensiveness aside, show some empathy, and try to be as objective as possible—no small task when emotions are riding high!

And react promptly—it's too easy to procrastinate or hope that something blows over. As a property manager, you need to be the "mother hen" who steps in and resolves a situation before it escalates. Taking a hands-on approach demonstrates that you care and keeps tenants happy.

So does that mean a tenant is always right? I don't think so. Operating your business with integrity and delivering outstanding customer service doesn't mean that you need to tolerate the worst behaviors.

THE CUSTOMER IS NOT ALWAYS RIGHT

Tenants are the kings and queens of the kingdom, but even royalty can sometimes do things bad enough to get dethroned. Leases are a partnership and the tenant has their own set of obligations to fulfill. It's not OK for a tenant to lower their neighbors' quality of life. And it's never OK for a tenant to disrespect your staff, break the law, or put others' health or safety in jeopardy.

Tenants are people and some are going to be dishonest. Even worse, some can be dangerous. You're engaged in business with a tenant, so you need to screen them as well as possible, and then, when necessary, be prepared to get rid of the bad ones that might slip through. This is part of doing the right thing, both for the sake of your other tenants as well as for your employees.

A tenant is also obligated to pay rent and respect the property. We take good care of our tenants and strive to provide them with an exceptional value. But if they don't hold up their end of the bargain, then it's time to part ways. Dragging your feet or giving second, third, and fourth chances to a tenant is almost always a bad idea.

PAYING RENT

One of the most common causes of inner turmoil for investors arises when tenants fall behind on paying rent. This situation can sometimes create a lot of stress for landlords—particularly for those who are managing their own properties and have developed personal attachments to their tenants. What the "right thing" is in some situations can become very confusing and present moral dilemmas.

One time we had a tenant who was experiencing a medical hardship and found him unable to pay rent with no idea of when he might be able to resume paying rent, if at all. The staff liked this tenant—by all accounts, he was a very nice person. My property manager confided in me: "I feel bad for this tenant—he's in a difficult position. Would you consider letting him stay without paying rent? He's always paid on time in the past and everybody likes him. I'm not sure how we can evict him."

"Let me ask you a question," I replied. "If you knew this was a nice person, but he lived in another apartment complex and found himself in the same position, do you think our staff would all pitch in to pay his rent?"

"No, probably not."

"If we let him stay without paying rent, that's the same situation," I said. "Except that the money would be coming from me. I'm not saying we shouldn't help, but it's going to cost us the same as making a donation."

Landlords face heart-wrenching situations like this all the time, and it's a challenge to determine what the right thing to do is. Complicating matters is that once you cut somebody a break, word spreads and the floodgates open. You don't want to be put in the position of trying to decide which situation is more compelling than the next. And in addition to concerns about a tenant's well-being, you have responsibilities to your business, your employees, and all the rest of your tenants.

As a real estate investor, you're probably already giving back in different ways. In our case, we provide quality apartments to tenants at very reasonable prices, and we take on challenging projects that improve the community. We make modest charitable donations when we can, but at times, it's been a challenge just to make payroll. Which of these commitments would be most appropriate to sacrifice for the sake of waiving rent? I'm not sure there is a right or wrong answer to this question.

Every investor needs to feel good about the decisions they make, but "doing the right thing" can be subjective, and I believe it's OK to set some limits when it comes to providing financial support to people in need. There are organizations and programs available in most communities, and helping direct tenants to such resources when they face hardship is definitely the right thing to do.

In the case of the tenant with the medical problems, shortly after the conversation took place regarding how to proceed, the tenant in question had a further decline in health and was admitted to the hospital, so we decided that the right thing to do in this circumstance was to let him stay. After a couple of months went by without hearing anything, we decided to reach out to the tenant's family and see if we could work out some kind of arrangement. After our numerous messages went unreturned, we eventually sent a warning notice. Unfortunately, right after our notice went out, we learned that the tenant had passed away.

The family removed the tenant's belongings from the apartment, but left us a note. Instead of thanking us for allowing him to stay rent-free, the note blamed us for his death. It said that our warning notice was what killed him!

Did we conduct ourselves with integrity in this case and do the right thing? I guess it depends who you ask, but I know we tried to.

MAKING EXCEPTIONS AND CONCESSIONS

When dealing with commercial tenants, there may be additional factors to take into consideration, as they are in effect your business partners. I say this because your ability to collect rent from them is directly dependent on the success of their business. And as the landlord, you sometimes have a role to play in that. Depending on how the lease is structured, how you maintain a property can affect their business's public image, what kind of experience their customers have, and the tenant's ability to focus on their actual business instead of dealing with a leaky ceiling, HVAC problems, etc.

Over the years, I have cooperated with commercial tenants on various occasions to help them get a business launched or to try to work through difficult situations. If a commercial tenant has a specific hardship that you're in a position to help them weather, it might be to everyone's benefit to find a solution. Even if that means working out an alternative payment plan, helping them sublet space, or making an investment in the property that will help them succeed.

All that said, on those occasions where tenants were allowed to fall behind on rent or where we have decided to cut tenants a break, it has rarely had a happy ending. Tenants falling into financial hardship tend to have downward momentum that a landlord may be able to slow, but can rarely reverse. This is just the reality and another reason why it can be extremely difficult to determine what the right course of action is. An emotional appeal can be powerful and you may have a strong desire to help, but know that any investment is more likely to slow the bleeding than to stop it.

A landlord's generosity can also be taken advantage of. Most tenants are people of high integrity, but unfortunately there are also too many people that fail to honor their commitments. Oftentimes they assume that as a landlord you must be wealthy, and they rationalize their amoral actions by telling themselves that it won't really harm anyone. Know that as a real estate investor, you've become "the man" who some people won't hesitate to stick it to.

Not too long ago, a tenant with a dance studio came to me with a very emotional appeal. His business was failing and he told us it was because of the low quality of his dance floor. He broke down in tears as he explained that he was losing students. If a new floor wasn't put in, he was going to go out of business.

He asked for my help. He had taken a chance on this location and now was asking me to take a chance on him. It was time for his lease to renew, and he promised to stay. My heart went out to him. He was an entrepreneur trying to keep his business afloat and seemed certain that a dance floor would make all the difference. So I agreed to pay for a new dance floor. He gave me a hug, and I felt good about the decision.

We installed the dance floor one week later and the tenant loved it. But less than a month after it went in, he notified us that he was leaving. He had found a new location that he liked better. Not only did he break his lease, but we had just spent several thousand dollars on a new dance floor. And now we'd have to pay to tear the dance floor out in order to lease the space to somebody else. There was little we could do. The lease was backed by his personal guarantee, but he had no assets to speak of.

Unfortunately, I could share numerous other similar stories. Heart-wrenching appeals for help, followed by expressions of gratitude, followed by knives in the back. My generosity has been taken advantage of on too many occasions, and I've learned to be much more cautious. But that doesn't mean I have regrets. In each instance, we've consistently weighed all the information and tried our hardest to do the right thing for everyone affected by the situation. If it didn't work out, it's not because we didn't try.

From a business standpoint, it's generally advisable to adhere to lease agreements, and on any occasions that you do choose to give a concession, you are better

> *"To succeed it is necessary to accept the world as it is and rise above it."*
> —MICHAEL KORDA

off just accepting that the gesture might not to be returned or appreciated in the manner you might hope.

It can be difficult when you feel betrayed, but try to remember that getting appreciation is not why you do the right thing. Just focus on weighing all the information and making the best decision you can. You can't control how other people feel and conduct themselves. But you *can* control how you conduct yourself.

Ultimately, it is your own choice. That is one of the great things about owning your own business—real estate or otherwise. You get to decide what you're willing to do and what you're not. You get to make up your own rules. If you want to take a chance on somebody, you can. If you don't, you don't.

Situations can and will get murky. But without exception, you should always try to conduct yourself with the highest level of integrity, and treat your tenants as royalty. It will reap rewards over the longer term and it's the right thing to do.

KEY POINTS

- ▶ Operating with a high level of integrity can be a competitive advantage and is imperative for long-term success.
- ▶ Acts of kindness and excellent customer service will consistently reap rewards over the long term.
- ▶ Tenants are your livelihood. They are the boss. Your fates are intertwined.
- ▶ People want to help other people who are doing the right thing. And the reverse is just as true. So don't be a jerk.
- ▶ It's generally advisable to adhere to the terms of lease agreements, and if you do choose to give concessions, accept that the gesture may not to be received as you might hope.

SECTION

GROWTH 3

CHAPTER 13

CREATING A FACTORY

"If you can't describe what you are doing as a process,
you don't know what you're doing."
—W. EDWARDS DEMING

"Quality is not an act, it is a habit."
—ARISTOTLE

■

FROM THE MOMENT I purchased my first property, I found myself facing the same challenges as most new business owners. As discussed in Chapter 9, any doubts about whether this was a passive investment were swiftly quashed.

But as I dug in and got to work, one of the things I noticed relatively early on was that I was taking steps along paths that I would walk again and again. And again and again and again.

Of course the specifics of the path would vary. For one thing, I made numerous mistakes, and I learned from them. I would also try new things sometimes or discover a better approach. Sometimes I'd pick up ideas from a book, a conversation, or a podcast. Sometimes the monotony of a task would motivate me to search out a more efficient process.

Eventually, I realized that I was feeling that sense of déjà vu all too often. I don't have a great memory, but I knew I was refiguring things out and not doing a good job of capturing everything I learned along the way. This was a particularly pronounced problem when I got big enough to hire employees. Once you have to train somebody, a lack of documentation or defined process becomes a more glaring deficiency.

PROCESS AND SCALABILITY

I was successfully running a business, but I had failed to figure out how to make it scale. And without taking steps to make the business more scalable, growth would be painful. By the time I had a couple of employees, I was starting to feel the effects of this. As somebody who adores efficiency and appreciates the value of learning from mistakes, I was remarkably slow to define processes in my real estate investing. Hopefully you can learn from the error of my ways!

With growth in my company came a necessity for a better focus on process. While it may not have emerged as early as it should have, I emphasized it in all areas of the company. Once we had 100 apartment units, I tried to create processes that would allow us to scale to 1,000. Or 10,000. When we are coming up with solutions, I will routinely ask my staff—if we acquire a 200-unit complex tomorrow, can our processes scale? Will it work? Or will it break down? Let's only have to solve this problem once!

My recommendation is to start building a factory from day one. Think big, and plan that way. Learn the steps you need to take as you go, and continue to refine them and make them better over time. And document them. You're learning every day, but if the knowledge isn't captured anywhere, much of it will inevitably be lost.

Processes and procedures are also what can establish routines and habits. They not only help train new employees, but they help ensure that important things don't get missed.

If you don't have the vision or patience to establish processes in your real estate company, the good news is that your business will eventually prompt you to do so. This is because growing without scalable processes inflicts pain. And when you feel pain enough times, eventually you look for a way to make it go away.

As with many rapidly growing companies, putting out fires is how too many problems were addressed in the early years of my business. Issues bubbled to the top of the priority list when they started to create enough pain. Then they got fixed. Then they happened again. And again. Until we came up with a process or system that ensured that the pain didn't come back.

> *"A startup is a temporary organization designed to search for a repeatable and scalable business model."*
> —STEVE BLANK

Processes will emerge over the full lifecycle of investing, starting from the identification and screening of new project opportunities and following all the way through the departure of a tenant or the sale of a property.

In order to stay organized and provide some structure, I recommend that you keep both a digital and physical binder, where you collect processes and procedures as they are developed.

FUNCTIONAL AREAS OF PROPERTY MANAGEMENT

From a high-level view, the management of a commercial property (or a portfolio of properties) can be broken down into the following buckets, each of which can benefit from some structure and process as your business grows:

- ▶ **Business Development**: This includes acquisitions, dispositions, and all marketing and leasing activities.
- ▶ **Routine and Preventative Maintenance**: Every property has a variety of ongoing routine maintenance needs including things like common area cleaning, snow removal, landscaping, servicing of mechanical systems, pest control treatments, etc. How much of these functions are your responsibility as the landlord will depend on the terms of your lease agreements.

- **Service Requests**: An important part of managing properties is addressing problems or complaints that arise on any given day, yet are somewhat unpredictable. This can be things like broken appliances, water leaks, or even little things like a squeaky door or a tenant who locks himself out. Service requests may be emergency or non-emergency and can occur during regular work hours or on nights and weekends. Processes need to be put in place for receiving such requests, determining their priority level, and responding accordingly.
- **Unit Turns**: When a space opens up, there are a series of repetitive tasks that need to be undertaken to prepare a space for the next tenant. For a residential property, having an efficient and thorough process will limit a unit's downtime and decrease vacancy losses.
- **Project Management**: Periodically a property owner will have to undertake projects of all scopes and sizes. Such projects typically involve replacing infrastructure, upgrades, build-outs, expansions, conversions, etc. Depending on the scope, executing projects can entail coordinating with an architect, soliciting contractor bids, contract management, and coordinating with local officials. If you serve as your own general contractor, projects can be demanding of your time.
- **Financial Management**: Operating a real estate business on a day-to-day basis includes a significant amount of bookkeeping, invoicing, rent collection, assessing late fees, paying the bills, loans, taxes, etc. These are repetitive tasks, for which processes should be established early on, both to maintain efficiency and minimize errors.
- **General Administrative**: There are a variety of administrative functions outside of the financial management associated with a real estate business. The scope of these expands significantly as you grow and can include payroll and human resources functions. There are also the general duties associated with scheduling, management of staff, and over-

sight of property management, which can extend into tenant-related issues.

The more structured all of these processes are the better off you'll be—both for efficiency's sake and to ensure the quality of your service.

SERVICE REQUEST EXAMPLE

One example of a task that is ripe for the creation of process and procedures is what we call "service requests," but which are more commonly referred to in the industry as "work orders." A work order, or service request, is when a residential or commercial tenant calls in with any type of request or complaint.

This is a basic description of how we handle service requests. When the call is received, we ask for details and make sure we understand what the situation is. We then confirm that we have permission to enter that tenant's space, or else schedule a time that works for them. The service request is now entered into an online software system, together with notes on the particulars. The service request is also assigned a priority, so that we are addressing the most important items before those that are less time sensitive.

Our service request software is accessible through a smartphone, and service requests are checked off as they are completed, together with any relevant notes about the problem's resolution. At any time, staff can review both open and closed service requests, showing a complete record. When any service request is closed, a follow-up call is placed to that tenant within 48 hours to confirm that the work was completed to their satisfaction.

For off-hours calls, we have a phone tree that takes messages. If the call is a low-priority item, the message is picked up the next morning and entered into the service request system. If the caller pushes a button indicating that it is a high-priority item, the call service automatically forwards their message to whoever is on call, and our on-call person returns their message. If the on-call person doesn't answer their phone, there is an automated chain of subsequent calls placed to backup people that will loop through until somebody responds.

It took a while to work the system out, but now it operates smoothly. It is cost-effective and it makes everyone's life easier while also maintaining a high level of responsiveness and efficiency. It means that when we add a new property, the process is already in place to accommodate the new tenants without having to figure everything out all over again.

BORROWING OTHER PEOPLE'S PROCESSES

The great news is that you shouldn't need to start from scratch when creating processes. Our service request system is based on a lengthy conversation I had with an experienced property manager from outside the area. We took what he had to offer, and then tweaked it to meet our particular needs.

Building a business is not like taking a closed book exam. Rarely should you have to create something from scratch. In fact, a quick Google search will generally yield dozens of free resources (articles, blogs, documents, videos, etc.) on almost any real estate or business process. Find one that best fits your individual needs and preferences, and use it as a starting point from which to build your own.

As an example, there is a particularly thorough 266-page document entitled the "Housing Manager's Procedures Manual" that is freely available online.[9] Developed by the U.S. Department of Housing and Urban Development, this tome includes step-by-step processes on everything from creating a budget to how you can organize your keys. Property investors tend to accumulate an astonishing number of keys!

---

9 U.S. Department of Housing and Urban Development, "Housing Manager's Procedures Manual," November 2005, http://portal.hud.gov/hudportal/documents/huddoc?id=DOC_9211.pdf.

This procedures manual includes entire sections on leasing, maintenance, security, energy conservation, and just about any other area you could possibly conceive of. While I don't recommend you adopt the document in its entirety, it does make a handy resource and any section can easily be adapted to suit your purposes. Though primarily designed for multifamily properties, much of the content is also relevant to other commercial investment properties. And it's free.

WHEN THE BOSS IS AWAY

Building a scalable business is also the path to handing off management as your portfolio grows. The more systems and procedures you have in place, the more smoothly things can operate when you or other key staff members are away.

In many respects, the processes and procedures are a reflection of the creator's priorities. For example, my commitment to high levels of customer service was the primary driver behind the creation and implementation of our process for handling service requests. An example of something that I added on my own was the follow-up calls, which I felt were important to ensure customer satisfaction.

Once a practice like this is made standard operating procedure, there is an element of customer service and quality control that is built in. If I am not around or take time off, I know that this aspect of the business is being run efficiently and in a way that reflects our company's values.

Over time, it has been a combination of this kind of structure, together with the hiring and development of excellent staff, that has allowed me to step further back from the day-to-day property management operations and focus more on other aspects of building the business, such as evaluating new investment opportunities and other pursuits where I can add more value.

If your long-term goal is to eventually be able to hand things over and be less involved, building a strong team and creating a factory will allow you to do that, while ensuring that your investments are continuing to operate at a level you are satisfied with.

THE SOLAR BUILDING PROJECT: PART VI

 Our research confirmed what we already suspected. We had some bad characters living in the Solar Building, and until they were gone, things weren't going to improve. So we began to get better leases in place, implemented new policies and procedures, and executed a series of changes designed to drive these people out.

It was pretty clear at this point that the decision to relocate our office into the building, while stressful, was already helping to make a difference. It forced everyone on the team to deal with situations head-on instead of avoiding them. Our constant presence had also created high levels of anxiety among the worst tenants, while kindling sparks of hope in the good ones.

Our staff was running around trying to fix problems and walking contractors through so we could get bids to have various work done. By the end of the first week or two, contractors were crawling all over the place.

 The top priority was security, though we also had crews working on cleaning and pest control issues. The first step was to light the whole place up. No more dark hallways or exterior—it was just too scary and dangerous, particularly at night. By the end of the first week, a contractor had installed wall pack lighting around the entire perimeter of the property. Then began the systematic installation of new lights in the entryway, the lobby, and throughout all of the hallways and other common areas. Simultaneously, we installed a lot of security cameras and a new solid front door with a key fob access system.

Installing the key fob system on the main entrance turned out to be an important step toward turning the property around because many of the problems going on in the building were caused by people who didn't even reside there. There were too many old keys to the building floating around in the community. Changing the locks wasn't a good solution because tenants with bad intentions would just make copies of the new keys and hand them out, or keep them after they were kicked out. We needed to control access to the property and didn't want to have to keep changing the locks. A fob system was the perfect solution because it allowed us to electronically deactivate fobs that were lost or stolen. So if we evicted somebody and they didn't turn the fob back in, for example, we could deactivate the fob in the system, rendering it useless.

Between the cameras and fob system we had video images of everyone who came and went, interior and exterior, combined with electronic records showing us the exact time of entry and whose key fob was used. Not surprisingly, we observed that this change resulted in some tenants using the fire escape, so we put a camera on that too.

These types of changes put a serious crimp in the resident drug trade, and greatly upset anyone else doing things they weren't supposed to be doing. In fact, anyone (tenants or otherwise) who had previously enjoyed lurking in the Solar Building's dark hallways was finding these changes quite distressing.

For the first couple of months, the resulting tension would bubble over on almost a daily basis, often creating enough drama to make us shake our heads in disbelief. Sometimes there were acts of reprisal, most often taking the form of screaming fits or petty vandalism. People shouted profanities at us, broke things, let their dogs relieve themselves in the hallways, or other crude acts of defiance. The day after Thanksgiving I came in to find turkey bones, leftover mashed potatoes, gravy, and all other kinds of food scraps and trash littered throughout the hallway and smeared on the walls.

Throughout this time I constantly reinforced that everyone on my staff was to continue to be careful not to put themselves in danger. If anyone felt threatened in any way, they were to leave immediately and not engage. Nobody was to enter alone, and we called on the police whenever a situation warranted. The police, while initially skeptical, were helpful and supportive when they could see what we were doing.

Despite any setbacks, we could see that progress was being made when some of the worst tenants began to move out. There was finally reason to feel some encouragement, and that glimmer of hope came at a good time. The project was starting to take a toll on everyone and nerves were frayed.

Was the optimism premature or misplaced? Would the positive momentum continue? I was convinced we had turned a corner, but so far I was the only one. To be continued...

KEY POINTS

- ▶ It is more efficient to create and capture processes than to refigure things out.
- ▶ Processes and procedures can create routines and good habits that fuel efficiency gains and help ensure that important things don't get missed.
- ▶ Growing without adequate processes and procedures in place inflicts pain. Start building a factory from day one by creating systems that will scale as your business grows.
- ▶ Creating a factory and hiring good people is the path to making yourself dispensable and transitioning management as your portfolio grows.

CHAPTER 14

BE PASSIONATE AND HAVE A PURPOSE

"A business that makes nothing but money is a poor business."
—HENRY FORD

*"Nothing great in the world has been accomplished
without passion."*
—GEORG WILHELM FRIEDRICH HEGEL

■

T TAKES A LOT of time, effort, and determination to do something really well and achieve a high level of success. What's going to get you through the difficult times? What's going to inspire you to achieve high standards? What's going to motivate you to go the extra mile and feel good doing it? What's going to pick you up when you get knocked down? And what's going to do all these things for your employees?

I would argue that a desire to get rich and make money isn't going to be enough. Neither is a desire to quit your current job. To build an empire, your real estate business needs to be something more than a path to riches and leisure.

The desire to build wealth might motivate you to get started, but it's going to take something bigger and more sustainable to keep you motivated over the longer term. You'll be devoting a significant part of your waking moments to this endeavor, so make sure it has meaning.

I would challenge you to closely examine everything about real estate that appeals to you personally. You could be considering a wide variety of investments, but something prompted you to read this book—so what was it? Of all things, why real estate?

What makes it interesting? Is it the idea of building a business? Creating jobs? Helping people? Providing others with a nice place to live and/or work? Making their lives better? Making them happy? Improving the community? Serving as a mentor? Do you like the idea of helping small business tenants and non-profit tenants be successful?

"True happiness is not attained through self-gratification, but through fidelity to a worthy purpose."

—HELEN KELLER

Perhaps you take pride in the physical properties themselves—the architecture, history, or uniqueness of every building. Or maybe you just like the idea of owning a tangible asset—something real that you can touch and improve. Some people take great joy and pride in maintaining a property or keeping it nice.

The list of possibilities is endless, and it's worth giving some thought. Even if you think you know now, your motivations might change as you grow and learn more about yourself.

You're making a lot of sacrifices when you start a small business—particularly if you're doing it while holding down another job. If you can take the time to define a mission or purpose besides just making money, it can help keep you motivated and contribute toward your success

When you can identify some of these intrinsic rewards, it will help you build something worthwhile over time. It will also allow you to take pride and satisfaction in what you're accomplishing. It is very important that you not gauge success by how much money you're able to pay yourself, particularly early on when you really shouldn't be pulling money out at all. Create a business that is a labor of love, and stay focused on making the investments necessary for long-term growth.

Identifying a purpose is not just important for these reasons, but also because the degree to which you care about properties or tenants will shine through in everything that you do.

"I never did a day's work in my life. It was all fun."
—THOMAS EDISON

If a tenant and/or a property represent just numbers and a paycheck, it will show on your face, be reflected in how you deal with things on a daily basis, and ultimately lead to bad, short-term decision-making. You'll lose the closeness that can give you a significant advantage over most investors who are too distanced and emotionally uninvested.

If you genuinely care, you'll always be ready to go that extra mile, and you'll have the will necessary to get up in the morning and keep chipping away, even when things aren't going your way. Your caring will be noticed—people will see that you're sincere in your desire to make things better, and they'll want to be a part of what you're doing. They will help you be successful.

"I've never felt like I was in the cookie business. I've always been in a feel-good feeling business. My job is to sell joy. My job is to sell happiness. My job is to sell an experience."
—DEBBI FIELDS

What motivates me? I am the first to admit that, like many who start investing in real estate, the potential financial rewards were a major driver when I got started, though not the only one. There were other underlying appeals of real estate that I hadn't examined the way I probably should have. Looking back, I was naive and underestimated almost every aspect of how starting a real estate investing business would affect my life.

It took a few years for me to appreciate how important it was to recognize and embrace the intrinsic rewards associated with being a landlord. And it took a few more years to realize how important it was to crystalize and communicate the company's values and our purpose.

COMPANY VALUES

I think it's more critical than ever to define and foster values as your company grows, because communicating an organization's values and purpose influences your employees' decision-making and behavior. Your values set the tone. They drive the culture and thereby influence the actions of everyone you and your employees interact with on a daily basis. Which means they ultimately define how you're perceived.

Everyone's values will be different, but after reflecting back over our first five years in business, I realized that the foundations of our success were rooted in things like integrity, excellence, value, and innovation.

At my company, we strive to make the world a better place—one square foot at a time. We improve the quality of life for our tenants, at work and at home. We demonstrate the highest level of integrity in all of our business dealings. We partner with our commercial tenants to help them be successful. We continuously strive to achieve the highest level of excellence in everything we do. We're committed to providing the best value to our tenants—nowhere will they find that they can get more for the same rent. We're able to deliver this value by being innovative in our projects and our problem-solving.

I take great pride in the projects where we create a lot of value by transforming a mismanaged or distressed asset into nice apartments or commercial space. Everybody wins. Not just my company, but also the tenants and our community. This is a rewarding way to conduct business and it keeps my employees and me motivated.

Even when times are tough, embracing our company values helps keep everyone on the right track, and helps us all find the joy in our work. This is how you build something extraordinary.

Despite all of this, there is no denying that everyone's motivations for entering the commercial real estate industry are different. If you're investing purely for the financial gain, or solely for the purpose of quitting your job, you'll be challenged to maintain your motivation when you have setbacks.

But you can still do it, and possibly make some good money if you're determined enough. It might not be much fun though, so everyone has to make their own decision about whether it's worth it.

I have a friend who has asked me several times, "How much is enough? How much money does your business need to be worth before you walk away?"

His question misses the point. I might have started my business for the extra income, but it became more than that with every hour of my time I put into growing it, as it does for most entrepreneurs. I've faced and overcome a lot of challenges and setbacks along the way. I learn something new every day. I feel good about what I'm doing and I find it fulfilling.

If I were motivated purely by money, and not by the more intrinsic rewards you can get from investing in real estate, I'm certain my business would not have grown into what it is today. And after some of the early success I experienced, I probably would have just sold my properties and walked away.

That day might come. But for now I'm still enjoying this journey.

KEY POINTS

▶ If you're investing purely for the financial gain, or solely for the purpose of quitting your job, you'll be challenged to maintain your motivation when you have setbacks.

▶ An investor should come up with a mission or purpose that will help keep them inspired and contribute toward a meaningful life. If you can create a business that is a labor of love, it will help you stay focused on making the investments necessary for long-term growth.

- ► Recognize and embrace the intrinsic rewards associated with being a landlord. The degree to which you care about properties or tenants will shine through in everything you do.
- ► Communicating the company's values and purpose will influence the decision-making and behavior of employees and drive the culture. This is how you build something extraordinary.

CHAPTER 15

BUY AND HOLD, FOR THE MOST PART

"Our favorite holding period is forever."
—WARREN BUFFETT

"Don't wait to buy real estate, buy real estate and wait."
—WILL ROGERS

■

THERE ARE A LOT of different ideas out there about when the right time is to sell a property. When I started investing I didn't have a preferred strategy for holding or selling. I was just focused on turning things around and adding value, which I knew would eventually open up more options. And after a couple years of ownership that's exactly what happened—I made enough progress that the prospect of selling for a profit was a realistic possibility.

At one point, I went so far as to discuss price with a potential buyer. That never really went anywhere, but the thought of selling was always in the back of my mind. I don't think this is unusual for anyone in business—especially when you're having one of those bad days that we all have where nothing seems to go right. But every time I ran through the pros and cons of selling, I came down squarely on the side of keeping the property. In hindsight I'm so glad I did.

The weighing of buying versus selling continues to this day as I am constantly assessing each property in my portfolio. But at this point, having looked at my options so many times, I've realized that buy-and-hold is the strategy that has worked best for me, and will likely do so in the majority of cases for the foreseeable future. You can sometimes make an attractive return by flipping a property, but over the long term, few people regret their decision to keep an investment.

The buy-and-hold approach is also the best strategy for achieving the highest level of growth. Selling creates inefficiencies that will slow you down and eat into your cash flow. If you want to build an empire, it's best to hold most of your properties for long periods of time.

LONG-TERM VALUE CREATION

There are numerous reasons to buy and hold. One is that this strategy fits perfectly with a commitment to long-term value creation. Adding value to a property takes time, especially if the improvements are financed through a property's cash flow. Even if you borrow in order to do most of the work up front, it's almost impossible to capture all the value-add in less than two years.

In most situations, achieving the full potential of a turnaround property is likely to take four or five years, and maybe longer. This is particularly true if you're doing it methodically and paying for improvements out of the property's cash flow. On top of that, if you want to get top dollar from a buyer, the property should be "seasoned" to the point that you can demonstrate two years of actual financials to support the full valuation.

> "I think the biggest single thing that causes difficulty in the business world is the short-term view. We become obsessed with it. But it forces bad decisions."
> —JAMES SINEGAL

The prospect of turning a quick profit on real estate can be very enticing. It puts cash in your pocket and it nails down a success that you can point to. But that doesn't mean it's the correct decision for maximizing long-term value. In fact, more often than not it's shortsighted. Better returns are generally realized with a buy-and-hold approach, where you keep reinvesting as long as possible.

Eventually your patience and diligent reinvestment will yield higher and higher cash flows and you can start to siphon some of that cash off to grow your portfolio or for some other purpose. But reinvestment can continue to reap solid returns for as long as you're willing to commit. The amount of value created is likely to slow down after the first year or two, but it's still there.

MINIMIZING TRANSACTION COSTS AND TAX LOSSES

A buy-and-hold strategy also minimizes transaction costs and avoids the potential tax consequences, all of which improve your portfolio's overall performance. Transaction costs associated with a sale can easily reach 5% to 10%, or higher in cases where there is a large broker commission due. When a sale results in a capital gain, you'll also need to pay income taxes, just like you would on income from the sale of stock.

As mentioned in Chapter 7, real estate investors in the U.S. can defer the capital gain associated with a sale by engaging in something called a "1031 Exchange," which is a provision under Section 1031 of the U.S. Internal Revenue Code (26 U.S.C. § 1031). Basically, this law allows an investor who sells a property to avoid paying capital gains by reinvesting the money in a property of equal or greater value within 180 days. There are a number of other specific requirements associated with a 1031 Exchange that a good commercial real estate attorney and tax accountant can help you understand and navigate.

Another consideration related to taxes is the effect of a sale on property taxes. Essentially, if you're a value-add investor, your properties are often more valuable to you than to a buyer. This is because when you sell the property for more than you paid for it, any value you have created is now reflected in the higher sale price, which is likely to trigger a reassessment by the taxing jurisdiction. This means that property taxes will go up, hurting the cash flow.

You may be wondering why you should care, since at this point you've already sold the property. It affects you because a savvy buyer will anticipate the jump in property taxes when they calculate the property's NOI and arrive at a purchase price.

Meanwhile, a buy-and-hold strategy keeps your assessment and associated property tax at a more reasonable level, which allows you to achieve a cash flow superior to any buyer and effectively makes the property more valuable to you than to anyone else. This dynamic is most pronounced in areas with rapidly appreciating property values and high property tax rates.

HIGH OPERATIONAL EFFICIENCIES

A buy-and-hold strategy allows the investor to achieve a host of efficiencies as you scale up. Once you've developed systems, trained employees, built relationships, and so forth, you're in a position to better leverage these across your portfolio—particularly when your properties are in close proximity. You're also more likely to establish a reputation and relationships, which helps generate referrals and can get you some positive publicity.

One of the greatest benefits we've achieved through this approach is the cross-pollination of leads. We get calls every day thanks to our property signs and word of mouth. Having developed a portfolio with a variety of locations and offerings in the area, we are better able to meet a broader spectrum of needs. As tenants outgrow their spaces or need to downsize, we're able to work with them to accommodate their wishes.

On the opposite end of the spectrum from the buy-and-hold approach is the investor who strives to improve a property's value with the goal of turning it around and selling it, progressively trading up to larger and larger properties. This approach can sometimes work, though it is not as likely to yield as large of a long-term return, in part due to its inherent inefficiencies.

Selling and buying properties in this fashion can be highly disruptive to your day-to-day operations. There tends to be a surge in workload before and after closings, interrupting any of those processes you may have put in place to efficiently manage operations.

As discussed in Chapter 9, real estate is a business just like any other. Yet the concept of flipping is relatively unique to investment real estate. It would be highly unorthodox to see a restaurateur, for example, focus on perfecting their business operation, only to keep flipping their restaurant so as to buy progressively larger ones. What is far more common is for a successful restaurateur to open additional locations, thereby leveraging the systems and model they have worked so hard to perfect. This is how a restaurateur can build an empire. The considerations with regard to real estate investing aren't as different as you might think.

REFINANCING

One of attractions of flipping a property is the quick cash, which can then be readily deployed in another opportunity. So how do you grow a portfolio when all of your cash is tied up in properties that you're constantly reinvesting in? Once you've created enough value, there are two primary paths. The conservative path is to set aside cash flow each month until you have saved enough to make your next acquisition. This is ideal because it avoids taking on more debt, but it can also take time.

The easiest way to secure cash after creating value in a property is to refinance. If you've added value, refinancing will be possible because, as you know, the numbers drive the property's valuation.

The proof is in the pudding, and in commercial real estate the pudding is the net operating income. Added value will be reflected in the NOI. So driving up that NOI opens the option of refinancing and pulling out some cash to grow your portfolio.

A Look at the Numbers

Let's look at an example based on one of my projects. Imagine you acquire a property that generates $100K per year in rental income and has $60K in annual expenses. So your NOI is the difference, which is $40K.

Income – Expenses (Excluding Debt Service) = NOI
$100K – $60K = $40K

If you negotiate to acquire it at a 10% cap rate, then you paid $400K for the property.

NOI / Cap Rate = Price
$40K / 0.10 = $400K

Now let's say that over the following two years you've fixed it up and have been able to raise the annual rental income by $20K, up to $120K. You've also been able to reduce the annual operating expenses by $10K, lowering them to $50K.

So our new NOI is $120K – $50K = $70K. The new value of the property at the same 10% cap rate is now $700K, *an increase in value of 75% over two years.*

$70,000 / 0.10 = $700,000

With $300K in newly created equity, you're now in a position, should you so choose, to refinance the property and pull some of this out. Let's assume you originally financed 90% of the acquisition, so you borrowed $360K. If you borrow 75% of the improved value of $700K, that equates to a new mortgage of $630K.

This would allow you to pull out $270K in cash, plus any principle that was paid down over the first two years of ownership. Depending on how you structure your next deal, you could use this $270K in cash to acquire a property valued as high as $1M to $2M or more!

Pulling this kind of cash out is definitely feasible and not uncommon, as long as the NOI and property valuation supports it. In the above scenario, you only borrowed 75% of the new value of the property, which leaves you some cushion.

The beauty of buy-and-hold investing is you still have this first property. Retaining properties in this fashion helps you build a portfolio with multiple income streams. Spreading your income across multiple properties reduces your risk. If a property fails, you will have others to help carry you through. This is in stark contrast to a growth strategy based on flipping properties in sequence, purchasing a larger one each time.

Meanwhile, the management of properties you hold should continue to get more efficient with time. And if you continue to strategically reinvest in your

> *"Never depend on a single income. Make investments to create a second source."*
> —WARREN BUFFETT

portfolio over the long term, the properties should show continuous improvement, further driving up your NOI, all the while paying down your debt.

PRINCIPAL PAY-DOWN

The power of buy-and-hold becomes more magnified as your portfolio grows. Every time you make a mortgage payment, part of your payment goes toward interest, and another portion of it goes to paying down your principal, which is the balance that you owe on the loan.[10] Eventually, the total principal you'll be paying down each year can grow to very respectable levels. This will decrease your risk exposure, and it's like putting money in the bank.

Principal pay-down is the most overlooked and boring form of return in real estate. But it can be a powerful way to accumulate equity. And this equity is like a stockpile of cash that can either be hoarded to hedge your risk, or be leveraged later on by refinancing to grow your portfolio.

Even if your real estate investment business is cash flow breakeven some months, you can always look at principal pay-down for reassurance that you're building wealth.

---

10   The notable exception being interest-only debt, where none of the payment is applied to the principal.

Does this mean I don't ever sell properties? Not at all, but it's the exception not the rule. As of the time I'm writing this, I've sold two properties in the nine years I've been an investor, and I'm sure I'll sell more. The first was a newly constructed Dollar General with a triple net (NNN) lease that I had acquired thinking that I should diversify my portfolio with an asset that was lower maintenance and low risk. It didn't take me long to realize that owning a Dollar General was both personally and financially unrewarding relative to my other investments. It just wasn't a good fit for me, and I realized that for this reason purchasing it had been a mistake.

So when a great value-add opportunity came along, I sold the Dollar General in order to pay for the new property acquisition. The second property was the small property referenced in Chapter 5 that I bought at auction for $24K and sold six months later for $60K.

Different strategies work for different people, and there might be opportunistic situations where selling makes sense—such as in my auction purchase, where I had no intent to hold the property long term. And even if you're a committed buy-and-hold investor, we all make mistakes sometimes, and you might end up with a property that isn't a good fit, like what happened to me with the Dollar General. But my position is that these should be the exceptions and not the rule.

> *"It's time for everyone to acknowledge that the term 'long-term investor' is redundant. A long-term investor is the only kind of investor there is."*
> —BENJAMIN GRAHAM

Weighing all the factors that come into play, I'm convinced that 9 times out of 10 it's in an investor's best interest to hold properties for the long term. My recommendation is for investors to go into commercial real estate with the idea of building a portfolio. Make up your mind *not* to sell. And when the opportunity to sell arises, your default should be to just say no. But if the opportunity is positively overwhelmingly—so compelling as to overcome all doubts, then revisit your stance.

THE SOLAR BUILDING PROJECT: PART VII

 While the contractors and staff were busy running around fixing things at the Solar Building, I strategically scoped out a project for myself. The main lobby finishes needed some work, so I decided I'd roll up my sleeves and spend a few hours in there each day doing it myself. I dressed in shabby clothes, threw on an old baseball cap, and worked on making minor repairs like patching holes, replacing and repairing wood trim, and even adding some chair rail, though these jobs were a real stretch for my meager carpentry skills.

The purpose wasn't to save money so much as a way to keep my finger on the pulse of what was going on at the most critical time of the building's transformation. Everybody was passing through the lobby all day—it was the only way in and out of the building other than the fire escape and the windows. Besides which it always feels good to get out of the office and do a little manual labor.

Working in the lobby, nobody besides my staff knew I was the owner, and I made sure it stayed that way. The things I heard and saw were fantastically helpful. Tenants would hang out there and talk among themselves about everything going on. So would the contractors. It was particularly entertaining to hear people talk about the owner right in front of me! They either loved him or they hated him! Nobody pays attention to the guy caulking, sanding, or painting.

I remember one of the worst tenants complaining animatedly to a friend about a new camera that had been installed near his apartment, and commenting that he saw one of the staff making notes in a little notebook. He seemed almost irrationally paranoid about what was being written down. Knowing it would make him crazy, the next day I told our entire team to start carrying notebooks with them in the building, and I told them to make frequent notations. It was amazing to see the effect this had. As with most of the changes we were implementing, it only alarmed the tenants engaged in nefarious activities. The rest assumed we were writing down repairs to be made or something equally innocuous.

The benefits of being a fly on the wall were too good to let go and I was having too much fun. After a couple weeks I had progressed beyond the trim and also adjusted and painted the drop ceiling grid, then changed out damaged ceiling tiles. I proceeded to paint the metal mailboxes, which looked like new when I was done. Then I went to work on the vestibule. It made me feel good to contribute to the project, and in the process, I overheard and observed dozens of other things that helped. Many of them were small, but helpful nonetheless.

For example, there was a trashcan in the lobby. It turns out this was used by the tenants for one thing only—they would carry a trash bag down from their apartment and drop it in there so that they wouldn't have to walk outside to the Dumpster. Then our staff would have to constantly empty the overflowing trashcan. So I simply removed the trashcan, and the tenants instead started using the Dumpster like they were supposed to. Of course this is a very small change, but there we so many more. It wasn't long before I knew every detail of what was going on in the building, which helped me make better decisions.

Over the ensuing months, our work continued and in addition to the initial security improvements, every unit in the building got a new steel door and doorframe, complete with deadbolts and peep-holes. Most of the old doors had been kicked in repeatedly over the years and were not secure. All of the common areas were refurbished and were now brightly lit. It was important to us that everyone felt safe.

Starting with the vacant units, we also began a methodical renovation of each apartment unit. Every time a unit opened up for lease, we would refurbish it with new appliances, fixtures, and finishes.

While the work progressed, it was becoming more and more clear that the changes were having the desired effect. Until eventually, we realized that the problem tenants were gone. The exact circumstances varied tenant by tenant. Some we notified that we would not be continuing their month-to-month leases, some we reported to the appropriate authorities, but most left on their own, avoiding any major confrontations or showdowns. It was actually all a bit anticlimactic given how things had started out. But that is a very good thing.

The better tenants were patient and encouraged as they saw the transition. We continued to make improvements and held rents in check. The majority of the good tenants remained, and while occupancy had dropped, it never fell below 50%. This was important because we were able to fund the improvements over time and pay for a good portion of them out of the building's own cash flow.

But as the building was transformed and problem tenants vacated, my concerns began to shift. We now had an entirely new challenge to face: 50% occupancy was not where we wanted to be, and the building's bad reputation remained and would be difficult to overcome. Would we be able to lease it back up? Or would we be left with nicely refurbished but empty apartments? Would any good tenants lease apartments in a building with such a poor reputation? To be continued…

KEY POINTS

- There is a wide variety of costs associated with selling a property that can be avoided by pulling equity out through a refinance.
- For patient investors who want to maximize long-term value creation, a buy-and-hold strategy will usually yield the best results.
- Principal pay-down is the most overlooked and unglamorous form of return, but it can be a powerful way to accumulate equity.
- Make up your mind *not* to sell. But if the opportunity is exceptional, then cautiously revisit your stance.

CHAPTER 16

STRIVE FOR BALANCE

"Wisdom is your perspective on life, your sense of balance,
your understanding of how the various parts and principles
apply and relate to each other."
—STEVEN R. COVEY

"A successful journey becomes your destination and is where
your real accomplishment lies."
—JOHN WOODEN

■

N THE BOOK'S INTRODUCTION, I shared that before becoming a teacher and part-time real estate investor, I had quit my job at a technology startup. The circumstances leading up to that decision taught me some valuable lessons; lessons that have profoundly affected the way I run my real estate business. Quitting that job wasn't easy, and I remember it vividly.

When I walked up to my boss's office door, I was filled with a great deal of determination and also some trepidation. Fresh off my first real vacation in recent memory, I had made up my mind to resign. After spending the past five years at a tech startup in Northern Virginia, and working my way up to vice president, it was time to make a change. I was working myself into an early grave.

My job had been a roller coaster of experiences, though one aspect remained constant throughout—it was all-consuming. I had lost touch with friends and family, grown apart from my spouse, and really let myself go. Working extreme hours contributed to an unhealthy lifestyle. I was overweight and started to have medical problems. Then one day at the ripe old age of 35, I found myself hospitalized with chest pains.

Sure, I had a lot of ambitions, but working myself to death before my 40th birthday was definitely not one of them. I wanted to achieve great things professionally and make a lot of money, but lying there staring at the EKG machine, I knew that there were more important things in life. The realization prompted me to schedule that long overdue vacation. The one where I decided it was time to step down.

This is how I found myself walking into the CEO's office on my first day back from vacation. I braced myself as I sat down and looked across the desk. Knowing him, I was going to have my hands full sticking to my decision. And I knew my fears were well founded the moment I broke the news. His eyebrows rose and his eyes got wide. My CEO had very different ideas about my departure.

"What?!" he erupted. "You can't leave now! We've worked so hard to get this company where it is today. We're so close… *You've swallowed the whole donkey except for the tail!!!*"

He leaned forward with a scowl, waiting to see how I would react.

What? Swallowed the donkey except for the tail? What the hell was that supposed to mean? He must have noticed my confusion because he proceeded to explain that this was some kind of a Greek proverb, and what he was trying to express was that the hardest work was already done. We were almost to the big payday!

Aha… now I understood. He was alluding to that ever-elusive acquisition or IPO that would make our stock options worth millions. It had been just around the corner for the past three years, but kept slipping out of our hands for one reason or another. I knew better than to argue this point, so I told him that the money no longer mattered to me. Then I braced myself for whatever argument he would throw at me next.

He leaned back and, studying me closely, seemed to accept that I was undeterred by his donkey-swallowing analogy. But my trepidation rose another notch under his steady gaze. Despite his wide, engaging smile, crinkly eyes, and folksy sayings, this man was as sharp as a razor and exceptionally cunning. I had learned a lot from him. He was always thinking strategically, and I marveled at his ability to turn any situation to his favor.

He kept at me, prying from every angle, and my resolve began to crumble, though not completely. In the end, I agreed to stay on through the end of the year to help smooth the transition. In return, he agreed to vest my remaining stock options.

Thanks to changes in the company's equity structure, a few years later my options netted me a "big payday" of about $13K when the company finally sold. Nothing to scoff at, but far from the millions I had once dreamed of when rationalizing my crazy work schedule.

THE BLACK HOLE

Values such as a strong work ethic and grit can help you be successful in whatever endeavor you choose to pursue—my personal experience and that of countless others backs this up. But how far are you willing to go, *and at what price?* If you're a highly motivated person, it's appropriate to be cautious about taking work to the extreme.

> *"Money often costs too much."*
> —RALPH WALDO EMERSON

One of the greatest challenges associated with being an entrepreneur is that your work can become a bottomless black hole that can slowly suck you in. The black hole is work that "needs" to get done. The problem is that in any growing business, there is *always* more work to be done. It really is a bottomless pit and you're better off just recognizing it as such up front. Failure to prioritize and set limits is a trap that many people fall into unfortunately, and often at a steep price.

Getting sucked into that black hole isn't fun. Working at a tech startup, I learned about the dangers firsthand. The culture of a startup can be like the force of gravity as it steadily reels you in. Especially if you're surrounded by others who are just as willing to sacrifice everything at the altar of work! If you're a driven person, and the workload is unrelenting, you can easily find yourself trying to do more and more. And more and more and more. And more…

Next thing you know, you're routinely working 16-hour days, you can't sleep when your head finally hits the pillow, and you're awake responding to emails at 3:00 a.m. Soon you're also gaining weight, self-medicating with alcohol

> *"I think that maybe inside any business, there is someone slowly going crazy."*
> —JOSEPH HELLER

or other addiction of choice, destroying your personal relationships, and doing an all-around outstanding job shutting out the rest of the world and shortening your lifespan.

The result? Well, there are a lot of directions that kind of thing can take you. In my case, it didn't end particularly well. But it could have been a lot worse. At least I made a change before I ended up dead, and it's an understatement to say I learned a lot from the experience.

In hindsight, I realize that the trap I had fallen into wasn't that I worked too hard. It was that I had allowed things to become so far out of balance—I'd become too narrowly focused on my job at the expense of other things that are too important to be ignored.

Hard work in itself wasn't to blame. I have been working hard my whole life, and I have seen over and over that it pays off. Grit and a commitment to excellence eventually lead to success in almost any endeavor.

The problems arise when you don't apply that same level of effort across all of the areas of your life that are critical to maintaining your overall well-being. Taking care of yourself and your loved ones needs to be done with the same level of determination as achieving success in your professional life. I had failed to strike that balance, and I was determined not to make the same mistake again.

Brian Dyson, former CEO of Coca-Cola, summed it up nicely in an analogy he shared during his Georgia Tech commencement speech:

Imagine life as a game in which you are juggling some five balls in the air. You name them—work, family, health, friends, and spirit—and you're keeping all of these in the air. You will soon understand that work is a rubber ball. If you drop it, it will bounce back. But the other four balls—family, health, friends, and spirit—are made of glass. If you drop one of these, they will be irrevocably scuffed, marked, nicked, damaged, or even shattered. They will never be the same. You must understand that and strive for balance in your life.[11]

 In this book, I suggest that you can improve the odds of successfully starting a commercial real estate business by doing such things as working a full-time job and actively managing your first properties at the same time. If you have a strong work ethic you *can* do this. But if you're not careful, such a demanding schedule can place a lot of stress on other areas of your life such as your health and personal relationships.

STARTING OVER IN REAL ESTATE

Everyone has his or her own priorities in life. In my case, I quit my tech company job because I wanted to see my kids grow up and to be around for them. I wanted to provide a better quality of life for my loved ones and myself. And I wanted to experience life and all it has to offer. So I decided to hit the "reset" button. I decided to walk away, and I started over.

The following years brought a torrent of change. After I quit my job, I took some much-needed time off, made futile efforts to repair damaged personal relationships, and did a lot of reflecting and soul-searching.

11 "Coca-Cola CEO's Secret Formula for Success: Vision, Confidence and Luck," The Georgia Tech Whistle, vol. 17, no. 27, September 30, 1991.

One of the first things I came to realize once I finally had some time off is that I didn't enjoy sitting around doing nothing. It became pretty clear that any dreams I had of one day lying on the beach and sipping fruity drinks all day was a fantasy that just wasn't going to work for me. The "beach life" is great in small doses, but lounging around wasn't fulfilling and wouldn't make me happy.

Personally, I take great enjoyment in being productive, helping others, challenging myself, learning and experiencing new things, and sharing those pursuits with my loved ones. So when I had the opportunity to work as a professor, I jumped at it. Teaching was something I had always liked, and it felt right. But even though I enjoyed teaching, I wanted more. Yes, I found it difficult to make ends meet on a teacher's salary, but I also missed the challenge of building a business.

This is when I finally discovered real estate investing, and it quickly proved to be a great path for me. Why? For one, the work schedule offered greater flexibility and I had more control. As I shared in Chapter 2, my daily routine wasn't easy, but for the most part real estate activities could be planned around my teaching job and other commitments. A lot of the work could even be done from home. And perhaps more importantly, I found it personally rewarding.

So I embraced work with a renewed, healthier perspective. I did it with a high level of motivation and determination to succeed. But I also took efforts to keep things in their proper perspective. I continued to address issues with my health through lifestyle changes, improving both my diet and my exercise routine. I worked through some very difficult personal relationship issues, and I committed to doing better moving forward. And years later, when it became too much to manage, I resigned from my faculty position and focused on real estate full-time.

My self-improvement efforts continue to this day. Though to be fair, I still manage to screw things up as much as the next guy. I'm far from perfect, and I will always be a work in progress. I make mistakes all the time. We all do, and that's OK. The goal is to learn from those mistakes and grow.

DELAYED GRATIFICATION

Depending on the extent to which you're experiencing joy in the day-to-day activities associated with building a business, it's also a path that, in many respects, can be one of delayed gratification. If you're not enjoying your job, and you allow work to interfere with the parts of your life that are most important, you're on the road to self-destruction.

To be the best at whatever you do, you need to make up your own mind about what will make you happy, and what's most important. This requires some introspection and can present some challenging questions. What motivates you? What is really most important to you? What sacrifices are you willing to make? The answers to these questions are different for everyone and well worth exploring.

Sacrificing time today for a better tomorrow is not consistent with everyone's personal values and philosophies. As such, making short-term sacrifices is a decision that should not be taken lightly, and the degree to which you're willing to do so is best examined ahead of time. It would be wise to reflect on the implications, and involve those close to you in weighing such matters. Creating extra income from any startup business can take time, and your decision will also affect those around you.

My experience is no exception. To this day I do not pay myself a salary. But the sacrifices are starting to pay off. Despite a decline in the local real estate market, my portfolio has stayed healthy. After many years of diligent reinvestment into the business, I have started taking periodic owner's draws not just to pay the bills, but also to do things like travel and share other rewarding experiences with my family. And in the not-too-distant future, I am hoping my real estate investments will help put my kids through college.

COME UP WITH A GAME PLAN

Real estate can create wealth and open the door to wonderful opportunities for you and your family, but it can also be demanding and you need to strive for balance. Otherwise you'll certainly lose the perspective and inspiration necessary to be the best. Rather than leave it to chance, come up with a plan that carves out enough time to take care of yourself and your personal relationships.

How you go about striking a healthy balance is entirely up to you, and only limited by your own creativity. It might mean getting up a little earlier or going to bed a little later, but don't forget what's important. Find ways to do your work, to go that extra mile, while protecting quality areas of time to stay physically and emotionally healthy.

The following are some practical strategies that might be effective as you strive for balance in different areas of your life, particularly if you have a family:

- Bring your work home in a positive way by involving family members in the business—make investments a topic of discussion, ask for your children's input, share entertaining stories, etc. Use real estate to help introduce your children to values that are important to you. Share stories of how your projects affect the community and the jobs you're creating.
- In addition to bringing your work home, you can bring your home to work. This might mean taking family members to see a project before and after, or even involving them to whatever extent makes sense given your situation. Bring your kids along to help out with small projects in an effort to show them that the financial rewards are the fruits of honest, hard work. Having family members hang out at work with you periodically might have a positive influence by providing exposure to an entrepreneurial environment or helping them understand and respect what you're doing.
- If you have a partner or close friend who shares your passion, consider bringing them into the business. This needs to be considered very carefully and entered into with caution, however, as it introduces a new dynamic into a rela-

tionship that can sometimes be destructive. That said, it can also sometimes be a great thing. I'm very fortunate that my wife shares my interest in real estate and left her job to work with me.

► Find gaps in the day and make them productive. This might be in the morning before anyone else gets up, in the early evenings when others are engaged in their routines, during breaks throughout the day, or at night after your spouse and children have gone to sleep. Find what works for you and your personal situation.

► Create a life for yourself in real estate that allows you to enjoy your work and gain fulfillment and happiness. Real estate is a broad field so find an area that you like. As discussed in Chapter 14, if you're going to invest a lot of time, it should be a labor of love. This may mean you trade off some profits in the short term, but if you're passionate about your work, you're destined for greater things in the long run.

► Find activities in your day that don't further your priorities and reduce or eliminate them. Commit to using this time in more meaningful ways. As observed by the Roman Emperor and Stoic philosopher Marcus Aurelius, "Most of what we say and do is not essential. If you can eliminate it, you'll have more time, and more tranquility. Ask yourself at every moment, 'Is this necessary?'"

► Commit to self-improvement in the same way you commit to improving properties. In your personal life, that can take the form of learning, growing, and healthy living. Fiercely protect and commit to time with your loved ones, just as you commit to your business.

These strategies are just a few that you might be able to harness, and they won't all work for everyone. Each situation is different, but in the end, you will be well served by staying mindful of the need for balance, regardless of your specific approach.

Life is a marathon and not a sprint. You need to work hard to be successful in real estate, but you also need to do it in a way that is rewarding and sustainable.

KEY POINTS

- Values such as a strong work ethic and grit play a key role in determining the outcome of a real estate venture, but taking work to the extreme can come at a high cost.
- If you give everything to your business and leave nothing for other areas of your life, you'll certainly lose the inspiration that is necessary to be the best.
- Real estate can provide greater flexibility and control than other occupations, offering the opportunity to strike a healthy balance.
- Don't leave things to chance. Create a plan that reflects your priorities and carves out adequate time for your wellness and personal relationships.

CHAPTER 17

KEEP LEARNING

"The more that you read, the more things you will know.
The more that you learn, the more places you'll go."
—DR. SEUSS

"Chance favors the prepared mind."
—LOUIS PASTEUR

■

F YOU'RE READY TO take the plunge and are motivated to build your wealth through commercial real estate, this book is a great start. The principles outlined here can provide a solid foundation for success. But this book should really be just one brick in your wall of real estate and business self-education.

The more knowledge you absorb, the greater competitive advantage you'll have, both in real estate and in life. If you can make a commitment to continuous learning, both you and your business will reap the rewards of self-improvement.

Books, courses, videos, articles, blogs, podcasts, discussion boards, conferences, and groups related to real estate in any form will be beneficial. I also recommend that you educate yourself on general business topics, which are just as relevant to real estate as they are to any other kind of business. There is a plethora of excellent resources out there on marketing, sales, customer service, accounting, and management that can all serve you well.

As you seek to educate yourself, remember to beware of inflated claims of easy money or "experts" charging exorbitant fees for workshops or advice. As mentioned in Chapter 1, unfortunately there are a lot of people out there preying on the dreams of prospective investors.

You don't need to have an MBA to be a real estate investor, or even a high school diploma for that matter. But you'll need an abundance of common sense, and if you don't already have an education or background in business, you'd be well served by making an effort to self-educate. Again, this book is an excellent start, but it should be one of many!

> *"No man was ever wise by chance."*
> —LUCIUS ANNAEUS SENECA

As mentioned earlier, another good resource is BiggerPockets.com. In addition to their online forums, they publish weekly podcasts featuring active investors.[12] Other informative podcasts include Michael Blank's "Apartment Building Investing," Joe Fairless's "Best Real Estate Investing Advice Ever," "Real Estate Investing for Cash Flow" with Kevin Bupp, "The Deal Farm" with Ken Corsini, "Epic Real Estate Investing" with Matt Theriault, and "Freedom Real Estate Investing" with Brock Collins. A careful listen to the full history of these and other podcasts can provide you with a ton of practical real estate investing advice. And they're all free!

I also recommend exploring business ideas and strategy beyond real estate. You can get inspiration and learn from best practices across almost any industry. I am a voracious reader and pick up tips all the time from general business books. Sometimes they can have a lasting impact on your business. I find autobiographies to be particularly valuable because they tend to be heavy on real-life lessons that you can apply to your own situation.

 For example, I recall being motivated by Zappos CEO Tony Hsieh's excellent book *Delivering Happiness: A Path to Profits, Passion, and Purpose.* Even though Zappos is in an entirely different industry, the core values espoused in the book really resonated with me. I could

---

12 After experiencing some success with my business, I was honored to be the featured guest on BiggerPockets.com's podcast, episode 126. In this podcast I share part of the Solar Building story.

see how the Zappos level of commitment to customer service could be just as effective in real estate as in any other industry, if not more so.

There was one anecdote in the book that I shared with my staff to help them better understand what we were striving for in terms of customer service. Tony Hsieh was in a hotel room with friends late one evening when one of them unsuccessfully tried to order a pepperoni pizza from room service, having missed the 11:00 p.m. deadline. At the urging of Hsieh, they called the Zappos customer service line to seek help with their pizza dilemma.

Even though Zappos sold shoes, not pizza, the friendly customer service rep asked them to hold for a moment, then returned to the line in short order with a list of the closest pizza places that were still open and delivering.

I challenged my staff to consider how they would handle a similar phone request. I'm still not sure how they would react, but what a great story to help me illustrate what we are striving for!

I also found inspiration in the book *Shoe Dog*, which is the autobiography of Phil Knight, the founder of Nike. Knight's account of the financial sacrifices and struggles associated with growing his nascent business really resonated with me. Sometimes when you're facing difficult challenges it's easy to forget that you're not the only one—there are entrepreneurs all over the world confronting similar circumstances. It can be inspiring to hear firsthand accounts from someone who persevered, in Knight's case, on the grandest scale.

The benefits I reaped from the books by Hsieh and Knight are two examples out of hundreds. Every time you crack open a book, read an article, or listen to a podcast, you never know what you're going to learn or how it might better you and your business. Or what kind of motivational boost you're going to get. It's all part of a commitment to learning and making yourself the best you can be.

FINDING A MENTOR

Another way to accelerate your education and learn from the experience of others is by finding a mentor. Those fortunate enough to have found a good mentor know there is no disputing how rewarding it can be. But finding such a person can be a great challenge.

Many successful real estate investors are generous with their time and eager to help. But like any entrepreneur, their time is often precious and their most valuable resource. So getting enough time with such an individual to guide you is often a challenge.

If you can find a way to offer value to a prospective mentor, your odds improve. But even if you're prepared to volunteer or offer services, recognize that mentorship is a great imposition on their time, and successful entrepreneurs are rarely able to mentor everyone they would like to. Personally, I would love to mentor more people, but the reality is there are only so many hours of the day and I'm just not able to fit any more in. So my advice is to always accept a no with grace and don't burn bridges.

The challenge of finding a mentor is compounded by the fact that the number of potential good mentors can be limited, particularly if you live in a smaller market. Having a mentor who is not local makes it difficult to build a relationship and greatly diminishes a mentor's effectiveness, so if you're in a very rural area, you might not have many options.

If you're fortunate enough to make such a valuable connection and establish a mentor–mentee relationship, it can be a wonderful resource. That said, I think there is entirely too much emphasis placed on mentorship, to the point that many aspiring investors see it as a prerequisite to success. The truth is, while mentorship can be a blessing, not everyone is in a position to secure such a relationship. And not all mentorships bear fruit. Quite honestly, the world is full of bad mentors who offer poor advice or take advantage of their mentees. Even worse, some of them charge for their disservice and call it coaching.

If you're unable to find the right person to take you under their wing, don't fret. I didn't have a mentor when I started and I'd like to think I did just fine. In fact, I think it helped me look at commercial real estate with a greater openness to doing things in a new and different way. Sure, I made my share of mistakes along the way (and

I continue to do so), but that's how I learned a lot of valuable lessons that made me a better investor.

Absent a mentor, I turned to books and a variety of online resources including articles, discussion boards, and podcasts, some of which I have already mentioned.

A complete list of resources can be found in Appendix D, but a few books that I found particularly helpful or that influenced me include:

> *The Bootstrapper's Bible* by Seth Godin
> *The Complete Guide to Buying and Selling Apartment Buildings* by Steve Berges
> *Don't Sweat the Small Stuff* by Richard Carlson
> *The E-Myth Revisited* by Michael Gerber
> *How to Build a Real Estate Empire* by Marcel Arsenault, et al.
> *The Millionaire Real Estate Investor* by Gary Keller
> *Multi-Family Millions* by David Lindahl
> *The Obstacle Is the Way* by Ryan Holiday
> *Rich Dad Poor Dad* by Robert Kiyosaki

I have also learned a lot from those around me, and continue to do so. Consider availing yourself of others in the industry or with ties to the industry. Get yourself in the mode of establishing a rapport with other investors, brokers, attorneys, contractors, and others with varied experiences and areas of expertise. Ask lots of questions and be a good listener. People enjoy sharing their knowledge and passions, and they appreciate being heard.

"The game of life is the game of everlasting learning. At least it is if you want to win."
—CHARLIE MUNGER

It's important to focus on saying less and listening more. Practically everyone you meet has something you can learn from if you're able to ask the right questions and are prepared to really listen.

BE A DISCRIMINATING SPONGE

Every bit of knowledge you can gain will improve your likelihood of success, so best to stack the deck as much in your favor as possible. Consume information on commercial real estate like a starving person at the buffet. Keep that appetite healthy, and feed it!

While it's very important to be a sponge, it's equally important to learn how to be discerning. Remember that most of what you absorb is laced with a healthy dose of opinion. It may be wrong. Or it may be right only in certain circumstances. Or it might not apply to you or your business at all. If you accept everything you read and hear as fact, you'll be immobilized by contradictions and confusion.

You need to be a discriminating sponge. Living life as a traditional sponge isn't going to work. A sponge is nonselective, absorbing and holding everything it comes into contact with. You can use a sponge to soak up water. But you can also use it to soak up vomit or sewage.

Be discriminating—think critically and use good judgment. Consider everything and be open to new ideas, but apply a filter and set things aside that don't ring true. Squeeze the bad stuff back out and retain the good stuff only!

Such an approach is easily said, but in reality much more difficult than one might realize. Being too rigid in your filters can quickly devolve into closed-mindedness and getting "set in your ways."

How to be discriminating without being inflexible? Use filters but don't be judgmental. The key is to stay open to new ideas and different approaches, while also applying a healthy dose of skepticism, common sense, and sound business principles. These are your filters.

So remember to soak it all in, but take everything you encounter with a grain of salt and use your best judgment regarding what will work best for you. And that includes this book!

MAKE LEARNING A HABIT

Your learning activities need to become a deeply ingrained habit—learning should be continuous. The worst thing that can happen is that you decide you know enough, or you don't need to keep learning. This would only mean you are deceiving yourself. There is always more to learn, and associated benefits to reap as we grow.

"He who knows best knows how little he knows."
—THOMAS JEFFERSON

In the end, a commitment to continuous learning will fuel self-improvement and allow you to reap dividends in more ways than you can imagine. Even if only 1 in 1,000 ideas or concepts you encounter is of some value to your situation, it's worth it. As with any effort expended toward your own betterment, it's an investment in your future.

This is an investment that you should continue to make in yourself, but recognize that it's a never-ending process and must be done in parallel with action. There is a large part of learning that can only be gained through experience and making mistakes. If you wait to make an investment until you feel that everything has been completely researched and you're 100% ready, then you'll gain a lot of book knowledge but never get started.

KEY POINTS

- You don't need an MBA to be a real estate investor, but the more knowledge you absorb, the greater competitive advantage you'll have.
- Good mentors can be highly beneficial, but are not prerequisites for success. Not all aspiring investors will find a mentor, and not all mentors are good mentors.
- When learning, be discriminating without being inflexible. Balance an openness to new ideas with a healthy dose of skepticism, common sense, and sound business principles.

▶ If you can make a commitment to continuous learning, both you and your business will reap the rewards of self-improvement.

CHAPTER 18

GETTING STARTED

*"The secret of getting ahead is getting started. The secret of
getting started is breaking complex overwhelming tasks into
small manageable tasks, and then starting on the first one."*
—MARK TWAIN

"The journey of a thousand miles begins with one step."
—LAO TZU

■

RECENTLY RAN INTO AN aspiring young investor who I hadn't
seen in almost a year. He had met with me a few times to talk
about how to get started, and I was curious to see how things
had gone.

"Actually, I never ended up doing anything," he said. "I really
wanted to invest in real estate, and I appreciate your taking the
time to meet with me. But I'm just too busy. Every time I thought
about it, I just got overwhelmed. I was thinking maybe my schedule
would open up and I would have a block of time, but it just never
happened."

The last time we spoke, I had given him some suggestions on
how to prepare himself, so I wondered if I had inadvertently overwhelmed him. I invited him for coffee later in the week and to see
if I couldn't help him get back on track.

Real estate investing certainly isn't for everyone, but in this case
it sounded like the problem had nothing to do with investing, or
even with lack of motivation. It sounded more like an inability to
break a large goal down into smaller ones.

Feeling overwhelmed is not specific to real estate. The magnitude of big goals can be daunting to almost anyone. It's natural to feel discouraged by something that seems too difficult. The key is to recognize that you are capable of making incremental progress every single day, and that these small steps will eventually add up— sometimes in ways that can surprise you. There is tremendous power in embracing this incremental approach toward reaching seemingly unattainable heights.

CLIMBING MOUNT EVEREST

Acquiring a commercial property might seem like climbing Mount Everest: overwhelming. And in many ways, you wouldn't be wrong to think this. As chronicled in this book, there is a lot of planning involved, and a lot of work to do. So much so that the average person is likely to discard the whole idea out of hand.

But let's try looking at things another way. What if instead of climbing Mount Everest, you were to climb three flights of stairs once per day? Would that be manageable? How much of a climb would that be? Well, let's say each stair is seven inches high, and that each flight of stairs has 24 steps. That works out to a total climb of 42 feet per day.

For most people, 42 feet doesn't seem unreasonable, even if they're not in shape. A far stretch from the tallest mountain on earth, you might say, but certainly doable. And it wouldn't take an exorbitant amount of time, even if you rest for a minute or two between each flight. You could probably fit the stairs in between other tasks. Or if you live or work on the second or third floor, maybe you take the stairs instead of the elevator each day.

Climbing three flights of stairs daily might not seem like much, but it can yield something substantial over time. Believe it or not, in less than two years you will have climbed enough steps to ascend over 30,000 feet, which is higher than the elevation of Mount Everest. This is the power of taking incremental steps.

If you're determined to reach a big goal, you don't need to do it all at once. In fact, you almost certainly can't. The best way to do it is by making a little progress every day. This is what I shared with that aspiring investor over coffee a few days later. He needed to stop looking at real estate investing as one large step, and start looking at it as a series of little ones. He needed to create a daily routine whereby he was putting one foot in front of the other and taking a few steps forward each and every day.

TAKING THE FIRST STEP

What is the hardest part? It's taking the very first step. If you can take that first step and then keep putting one foot in front of the other, you can accomplish extraordinary things. Yet most people never take that step. They see a big goal or great accomplishment as unattainable. They see it as Mount Everest.

"Have a bias toward action— let's see something happen now. You can break that big plan into small steps and take the first step right away."
—INDIRA GANDHI

As with most audacious goals, building a commercial real estate portfolio can be broken down into more manageable chunks. If you want to be a real estate investor, you need to get started. Action is what sets an investor apart from a dreamer.

How do you break it down? Pick up a book and read. Listen to a podcast on the way to work. Browse properties online. Ask for financials. Create a buyer's proforma. Do your homework. But don't research and do homework forever. You'll never be 100% ready. Eventually, after you've researched enough properties, make an offer. Buy that first property. Make mistakes and learn from them. Make more mistakes and keep learning.

You'll never reach your goal unless you start chipping away at it. And to do that, you need to start. Once you take that first step, make a commitment to taking steps forward every single day. Make it a routine. If you can do this, you're likely to look back in a few years and be positively *amazed* at what you've learned and how far you've come. You'll be looking down from the summit of your own personal Mount Everest.

> *"If you have a dream, you can spend a lifetime studying, planning, and getting ready for it. What you should be doing is getting started."*
> —DREW HOUSTON

THE SOLAR BUILDING PROJECT: PART VIII

 While my resolve was tested, and it was hard work for everyone involved, the Solar Building was eventually completely turned around. The tenants who stayed through it all were enormously grateful for the improvements in their living conditions, and their acts of kindness continue to this day. One of them shows up in our office with cupcakes at each major holiday. Another stops by regularly with treats for the dogs in our office. Others just extend warm smiles. No matter how small the gesture, it's rewarding to know that we made a difference and improved their quality of life.

Thankfully, my fears about whether we could lease out the vacant units proved unfounded. The low acquisition price gave us enough flexibility to charge rents that were too compelling for value-conscious tenants to pass up. We rewarded the legacy tenants by locking in their old rent, but every time another apartment opened up for lease, it commanded slightly higher rent, until 18 months later when the gross income from the property had more than doubled.

As the property filled, other income streams besides rent kicked in as well. Higher occupancy and safer conditions resulted in a significant jump in laundry income. We also implemented a revenue-sharing agreement with the local cable company.

On the expense side, we completed a full energy audit and implemented a wide range of improvements to help reduce energy costs and water consumption. As a result, we were able to secure utility incentives and reduce operating expenses.

It took a while, but word of the changes slowly spread through the community and the property's reputation improved. That said, the building's history is emblazoned in some people's memories, so sometimes it can still present a challenge. In most instances, any reservations a prospective renter might have can be overcome by giving them a tour.

The Solar Building was definitely one of our most successful and rewarding projects by any measure. There was an enormous amount of value created for everyone involved—not just through the improved cash flow, but also through a better quality of life for the tenants and the surrounding community. It was humbling and gratifying for everyone involved when the Solar Building project was later featured in a *Community Investor* magazine cover story about our company.

This was a project that challenged my staff and our partners like no other project had. Fortunately, we have a great team that worked together and rose to the occasion. We called on all of the principles espoused in this book to make it happen.

It is my sincerest hope that you can call on some of these principles for your own benefit, as well as for the benefit of your community.

Now get out there, roll up your sleeves, and *crush it*.

▶ The magnitude of big goals can be overwhelming. The key to achieving them is breaking them down into more manageable chunks.

▶ Taking the first step is the hardest part and what sets successful investors apart from those who never get started.

▶ Make a commitment to taking steps forward every single day. If you can do this, you're likely to look backward in a few years and be amazed at your progress.

▶ Doing the hard work necessary to tackle a challenging project can be very rewarding.

FINANCIAL FORMULAS

Annual Income – Annual Expenses (Excluding Debt Service) =
Net Operating Income (NOI)

▓

Cash-on-Cash Return = Annual Cash Flow / Initial Cash
Investment (expressed as a percent)

▓

Payback Period = Initial Cash Investment / Annual Cash Flow

▓

Cap Rate = NOI / Purchase Price (expressed as a percent)

▓

NOI / Cap Rate = Purchase Price

▓

Value-Added = Incremental NOI / Cap Rate

▓

Debt Service Coverage Ratio = NOI / Mortgage Payments

▓

LTV = Loan Amount / Appraised Value (expressed as a percent)

TEAM MEMBERS

THE FOLLOWING IS A list of the team members that a typical real estate investor might need to have:

ACCOUNTANT: Unless you are an experienced accountant, you should seriously consider using the services of a certified public accountant (CPA)—at least for generating financial statements and handling your tax returns. A good CPA will pay for themselves by sharing advice and strategies on how to minimize your tax burden.

ANSWERING SERVICE: In commercial real estate, you need to be available 24/7 in case of emergencies. But as you grow, after-hours calls can become a pain, particularly when they are unimportant. An answering service can be a way to filter incoming calls so that you're only bothered in real cases of emergency. Non-emergency calls and messages can then be responded to on your desired schedule.

APPLIANCE REPAIR: If you own apartments, you'll be dealing with appliances. It's often cheaper to make repairs than to make replacements.

ARCHITECT: Experienced architects can help you navigate local code issues and avoid unexpected problems with the projects you undertake. They can also help with cost estimates and securing project bids. The best architects are also magicians at maximizing space utility and design.

ASPHALT/PAVING/STRIPING CONTRACTOR: If your property includes a driveway or parking lot, the asphalt and striping will need to be maintained and eventually resurfaced.

ATTORNEY: It's best to have a good commercial real estate attorney, particularly for real estate transactions or significant lease negotiations. As your business grows, you may end up with multiple attorneys, perhaps using separate counsel for things like evictions, labor issues, or lawsuits.

BACKGROUND CHECK COMPANY: If you're an apartment owner, you'll want to find a service provider through which you can run security and credit checks to screen your prospective tenants.

BANK: This is perhaps the most important partner of all. This is why there is an entire chapter dedicated to it.

BOOKKEEPER: Many investors elect to do their own bookkeeping, at least early on. But if you're short on time, this is a task that can be somewhat menial and is a candidate for outsourcing. You can also have your accountant handle bookkeeping.

CARPENTER/DRYWALL: Any commercial property will periodically require the services of somebody with basic carpentry or drywall skills.

COLLECTION AGENCY: There is a limit to how much time and effort it is worthwhile to expend on the unpleasant task of collecting back rent. Once a tenant leaves or is evicted, it's often best to hand this off to the professionals that will work off of a commission on what they collect. Since these agencies report uncollected debt to credit agencies, it can provide additional incentive for tenants to pay up.

COMMERCIAL CLEANER: Depending on the size and nature of your properties, it can sometimes be economical or necessary to outsource cleaning services. Cleaning services can be contracted on an as-needed or longer-term basis.

DEMOLITION: If you want to gut a space or demolish a building, you will typically get the best price from a contractor that specializes in demolition. For smaller jobs, you may be able to contract with a roofer (contracting for interior demolition can be a way for roofing companies to keep their crews busy when weather prevents them from working on roofing jobs).

ELECTRICIAN: Working with electricity can be a very dangerous proposition for do-it-yourselfers. Best to establish a good working relationship with a properly trained electrician.

ELEVATOR CONTRACTOR: If your property has an elevator, you'll want to have it serviced and tested periodically. You'll also need to have somebody to call when it breaks down or malfunctions.

EMERGENCY CLEANUP/RESTORATION: Fire/flood/emergency cleanup is something you might not want to think about, but it's better to know in advance who you'll call and establish a relationship in case of an emergency. If you stay in the business for a while, it's not a question of if, it's a question of when.

ENERGY PROGRAM CONTRACTOR: Energy consultants versed in regional programs can help you navigate and implement a wide variety of value-add improvements that might be subsidized by government entities or utility companies. Oftentimes their fees are covered in part or full by the agency sponsoring the programs.

ENGINEER: If you have a project with significant structural or mechanical issues, it is best to call on the services of an engineer working in the associated discipline.

ENVIRONMENTAL ABATEMENT: If you do a significant amount of work on older properties, you are likely to encounter hazardous materials such as asbestos that will need to be abated.

ENVIRONMENTAL ENGINEER: Many lenders will require you to complete an environmental survey, or a Phase I or Phase II environmental report prior to lending.

EXTERMINATOR/PEST CONTROL: Commercial real estate owners must be mindful of the importance of keeping pests at bay. Routine, preventative treatments should be established with a pest control company that is also available for emergency situations.

FENCING: Fencing is usually most economically supplied by a company that specializes in fencing.

FIRE/ALARM CONTRACTOR: Most commercial properties have fire extinguishers that need to be inspected regularly, sprinkler systems that need to be maintained, and alarm systems that might need to be serviced.

FLOORING CONTRACTOR: The build-out of most spaces includes flooring work. This is particularly true for apartments, where carpets must be changed out regularly.

GENERAL CONTRACTOR (GC): Larger projects are sometimes too much for you to oversee all the individual trades yourself, or you may not yet be ready to undertake something of such magnitude. A good general contractor is like the conductor of the orchestra; they will organize all elements of a construction project and alleviate the hassles of being your own GC.

HVAC CONTRACTOR: Problems with heating, ventilation, or air-conditioning are routine in a commercial property. It's best to have the systems maintained by a professional, preferably a responsive contractor you can call whenever there is a problem. You can generally secure annual maintenance contracts and/or negotiate on a project basis.

INSURANCE BROKER: It's important to maintain the proper insurance at competitive rates. A good insurance broker can help you navigate these waters and simplify the process.

IT CONTRACTOR: As your company grows, so will your computers, printers, and IT infrastructure. When the time comes, you'll need somebody to call with problems if you're not technologically inclined.

LANDSCAPER: If your business can afford it, having a professional landscaper spruce up a property can really make it pop, even if you intend to maintain it yourself.

LAUNDRY: Apartment owners can boost revenues through laundry income. If the laundry machines are owned, they will need to be repaired periodically. The other option is to outsource laundry to a third party. In this case, a third-party company provides and maintains the machines, then gives you a percentage of their sales.

LOCKSMITH: Locks and keys are a whole process unto themselves when you're in the commercial real estate business. It's best to identify a good locksmith, plan ahead, and have a system for tracking and labeling keys. Stay organized.

MASON: Concrete, brick, and stonework are best done by a contractor that specializes in masonry.

MORTGAGE BROKER: If you want help shopping around for mortgages, there are brokers out there ready and willing to help you. This is most appropriate for larger deals and national lenders, including banks and insurance companies.

PAINTER: A good, reliable painter is a valuable contractor to have. Most people underestimate the difference you can make at most properties with a fresh coat of paint! It's also something you may be able to do on your own sometimes—particularly in apartments.

PAYMENT PROCESSOR: The ability to process credit card payments or electronic funds transfers can make things a lot more convenient for both you and your tenants, particularly if you're managing an apartment complex.

PAYROLL COMPANY: Doing your own payroll is definitely possible, but also fraught with potential perils. Take it from somebody who was the victim of errors in do-it-yourself payroll taxes—it's not fun to deal with state and federal fines if you get it wrong!

PLUMBER: Establishing a good relationship with one or more licensed plumbers is very important. Plumbing emergencies are not uncommon, and water leaks can rapidly cause significant damage. A responsive and reasonably priced plumber is one of the best partners you can have.

PROPERTY MANAGEMENT COMPANY: If you are unable to manage your own property, you can outsource this function to a property management firm. In this case, you serve as the asset manager, which includes the oversight of the property management firm.

PROPERTY MANAGEMENT SOFTWARE SERVICE: For my first few properties, I did everything in a spreadsheet. But a good software service can make property management a lot more efficient and set a better foundation for growth and expansion.

REAL ESTATE BROKER: Establishing positive and fruitful relationships with area commercial real estate brokers is a critical part of most investors' success. Brokers can assist you not only in identifying new properties, but also in securing tenants, commercial and residential. Good brokers earn their commission, so don't be stingy. If you treat them right, you can expect the goodwill to be reciprocated.

ROOFER: Even if you don't expect to have roof work done, damage can be done. Roofers are licensed to do the work properly. See also

Demolition.

SIDING CONTRACTOR: If your property has siding or masonry, it will require a contractor with the appropriate knowledge and skills to make any repairs or upgrades.

SIGN COMPANY: Signage is one of the most powerful and cost-effective mediums for marketing. It's also critical to your tenants for the promotion of their business and to help their patrons find them. A good sign company will not only be able to fabricate signs for you but also be familiar with local ordinances and facilitate the permitting process.

SNOW REMOVAL CONTRACTOR: Depending on the size of your property, removing snow yourself can be impossible without the right equipment. Having a reliable contractor under contract to remove snow is imperative to keeping tenants happy if you're located in an area that experiences difficult winter conditions.

STAFFING/TEMP AGENCY: A staffing company can ease the burden of hiring by taking care of the advertising and prescreening prospective employees. They also offer the benefit of not having to put somebody on your payroll. It can be a convenient way to "try out" a prospective employee and ease the process of getting rid of them if they're not a good fit.

SUPPLY COMPANY: As you grow, you'll want to establish relationships with a variety of companies for general supplies and inventory. This might include office supplies, maintenance materials, equipment, paint, etc. Some of these can be secured from retail stores, while other things, like plumbing parts, might need to be obtained from specialty suppliers.

TRASH COLLECTOR: For properties where the landlord is responsible for trash removal, you will need to contract with a waste collection company. There are also brokers who specialize in putting waste collection needs out to bid and securing the best terms.

TREE REMOVAL: As your portfolio grows, there will inevitably be trees and shrubs to remove. The larger the job, the smarter it is to hire a pro. The terms "experiment" and "chainsaw" don't go particularly well together.

WINDOW WASHER: Oddly enough, many commercial cleaners don't do windows! There are typically separate vendors that specialize in window cleaning. This is particularly important if you have a multi-story property. Best not to break out the bungee cord or scale down the walls and do it yourself.

WINDOW/DOOR CONTRACTOR: Repair or replacement of windows and doors can be a regular activity as your portfolio grows.

UNDERWRITING CONSIDERATIONS BY PROPERTY TYPE

EXAMINERS SHOULD UNDERSTAND THE unique characteristics and risks associated with various types of properties, and banks should establish prudent policies that consider these characteristics and risks for each loan type they finance. General considerations for the primary property types are discussed in this section. Underwriting metrics are provided only for general guidance and vary by market, property type, and building characteristics. Appraisals of similar properties and third-party surveys can provide information that is more specific to a property's characteristics and market.

OFFICE

Office buildings can be classified as suburban or central business district (CBD) properties and graded in terms of quality from A to C. Class A properties are newer, recently rehabilitated, or very well-maintained properties built of high-quality materials offering retail and other amenities. Class B properties are older or of average construction with few or no amenities and average desirability, while Class C offers space that may be outdated or plain but functional.

Important characteristics to consider when evaluating an office property are the aesthetics of the design and quality of materials, availability of parking, access to public transportation or major roads, and proximity to hotels, shopping, and other amenities. Also important are the size and configurability of the floors (the floor plate) to accommodate tenants requiring various amounts of space, adequacy of elevator service, and the ability to meet current and future technology requirements.

Medical office buildings have unique requirements, including additional plumbing and wiring to accommodate examination room fixtures and equipment. Consequently, costs for construction and tenant improvements are higher than conventional office buildings. These buildings are often located near other medical service providers, such as hospitals, and may feature pharmacies and lab facilities.

Office buildings are usually leased on a gross basis (expenses paid by the landlord) with the tenant typically responsible for expenses directly related to occupancy such as utilities and janitorial. Because terms can vary from lease to lease, however, lease agreements should always be reviewed to determine which expenses are the landlord's responsibility. Lease terms are typically for periods of three, five, or seven years.

Replacement reserves for office properties are underwritten on an annual, per-square-foot basis and vary depending on the property's age and condition. Management fees are typically underwritten from 3 to 5 percent of effective gross income, depending on the number of tenants.

Costs to re-lease space are important underwriting considerations. These costs include leasing commissions and the cost of tenant improvements for new and renewing tenants. Leasing commissions are calculated as a percentage of total lease payments with typical underwriting assumptions of 4 percent for new leases and 2 percent for renewals. Expenses for tenant improvements are higher for new tenants than for renewing tenants and can vary widely depending on the market and building class. The re-leasing costs can be projected by an analysis of the rent roll and utilizing an assumption about the probability of renewals with 60 to 65 percent being typical. Re-leasing costs are not always considered as an operating expense in calculating NOI but are an important consideration when analyzing cash flow.

Source: The Office of the Comptroller of the Currency (OCC) Comptroller's Handbook, "Commercial Real Estate Lending," August 2013, http://www.occ.gov/publications/publications-by-type/comptrollers-handbook/cre.pdf.

RETAIL

There are many types of retail properties. They may be anchored, with major tenants that generate traffic for other tenants and provide financial stability, or unanchored. They range in size from very small neighborhood centers serving their immediate communities to super regional malls that may have 1 million square feet or more drawing from very large trade areas.

Demographics, including population concentration and income levels, along with vehicular traffic volume, site configuration, ease of ingress and egress, parking, surrounding residential density, and tenant mix are all important in determining the success of retail properties.

Appropriate site characteristics are critical to the success of retail properties. Some things to consider include the following:

▶ The traffic count should be suitable for the retail type; small neighborhood centers can be successful on tertiary or secondary roads while larger properties, such as power centers or major malls, require location on or access to primary arteries.

▶ Properties and signage should be readily visible to passing traffic; sites that are parallel to the primary source of traffic flow are generally superior to sites that are perpendicular to the road, having less frontage and visibility.

▶ Traffic control devices and turning lanes should permit easy access for vehicles passing in either direction at all times of the day.

▶ Lease terms generally vary by retail type and tenant. Considerations include the following.

▶ Lease terms typically range from five to 10 years with anchor tenants often signing leases of 20 to 25 years with options to renew.

▶ Leases are commonly written on a net basis with tenants reimbursing the landlord for common area maintenance (CAM), including landscaping, refuse collection, taxes, insurance, and lighting of parking lots and walkways, with the landlord usually responsible for the roof and outer walls. Because terms can vary from lease to lease, however, lease agreements should always be reviewed to determine which expenses are the landlord's responsibility.

▶ Anchor tenants may pay a flat rate plus a percentage of their annual sales (percentage rent). Percentage rents may vary considerably and are inherently less predictable. The flat rate should be high enough to dissuade the tenant from ceasing operations while maintaining possession in order to prevent the landlord from leasing to a competitor. It is desirable for an anchor tenant's lease to require continued operations so that the tenant may be replaced if it ceases to operate.

▶ Some lease clauses may call for a decrease in rents or permit termination if an anchor tenant ceases operations (co-tenancy clauses). These clauses make the success of anchor tenants even more critical to the viability of the property.

Tenant improvements provided for retail tenants tend to be minimal, with the landlord usually delivering a so-called white box (primed drywall and a concrete floor) to the tenant who is responsible for finishing the space.

Replacement reserves for retail properties are underwritten on an annual per-square-foot basis and vary depending on the property's age and condition. Management fees are typically underwritten at 3 to 5 percent of effective gross income, exclusive of reimbursements.

Re-leasing costs consist mostly of leasing commissions, which are usually underwritten at 4 percent of the total lease payments for new tenants and 2 percent for renewing tenants as determined by the underwriting assumptions with respect to tenant renewal.

INDUSTRIAL

Industrial properties include manufacturing, light industrial, warehouse, and distribution facilities. While industrial properties can be located in older or redeveloped urban areas or in the suburbs, their proximity to transportation is an important factor. This is also true of distribution facilities where access to major highways is of crucial importance.

Industrial buildings can vary widely in size, typically ranging from several thousand to several hundred thousand square feet and may be single tenant or multitenant. Office space usually comprises about 10 to 20 percent of the total square footage of these properties.

Physical characteristics that can accommodate the operations of prospective tenants are critical considerations. Industrial properties usually feature ceiling heights that range from 18 to 30 feet and require sufficient truck bays with a site large enough to permit the maneuvering of large trucks. Electrical capacity and floor thickness are important considerations. Properties that do not meet these criteria may be at a significant disadvantage relative to competing properties.

Industrial properties having a higher percentage of office space, sometimes 50 percent or more, are commonly referred to as flex, research and development, or high-tech. The industrial portions of these buildings tend to have office-like ceiling heights with few or no truck bays. These properties share many characteristics with office properties, and these characteristics should be considered when the properties are underwritten.

Industrial properties as a group pose the highest risk of environmental contamination and merit close review of past and intended uses and investigation of their current environmental condition.

Manufacturing facilities are often built to accommodate a specific user's needs. The adaptability of the building to meet the needs of other potential users is an important underwriting consideration.

Leases for single-tenant industrial properties are usually written on a net basis with the landlord responsible for maintenance of the roof and outer walls only. Because terms can vary from lease to lease, however, lease agreements should always be reviewed to determine which expenses are the landlord's responsibility.

Landlords for multitenant properties would typically be responsible for CAM and require reimbursement for this from the tenant.

Lease terms of three to five years are common. Replacement reserves for industrial properties are underwritten on an annual per-square-foot basis and vary depending on the age and condition of the property. Management fees typically range from 3 to 4 percent, depending on the number of tenants.

MULTIFAMILY

Multifamily rental properties fill an important need in many communities; they can be more affordable than owner-occupied housing and offer relatively short-term housing solutions. Multifamily, or apartment, properties have historically been one of the most stable property types, despite typical leases of one year and higher rates of tenant turnover than other property types.

Management ability is critical to the success of these properties; inept or inexperienced management is a major cause of difficulty for loans financing multifamily dwellings. Mitigating tenant turnover requires a constant marketing effort and management must retain tenants when possible by being attentive to their needs. In addition to attracting and retaining tenants, management must do an effective job of collecting rents. Even though a review of the rent roll might indicate a high rate of occupancy, actual collections should be examined to determine the true economic occupancy and evaluate the competency of management and the effectiveness of its collection efforts. Whether properties are self-managed or managed by a third party, the manager's ability and experience should be carefully evaluated.

Important general considerations for multifamily properties include:

▶ **Demographics**: Income levels, age distribution, rate of household formations, and household sizes.
▶ **Economic Factors**: Affordability of entry-level single-family housing versus renting, strength of local economy, local employment conditions including current levels and trends, trends in the value of single-family housing, current levels and trends for local rents, and vacancy.

- **Location Factors**: Local quality of life; proximity to shopping, recreation, and employment; school system; and availability of land for future residential development.
- **Local and State Laws**: Rent control and/or stabilization programs, co-op/condominium conversion rules, low income housing programs.

Property-specific considerations include:

- Occupancy history
- Collection losses
- Rents as compared with competitive properties
- Management quality
- Ingress and egress
- Quality of construction, age, and condition of improvements
- Parking availability and convenience
- Amenities as compared with competitive properties
- Availability of individual unit metering for utilities

Lack of proper maintenance can pose a significant risk to the viability of multifamily properties. Undercapitalized borrowers may neglect needed maintenance when cash flows are inadequate which can result in increased turnover and vacancies. Deferred maintenance can significantly affect loan losses and expenses in the event of foreclosure. An inspection of the property should determine how many of the vacant units are rentable in their current condition; cash-strapped borrowers sometimes "cannibalize" vacant units of appliances, heating units, and other items when replacements are needed. It is important that banks monitor property maintenance and improvements to ensure they are timely and appropriate. Banks should ensure that cash flow is adequate to provide for necessary replacements and upgrades over time.

Historical operating expenses should be carefully analyzed. Operating expenses would usually be expected to range from 35 to 45 percent of revenue. Older properties, those with more amenities, and properties where the landlord provides heat, water, or electricity as part of the rent (usually because of lack of separate metering) represent the upper end of the range.

A multifamily property is typically underwritten with management fees of 5 percent of revenues. Replacement reserves for multifamily properties are underwritten on an annual per-unit basis and vary based on the age and condition of the property.

HOSPITALITY

The hospitality industry is highly sensitive to trends in leisure and business spending. Hospitality properties have historically experienced considerable volatility in income and value. Hotel operations can be complex and may have a sizable non-real estate component. Successful hotel lending requires specialized knowledge and should not be undertaken without an adequate understanding of the hospitality business.

Hotels may be full or limited service. Full service hotels offer a number of amenities including dining and room service, convenience retail, higher service-staff levels, banquet and convention facilities, recreational facilities, and business support services. Consequently, full service hotels derive a significant portion of their income from non-room-related activities. Non-room revenue and expense centers include banquet, food and beverage, and others.

Limited service hotels and motels offer no or limited food service and limited meeting space. Location in close proximity to restaurants is an important consideration for limited service hotels.

A hotel's franchise, or "flag," can be an important factor in the success of a hotel. Flagged hotels benefit from a central reservation service and guest loyalty programs. Other franchise benefits include brand identity, operating guidance, strategic support, uniform standards, training, and marketing and sales support.

In addition to economic conditions, the following property-specific factors should be considered:

- Current and historical profitability and trends
- Management quality
- Reputation of the franchisor
- Franchise agreement including duration and termination rights
- Property age, condition, and amenities
- Age, condition, and quality of furniture, fixtures, and equipment (FF&E) and replacement needs
- Revenue seasonality
- Proximity to transportation and demand generators such as office and recreational facilities
- Adequacy and convenience of parking

Common performance metrics for hotels are occupancy and average daily rate (ADR) and revenue per available room (RevPAR). The ADR is calculated by dividing the room revenue by the number of rooms occupied for a given period. This calculation should exclude complimentary rooms or other occupancy that do not generate revenue. RevPAR is calculated by multiplying a hotel's ADR by its occupancy rate.

Other income and expenses, such as for food and beverage, banquet, telephone, or Internet use, are segregated into separate departments. Expenses that are not directly attributable to a department, such as management, franchise, sales and marketing fees, and repairs and maintenance, are recorded as unallocated expenses. Real estate taxes and insurance are allocated to fixed expenses.

Studies of industry performance metrics provide an important comparative reference in underwriting hotels. These studies are commercially available and should be utilized in the bank's underwriting process. While an analysis of historical income and expenses should include a comparison with industry benchmarks to test for reasonableness, the following underwriting considerations provide guidance in analyzing a hotel's income and expenses:

- **Franchise Fees**: Usually underwritten at the higher of actual or 4 to 6 percent of total revenues.

- **Management Fees**: Typically expected to be 4 to 5 percent of gross revenues.
- **Fixed Expenses**: Expenses for property taxes, real and personal, should reflect the actual property tax assessment. Insurance should reflect the actual expense and include premiums for insuring the real and personal property.
- **Replacement Reserves**: Reserves for FF&E typically range from 4 to 6 percent of total revenues.
- **Profit Margins**: Vary according to type, franchise, and location. Margins for full service properties typically range from 20 to 30 percent while limited service properties generally range from 30 to 40 percent. Luxury resorts typically range from 20 to 25 percent with extended-stay suites usually ranging from 35 to 42 percent.

Appraisals of hotel properties, in addition to the market value of the real estate, may also include values of personal property, such as FF&E, and intangibles, such as goodwill. The sum of these values is sometimes referred to as the "going-concern value." The value, however, of non-real property, such as personal property and intangibles, cannot be used to support federally related transactions; value opinions, such as "going-concern value," "value in use," or a special value to a specific property user may not be used as market value for federally related transactions. An appraisal report that elicits a value of the enterprise, such as "going-concern value," must allocate that value among the components of the total value. Traditionally, the three components are described as: (1) market value of the real estate, (2) personal property value, and (3) value of intangibles. The bank may rely only on the real estate's market value in these appraisals to support the federally related transaction. A separate loan may be used to finance the personal property or intangibles. For further information, see OCC Bulletin 2010–42, "Sound Practices for Appraisals and Evaluations: Interagency Appraisal and Evaluation Guidelines."

RESIDENTIAL HEALTH CARE

Residential health care facilities typically include independent living, assisted living, and nursing homes. The most significant distinction among these is the level of care provided. While facilities are most often dedicated to one level of care, some may provide a continuum of services.

Independent living, sometimes referred to as congregate care, provides the lowest level of care. The residents do not require daily assistance with living activities and enjoy a high degree of mobility. The facilities share many of the features and amenities of multifamily properties with such additional features as dining rooms and communal living areas. The facilities may offer meals, laundry, and housekeeping. No health care is provided. These properties are not regulated and do not qualify for government reimbursement. Income is generated mostly from unit rental.

Assisted-living facilities provide a range of services for the elderly and disabled that can include meals, laundry, housekeeping, transportation, and assistance with daily living activities, such as dressing and bathing. Assisted-living facilities may be subject to state regulation with varying levels of health care permitted. When more acute medical care is permitted and provided, government reimbursement may be available.

Nursing homes provide 24-hour non-acute medical care and provide the highest level of living assistance and medical care. Nursing homes are highly regulated and, like hospitals, are subject to state certificates of need. Government reimbursement is a common source of payment.

The demand for residential health care facilities is strongly correlated with local demographics; residents want to live in locations convenient to their families, with older populations generating greater demand. The bank should consider the quality, reputation, and experience of management. Other considerations are adequacy of staffing, staff turnover, the condition and location of the facility, and the quality of care and services.

Assisted-living facilities and nursing homes are sensitive to government reimbursement programs; state and federal policies affecting qualification criteria and reimbursement rates are important considerations in the analysis of these properties. The mix of private and government pay can be a useful measurement in determining the sensitivity of these properties to changes in government reimbursement policies.

RESOURCES

Books on Real Estate Investing

The Book on Investing in Real Estate with No (and Low) Money Down by Brandon Turner

The Book on Managing Rental Properties by Brandon Turner and Heather Turner

The Book on Rental Property Investing by Brandon Turner

Commercial Mortgages 101 by Michael Reinhard

Commercial Real Estate 101 by Mark Flores

Commercial Real Estate for Beginners by Peter Harris

Commercial Real Estate Investing for Dummies by Peter Conti and Peter Harris

The Complete Guide to Buying and Selling Apartment Buildings by Steve Berges

Confessions of a Real Estate Entrepreneur by James A. Randel

The Due Diligence Handbook for Commercial Real Estate by Brian Hennessey

Getting Started in Commercial Real Estate by Adam Von Romer and Patricia O'Connor

How to Build a Real Estate Empire by Marcel Arsenault, et al.

How to Read a Rent Roll by John Wilhoit Jr.

How to Succeed in Commercial Real Estate by John L. Bowman

How to Win in Commercial Real Estate Investing by R. Craig Coppola

How We Bought a 24-Unit Apartment Building for (Almost) No Money Down by Brandon Turner

Investing in Apartment Buildings by Matthew Martinez

The Millionaire Real Estate Investor by Gary Keller

Multi-Family Millions by David Lindahl

The Real Book of Real Estate by Robert Kiyosaki

Real Estate: Investing Successfully for Beginners by F. R. Commerce

The Wall Street Journal Complete Real-Estate Investing Guidebook by David Crook

*What Every Real Estate Investor Needs to Know About Cash Flow…
And 36 Other Key Financial Measures* by Frank Gallinelli

Books on Commercial Leasing and Sales

The Art of Commercial Real Estate Leasing by R. Craig Coppola

The Fundamentals of Listing and Selling Commercial Real Estate by Keim K. Loren

Getting Started in Commercial Real Estate by Adam Von Romer and Patricia O'Connor

How to Succeed in Commercial Real Estate by John L. Bowman

How to Win in Commercial Real Estate Investing by R. Craig Coppola

Negotiating Commercial Real Estate Leases by Martin I. Zankel

Books on Property Management

The ABCs of Property Management by Ken McElroy

Be a Successful Property Manager by Roger Woodson

Professional Property Management by Zenya Allen

Property Management by Robert C. Kyle

Property Management by Kathryn Haupt

Property Management Accounting by Marc Levetin

Property Management Kit for Dummies by Robert S. Griswold

The Property Management Tool Kit by Mike Beirne

Your Quick Guide to Commercial Property Management by John Highman

General Business Books

The 4-Hour Workweek by Timothy Ferriss

The Bootstrapper's Bible by Seth Godin

Competitive Strategy by Michael E. Porter

David and Goliath by Malcolm Gladwell

Delivering Happiness by Tony Hsieh

Don't Sweat the Small Stuff by Richard Carlson

Dr. Deming by Rafael Aguayo

The E-Myth Revisited by Michael E. Gerber

The Essays of Warren Buffett by Warren Buffett and Lawrence Cunningham

Good to Great by Jim Collins

Grit by Angela Duckworth

The Hard Thing About Hard Things by Ben Horowitz

The Obstacle Is the Way by Ryan Holiday

Rich Dad Poor Dad by Robert Kiyosaki
The Richest Man in Babylon by George S. Clason
Think and Grow Rich by Napoleon Hill
Wooden by Coach John Wooden
Zero to One by Peter Thiel

Websites

www.auction.com
www.biggerpockets.com
www.boma.org
www.ccim.com
www.irei.com
www.irem.org
www.loopnet.com
www.multifamilyexecutive.com

Podcasts

"Best Real Estate Investing Advice Ever" with Joe Fairless
BiggerPockets' "Real Estate Investing & Wealth Building Podcast"
"Apartment Building Investing Podcast" with Michael Blank
"The Commercial Real Estate Show" with Michael Bull
"The Deal Farm" with Ken Corsini
"Epic Real Estate Investing" with Matt Theriault
"Freedom Real Estate Investing" with Brock Collins
"LandAcademy" with Jack Butala and Jill DeWit
"The Real Estate Guys Radio Show"
"Real Estate Investing for Cash Flow" with Kevin Bupp
"Real Estate Investing Mastery" with Joe McCall
"Real Estate Realities" with Robert "The Rebel Broker" Whitelaw
"The Ultimate Real Estate Investing Podcast" by Sean Terry

GLOSSARY

THE FOLLOWING GLOSSARY CONTAINS commonly used terms in commercial real estate. It is provided as a quick reference and is not comprehensive.

The definitions are courtesy of Institutional Real Estate Inc. (IREI). Since 1987, IREI has been a leading force in industry knowledge, providing institutional real estate and infrastructure investors with decision-making tools via its publications, conferences, and consulting services.

Readers are encouraged to visit the organization's website (www.irei.com) for complimentary access to a more complete and updated glossary of terms, as well as a host of excellent educational resources for commercial real estate professionals.

ABATEMENT: Often referred to as free rent or early occupancy and may occur outside or in addition to the primary term of the lease.

ABOVE BUILDING STANDARD: Upgraded finishes and specialized designs necessary to accommodate a tenant's requirements.

ABSORPTION RATE: The rate at which rentable space is filled. Gross absorption is a measure of the total square feet leased over a specified period with no consideration given to space vacated in the same geographic area during the same time period. Net absorption is equal to the amount occupied at the end of a period minus the amount occupied at the beginning of a period and takes into consideration space vacated during the period.

ADMINISTRATIVE FEE: Usually stated as a percentage of assets under management or as a fixed annual dollar amount.

ADVANCES: Payments made by the servicer when the borrower fails to make a payment.

ADVISER: A broker, consultant or investment banker who represents an investor in a transaction. Advisers may be paid a retainer and/or a performance fee upon the close of a financing or sales transaction.

ALTERNATIVE OR SPECIALTY INVESTMENTS: Property types that are not considered conventional institutional-grade real estate investments. Examples include congregate care facilities, self-storage facilities, mobile homes, timber, agriculture and parking lots.

AMORTIZATION: The liquidation of a financial debt through regular periodic installment payments. For tax purposes, the periodic deduction of capitalized expenses such as organization costs.

ANCHOR: The tenant that serves as the predominant draw to a commercial property, usually the largest tenant in a shopping center.

ANNUAL PERCENTAGE RATE (APR): The actual cost of borrowing money. It may be higher than the note rate because it represents full disclosure of the interest rate, loan origination fees, loan discount points and other credit costs paid to the lender.

APPRAISAL: An estimate of a property's fair market value that is typically based on replacement cost, discounted cash flow analysis and/or comparable sales price.

APPRECIATION: An increase in the value or price of an asset.

APPRECIATION RETURN: The portion of the total return generated by the change in the value of the real estate assets during the current quarter, as measured by both appraisals and sales of assets.

AS-IS CONDITION: The acceptance by the tenant of the existing condition of the premises at the time a lease is consummated, including any physical defects.

ASSESSMENT: A fee imposed on property, usually to pay for public improvements such as water, sewers, streets, improvement districts, etc.

ASSET MANAGEMENT: The various disciplines involved with managing real property assets from the time of investment through the time of disposition, including acquisition, management, leasing, operational/financial reporting, appraisals, audits, market review and asset disposition plans.

ASSET MANAGEMENT FEE: A fee charged to investors based on the amount invested into real estate assets for the fund or account.

ASSET TURNOVER: Calculated as total revenues for the trailing 12 months divided by the average total assets.

ASSETS UNDER MANAGEMENT: The current market value of real estate assets for which a manager has investment and asset management responsibilities.

ASSIGNEE NAME: The individual or entity to which the obligations of a lease, mortgage or other contract have been transferred.

ASSIGNMENT: A transfer of the lessee's entire stake in the property. It is distinguishable from a sublease where the sublessee acquires something less than the lessee's entire interest.

ATTORN: To agree to recognize a new owner of a property and to pay him/her rent.

AVERAGE DOWNTIME: Expressed in months, the amount of time expected between the expiration of a lease and the commencement of a replacement lease under current market conditions.

AVERAGE FREE RENT: Expressed in months, the rent abatement concession expected to be granted to a tenant as part of a lease incentive under current market conditions.

AVERAGE OCCUPANCY: The average occupancy rate of each of the preceding 12 months.

BALLOON RISK: The risk that a borrower will not be able to make a balloon (lump sum) payment at maturity due to a lack of funding.

BALLOON OR BULLET LOAN: A loan with a maturity that is shorter than the amortization period.

BANKRUPT: The state of an entity that is unable to repay its debts as they become due.

BANKRUPTCY: Proceedings under federal statutes to relieve a debtor who is unable or unwilling to pay its debts. After addressing certain priorities and exemptions, the bankrupt entity's property and other assets are distributed by the court to creditors as full satisfaction for the debt.

BASE RENT: A set amount used as a minimum rent with provisions for increasing the rent over the term of the lease.

BASE YEAR: Actual taxes and operating expenses for a specified year, most often the year in which a lease commences.

BASIS POINT: 1/100 of 1 percent.

BELOW-GRADE: Any structure or portion of a structure located underground or below the surface grade of the surrounding land.

BID: An offer, stated as a price or spread, to buy whole loans or securities.

BLIND POOL: A commingled fund accepting investor capital without prior specification of property assets.

BROKER: A person who acts as an intermediary between two or more parties in connection with a transaction.

BUILD-OUT: Space improvements put in place per the tenant's specifications. Takes into consideration the amount of tenant finish allowance provided for in the lease agreement.

BUILD-TO-SUIT: A method of leasing property whereby the developer/landlord builds to a tenant's specifications.

BUILDABLE ACRES: The area of land that is available to be built on after subtracting for roads, setbacks, anticipated open spaces and areas unsuitable for construction.

BUILDING CODE: The various laws set forth by the ruling municipality as to the end use of a certain piece of property. They dictate the criteria for design, materials and types of improvements allowed.

BUILDING STANDARD PLUS ALLOWANCE: The landlord lists, in detail, the building standard materials and costs necessary to make the premises suitable for occupancy. A negotiated allowance is then provided for the tenant to customize or upgrade materials.

CALL DATE: Periodic or continuous rights given to the lender to cause payment of the total principal balance prior to the maturity date.

CAPITAL APPRECIATION: The change in market value of a property or portfolio adjusted for capital improvements and partial sales.

CAPITAL EXPENDITURES: Investment of cash or the creation of a liability to acquire or improve an asset, as distinguished from cash outflows for expense items that are considered part of normal operations.

CAPITAL GAIN: The amount by which the net proceeds from the sale of a capital item exceeds the book value of the asset.

CAPITAL IMPROVEMENTS: Expenditures that arrest deterioration of property or add new improvements and appreciably prolong its life.

CAPITAL MARKETS: Public and private markets where businesses or individuals can raise or borrow capital.

CAPITALIZATION: The total dollar value of various securities issued by a company.

CAPITALIZATION RATE: The rate at which net operating income is discounted to determine the value of a property. It is the net operating income divided by the sales price or value of a property expressed as a percentage.

CARRYING CHARGES: Costs incidental to property ownership that must be absorbed by the landlord during the initial lease-up of a building and thereafter during periods of vacancy.

CASH FLOW: The revenue remaining after all cash expenses are paid.

CASH-ON-CASH YIELD: The relationship, expressed as a percentage, between the net cash flow of a property and the average amount of invested capital during an operating year.

CERTIFICATE OF OCCUPANCY: A document presented by a local government agency or building department certifying that a building and/or the leased area has been satisfactorily inspected and is in a condition suitable for occupancy.

CHAPTER 11: That portion of the federal bankruptcy code that deals with business reorganizations.

CHAPTER 7: That portion of the federal bankruptcy code that deals with business liquidations.

CIRCULATION FACTOR: Interior space required for internal office circulation not accounted for in the net square footage.

CLASS A: A real estate rating generally assigned to properties that will generate the highest rents per square foot due to their high quality and/or superior location.

CLASS B: Good assets that most tenants would find desirable but lack attributes that would permit owners to charge top dollar.

CLASS C: Buildings that offer few amenities but are otherwise in physically acceptable condition and provide cost-effective space to tenants who are not particularly image-conscious.

CLEAR-SPAN FACILITY: A building, most often a warehouse or parking garage, with vertical columns on the outside edges of the structure and a clear span between columns.

CMBS (COMMERCIAL MORTGAGE-BACKED SECURITIES): Securities backed by loans on commercial real estate.

CMO (COLLATERALIZED MORTGAGE OBLIGATION): Debt obligations that are collateralized by and have payments linked to a pool of mortgages.

COLLATERAL: Asset(s) pledged to a lender to secure repayment of a loan in case of default.

COMMERCIAL REAL ESTATE: Buildings or land intended to generate a profit for investors, either from rental income or capital gain. Types of commercial real estate include office buildings, retail properties, industrial properties, apartments and hotels, as well as specialty niche property categories such as healthcare, student housing, senior housing, self-storage, data centers and farmland.

COMMON AREA: For lease purposes, the areas of a building and its site that are available for the non-exclusive use of all its tenants, e.g., lobbies, corridors, etc.

COMMON AREA MAINTENANCE (CAM): Rent charged to the tenant in addition to the base rent to maintain the common areas. Examples include snow removal, outdoor lighting, parking lot sweeping, insurance, property taxes, etc.

COMPARABLES: Used to determine the fair market lease rate or asking price, based on other properties with similar characteristics.

CONCESSIONS: Cash or cash equivalents expended by the landlord in the form of rental abatement, additional tenant finish allowance, moving expenses or other monies expended to influence or persuade a tenant to sign a lease.

CONDEMNATION: The process of taking private property, without the consent of the owner, by a governmental agency for public use through the power of eminent domain.

CONSTRUCTION LOAN: Interim financing during the developmental phase of a property.

CONSTRUCTION MANAGEMENT: The act of ensuring the various stages of the construction process are completed in a timely and seamless fashion.

CONSUMER PRICE INDEX (CPI): Measures inflation in relation to the change in the price of goods and services purchased by a specified population during a base period of time. The CPI is commonly used to increase the base rent periodically as a means of protecting the landlord's rental stream against inflation or to provide a cushion for operating expense increases for a landlord unwilling to undertake the record-keeping necessary for operating expense escalations.

CONTIGUOUS SPACE: Multiple suites/spaces within the same building and on the same floor that can be combined and rented to a single tenant, or a block of space located on multiple adjoining floors in a building.

CONTRACT DOCUMENTS: The complete set of design plans and specifications for the construction of a building.

CONTRACT RENT: The rental obligation, expressed in dollars, as specified in a lease. Also known as face rent.

CONVERTIBLE DEBT: A mortgage position that gives the lender the option to convert to a partial or full ownership position in a property within a specified time period.

CONVEYANCE: Most commonly refers to the transfer of title to property between parties by deed. The term may also include most of the instruments with which an interest in real estate is created, mortgaged or assigned.

CORE: Typically includes the four major property types—specifically office, retail, industrial and multifamily. Core assets are high-quality, multitenanted properties typically located in major metropolitan areas and built within the past five years or recently renovated. They are substantially leased (90 percent or better) with higher-credit tenants and well-structured, long-term leases with the majority fairly early in the term of the lease. Core investments are unleveraged or very low leveraged and generate good, stable income that, together with potential appreciation, is historically expected to generate total returns in the 8 to 10 percent range. (Note: In today's low-yield environment, many investors are willing to accept core property returns below 8 percent.)

CORE-PLUS: These investments possess similar attributes to core properties—providing moderate risk and moderate returns—but these assets offer an opportunity for modest value enhancement, typically through improved tenancy/occupancy or minor property improvements. This strategy might employ leverage in the range of 30 to 50 percent with return expectations of 9 to 12 percent.

COST-APPROACH IMPROVEMENT VALUE: The current cost to construct a reproduction of, or replacement for, the existing structure less an estimate for accrued depreciation.

COST-APPROACH LAND VALUE: The estimated value of the fee simple interest in the land as if vacant and available for development to its highest and best use.

COST-OF-SALE PERCENTAGE: An estimate of the costs to sell an investment representing brokerage commissions, closing costs, fees and other necessary disposition expenses.

COUPON: The nominal interest rate charged to the borrower on a promissory note or mortgage.

COVENANT: A written agreement inserted into deeds or other legal instruments stipulating performance or non-performance of certain acts, or use or non-use of a property and/or land.

CROSS-COLLATERALIZATION: A grouping of mortgages or properties that serves to jointly secure one debt obligation.

CROSS-DEFAULTING: Allows the trustee to call all loans in a group into default when any single loan is in default.

CUMULATIVE DISCOUNT RATE: Expressed as a percentage of base rent, it is the interest rate used in finding present values that takes into account all landlord lease concessions.

CURRENT OCCUPANCY: The current leased portion of a building or property expressed as a percentage of its total area or units.

DEAL STRUCTURE: With regard to the financing of an acquisition, deals can be unleveraged, leveraged, traditional debt, participating debt, participating/convertible debt or joint ventures.

DEBT SERVICE: The outlay necessary to meet all interest and principal payments during a given period.

DEBT SERVICE COVERAGE RATIO (DSCR): The annual net operating income from a property divided by annual cost of debt service. A DSCR below 1 means the property is generating insufficient cash flow to cover debt payments.

DEDICATE: To appropriate private property to public ownership for a public use.

DEED: A legal instrument transferring title to real property from the seller to the buyer upon the sale of such property.

DEED IN LIEU OF FORECLOSURE: A deed given by an owner/borrower to a lender to satisfy a mortgage debt and avoid foreclosure.

DEED OF TRUST: An instrument used in place of a mortgage by which real property is transferred to a trustee to secure repayment of a debt.

DEFAULT: The general failure to perform a legal or contractual duty or to discharge an obligation when due.

DEFERRED MAINTENANCE ACCOUNT: An account a borrower is required to fund that provides for maintenance of a property.

DEFICIENCY JUDGMENT: Imposition of personal liability on a borrower for the unpaid balance of mortgage debt after a foreclosure has failed to yield the full amount of the debt.

DEMISING WALL: The partition wall that separates one tenant's space from another or from the building's common areas.

DEPRECIATION: A decrease or loss in property value due to wear, age or other cause. In accounting, depreciation is a periodic allowance made for this real or implied loss.

DESIGN/BUILD: A system in which a single entity is responsible for both the design and construction.

DISCOUNT RATE: A yield rate used to convert future payments or receipts into present value.

DISTRAINT: The act of seizing personal property of a tenant in default based on the right and interest a landlord has in the property.

DIVERSIFICATION: The process of consummating individual investments in a manner that insulates a portfolio against the risk of reduced yield or capital loss, accomplished by allocating individual investments among a variety of asset types, each with different characteristics.

DOLLAR STOP: An agreed dollar amount of taxes and operating expense each tenant will pay on a prorated basis.

DUE DILIGENCE: Activities carried out by a prospective purchaser or mortgager of real property to confirm that the property is as represented by the seller and is not subject to environmental or other problems. In the case of an IPO registration statement, due diligence is a reasonable investigation by the parties involved to confirm that all the statements within the document are true and that no material facts are omitted.

DUE ON SALE: A covenant that makes a mortgage due if the property is sold before the maturity date.

EARNEST MONEY: The monetary advance of part of the purchase price to indicate the intention and ability of the buyer to carry out the contract.

EASEMENT: A right created by grant, reservation, agreement, prescription or necessary implication to use someone else's property.

ECONOMIC FEASIBILITY: The feasibility of a building or project in terms of costs and revenue, with excess revenue establishing the degree of viability.

ECONOMIC RENT: The market rental value of a property at a given point in time.

EFFECTIVE DATE: The date on which a registration statement becomes effective and the sale of securities can commence.

EFFECTIVE GROSS INCOME (EGI): The total income from a property generated by rents and other sources, less a vacancy factor estimated to be appropriate for the property. EGI is expressed as collected income before expenses and debt service.

EFFECTIVE GROSS RENT (EGR): The net rent generated, after adjusting for tenant improvements and other capital costs, lease commissions and other sales expenses.

EFFECTIVE RENT: The actual rental rate to be achieved by the landlord after deducting the value of concessions from the base rental rate paid by a tenant, usually expressed as an average rate over the term of the lease.

EMINENT DOMAIN: A power to acquire by condemnation private property for public use in return for just compensation.

ENCROACHMENT: The intrusion of a structure that extends, without permission, over a property line, easement boundary or building setback line.

ENCUMBRANCE: A right to, or interest in, real property held by someone other than the owner that does not prevent the transfer of fee title.

ENVIRONMENTAL IMPACT STATEMENT: Documents required by federal and state laws to accompany proposals for major projects and programs that will likely have an impact on the surrounding environment.

EQUITY: The residual value of a property beyond mortgage or liability.

ESCALATION CLAUSE: A clause in a lease that provides for the rent to be increased to reflect changes in expenses paid by the landlord such as real estate taxes and operating costs.

ESCROW AGREEMENT: A written agreement made between an escrow agent and the parties to a contract setting forth the basic obligations of the parties, describing the money (or other things of value) to be deposited in escrow, and instructing the escrow agent concerning the disposition of the monies deposited.

ESTOPPEL CERTIFICATE: A signed statement certifying that certain statements of fact are correct as of the date of the statement and can be relied upon by a third party, including a prospective lender or purchaser.

EXCLUSIVE AGENCY LISTING: A written agreement between a real estate broker and a property owner in which the owner promises to pay a fee or commission to the broker if specified real property is leased during the listing period.

EXIT STRATEGY: Strategy available to investors when they desire to liquidate all or part of their investment.

FACE RENTAL RATE: The asking rental rate published by the landlord.

FACILITY SPACE: The floor area in hospitality properties dedicated to operating departments such as restaurants, health clubs and gift shops that service multiple guests or the general public on an interactive basis not directly related to room occupancy.

FAD (FUNDS AVAILABLE FOR DISTRIBUTION): Funds from operations less deductions for cash expenditures for leasing commissions and tenant improvement costs.

FAIR MARKET VALUE: The sale price at which a property would change hands between a willing buyer and willing seller, neither being under any compulsion to buy or sell and both having reasonable knowledge of the relevant facts.

FANNIE MAE (THE FEDERAL NATIONAL MORTGAGE ASSOCIATION, FNMA): A quasi-governmental corporation authorized to sell debentures in order to supplement private mortgage funds by buying and selling FHA (Federal Housing Administration) and VA (Veterans Affairs) loans at market prices.

FEE SIMPLE INTEREST: When an owner owns all the rights in a real estate parcel.

FFO (FUNDS FROM OPERATIONS): A ratio intended to highlight the amount of cash generated by a company's real estate portfolio relative to its total operating cash flow. FFO is equal to net income, excluding gains (or losses) from debt restructuring and sales of property, plus depreciation and amortization.

FINANCE CHARGE: The amount paid for the privilege of deferring payment of goods or services purchased, including any charges payable by the purchaser as a condition of the loan.

FIRST MORTGAGE: The senior mortgage that, by reason of its position, has priority over all junior encumbrances. The holder has a priority right to payment in the event of default.

FIRST REFUSAL RIGHT OR RIGHT OF FIRST REFUSAL: A lease clause giving a tenant the first opportunity to buy a property or lease additional space in a property at the same price and on the same terms and conditions as those contained in a third-party offer that the owner has expressed a willingness to accept.

FIRST-GENERATION SPACE: Generally refers to new space that is currently available for lease and has never before been occupied by a tenant.

FIRST-LOSS POSITION: The position in a security that will suffer the first economic loss if the underlying assets lose value or are foreclosed on. The first-loss position carries a higher risk and a higher yield.

FIXED RATE: An interest rate that remains constant over the term of the loan.

FLAT FEE: A fee paid to an adviser or manager for managing a portfolio of real estate assets, typically stated as a flat percentage of gross asset value, net asset value or invested capital.

FLEX SPACE: A building that provides a configuration allowing occupants a flexible amount of office or showroom space in combination with manufacturing, laboratory, warehouse, distribution, etc.

FLOOR AREA RATIO (FAR): The ratio of the gross square footage of a building to the square footage of the land on which it is situated.

FORCE MAJEURE: A force that cannot be controlled by the parties to a contract and prevents them from complying with the provisions of the contract. This includes acts of God such as a flood or a hurricane, or acts of man such as a strike, fire or war.

FORECLOSURE: The process by which the trustee or servicer takes over a property from a borrower on behalf of the lender.

FORWARD COMMITMENTS: Contractual obligations to perform certain financing activities upon the satisfaction of any stated conditions. Usually used to describe a lender's obligation to fund a mortgage.

FREDDIE MAC (FEDERAL HOME LOAN MORTGAGE CORP., FHLMC): A corporation established by the Federal Home Loan Bank to issue mortgage-backed securities.

FULL RECOURSE: A loan on which an endorser or guarantor is liable in the event of default by the borrower.

FULL-SERVICE RENT: An all-inclusive rental rate that includes operating expenses and real estate taxes for the first year. The tenant is generally still responsible for any increase in operating expenses over the base year amount.

FUTURE PROPOSED SPACE: Space in a proposed commercial development that is not yet under construction or where no construction start date has been set. It also may refer to the future phases of a multi-phase project not yet built.

GENERAL CONTRACTOR: The prime contractor who contracts for the construction of an entire building or project, rather than just a portion of the work. The general contractor hires subcontractors, coordinates all work and is responsible for payment to subcontractors.

GENERAL PARTNER: A member of a partnership who has authority to bind the partnership and shares in the profits and losses of the partnership.

GOING-IN CAPITALIZATION RATE: The capitalization rate computed by dividing the projected first year's net operating income by the value of the property.

GRADUATED LEASE: A lease, generally long-term in nature, in which rent varies depending upon future contingencies.

GRANT: To bestow or transfer an interest in real property by deed or other instrument.

GRANTEE: One to whom a grant is made.

GRANTOR: The person making the grant.

GROSS BUILDING AREA: The sum of areas at each floor level, including basements, mezzanines and penthouses included within the principal outside faces of the exterior walls and neglecting architectural setbacks or projections.

GROSS INVESTMENT IN REAL ESTATE (HISTORIC COST): The total amount of equity and debt invested in real estate investments, including the gross purchase price, all acquisition fees and costs, plus subsequent capital improvements, less proceeds from sales and partial sales.

GROSS LEASABLE AREA: The portion of total floor area designed for tenants' occupancy and exclusive use, including storage areas. It is the total area that produces rental income.

GROSS LEASE: A lease in which the tenant pays a flat sum for rent out of which the landlord must pay all expenses such as taxes, insurance, maintenance, utilities, etc.

GROSS REAL ESTATE ASSET VALUE: The market value of the total real estate investments under management in a fund or individual accounts. It typically includes the total value of all equity positions, debt positions and joint venture ownership positions, including the amount of any mortgages or notes payable related to those assets.

GROSS REAL ESTATE INVESTMENT VALUE: The market value of real estate investments held in a portfolio without regard to debt, equal to the total of real estate investments as shown on a statement of assets and liabilities on a market-value basis.

GROSS RETURNS: Returns generated from the operation of real estate without dilution for adviser or manager fees.

GROUND RENT: Rent paid to the owner for use of land, normally on which to build a building. Generally, the arrangement is that of a long-term lease (e.g., 99 years) with the lessor retaining title to the land.

GUARANTOR: One who makes a guaranty.

GUARANTY: Agreement whereby the guarantor assures satisfaction of the debt of another or performs the obligation of another if and when the debtor fails to do so.

HARD COST: The cost of actually constructing property improvements.

HIGH-RISE: In the central business district, this could mean a building higher than 25 stories above ground level, but in suburban markets, it generally refers to buildings higher than seven or eight stories.

HIGHEST AND BEST USE: The reasonably probable and legal use of vacant land or an improved property that is physically possible, appropriately supported, financially feasible and that results in the highest value.

HOLD-OVER TENANT: A tenant retaining possession of the leased premises after the expiration of a lease.

HOLDBACKS: A portion of a loan commitment that is not funded until an additional requirement is met, such as completion of construction.

HOLDING PERIOD: The length of time an investor expects to own a property from purchase to sale.

HVAC: The acronym for heating, ventilating and air conditioning.

HYBRID DEBT: A mortgage position with equity-like participation features in both cash flow and the appreciation of the property at the time of sale or refinance.

IMPLIED CAP RATE: Net operating income divided by the sum of a REIT's equity market capitalization and its total outstanding debt.

IMPROVEMENTS: In the context of leasing, the term typically refers to the improvements made to or inside a building but may include any permanent structure or other development, such as a street, sidewalk, utilities, etc.

INCENTIVE FEE: Applies to fee structures where the amount of the fee that is charged is determined by the performance of the real estate assets under management.

INCOME CAPITALIZATION VALUE: The indication of value derived for an income-producing property by converting its anticipated benefits into property value through direct capitalization of expected income or by discounting the annual cash flows for the holding period at a specified yield rate.

INCOME PROPERTY: Real estate that is owned or operated to produce revenue.

INCOME RETURN: The percentage of the total return that is generated by the income from operations of a property, fund or account.

INDIRECT COSTS: Development costs other than direct material and labor costs that are directly related to the construction of improvements, including administrative and office expenses, commissions, architectural, engineering and financing costs.

INDIVIDUAL ACCOUNT MANAGEMENT: Accounts established for individual plan sponsors or other investors for investment in real estate, where a firm acts as an adviser in acquiring and/or managing a direct real estate portfolio.

INFLATION: The annual rate at which consumer prices increase.

INFLATION HEDGE: An investment that tends to increase in value at a rate greater than inflation and helps contribute to the preservation of the purchasing power of a portfolio.

INITIAL PUBLIC OFFERING (IPO): The first time a private company offers securities for sale to the public.

INSTITUTIONAL-GRADE PROPERTY: Various types of real estate properties generally owned or financed by institutional investors. Core investments typically include office, retail, industrial and apartments. Specialty investments include hotels, healthcare facilities, senior housing, student housing, self-storage facilities, and mixed-use properties (i.e., a property containing at least two property types).

INTEREST: The price paid for the use of capital.

INTERNAL RATE OF RETURN (IRR): A discounted cash-flow analysis calculation used to determine the potential total return of a real estate asset during an anticipated holding period.

INVENTORY: All space within a certain proscribed market without regard to its availability or condition.

INVESTMENT MANAGER: Any company or individual that assumes discretion over a specified amount of real estate capital, invests that capital in assets via a separate account, co-investment program or commingled fund, and provides asset management.

INVESTMENT POLICY: A document that formalizes an institution's guidelines for investment and asset management. An investment policy typically will contain goals and objectives; core and specialty investment criteria and methodology; and guidelines for asset management, investment advisory contracting, fees and utilization of consultants and other outside professionals.

INVESTMENT STRATEGY: The investment parameters used by the manager in structuring the portfolio and selecting the real estate assets for a fund or account. This includes a description of the types, locations and sizes of properties to be considered, the ownership positions that will be used, and the stages of the investment lifecycle.

INVESTMENT STRUCTURES: Unleveraged acquisitions, leveraged acquisitions, traditional debt, participating debt, convertible debt, triple-net leases and joint ventures.

JOINT VENTURE: An investment entity formed by one or more entities to acquire or develop and manage real property and/or other assets.

JUST COMPENSATION: Compensation that is fair to both the owner and the public when property is taken for public use through condemnation (eminent domain).

LANDLORD'S WARRANT: A warrant from a landlord to levy upon a tenant's personal property (e.g., furniture, etc.) and to sell this property at a public sale to compel payment of the rent or the observance of some other stipulation in the lease.

LEASE: An agreement whereby the owner of real property gives the right of possession to another for a specified period of time and for a specified consideration.

LEASE AGREEMENT: The formal legal document entered into between a landlord and a tenant to reflect the terms of the negotiations between them.

LEASE COMMENCEMENT DATE: The date usually constitutes the commencement of the term of the lease, whether or not the tenant has actually taken possession, so long as beneficial occupancy is possible.

LEASE EXPIRATION EXPOSURE SCHEDULE: A listing of the total square footage of all current leases that expire in each of the next five years, without regard to renewal options.

LEASEHOLD INTEREST: The right to hold or use property for a fixed period of time at a given price, without transfer of ownership.

LEGAL DESCRIPTION: A geographical description identifying a parcel by government survey, metes and bounds, or lot numbers of a recorded plat including a description of any portion that is subject to an easement or reservation.

LEGAL OWNER: The legal owner has title to the property, although the title may actually carry no rights to the property other than as a lien.

LETTER OF CREDIT: A commitment by a bank or other person that the issuer will honor drafts or other demands for payment upon full compliance with the conditions specified in the letter of credit. Letters of credit are often used in place of cash deposited with the landlord in satisfying the security deposit provisions of a lease.

LETTER OF INTENT: A preliminary agreement stating the proposed terms for a final contract.

LEVERAGE: The use of credit to finance a portion of the costs of purchasing or developing a real estate investment. Positive leverage occurs when the interest rate is lower than the capitalization rate or projected internal rate of return. Negative leverage occurs when the current return on equity is diminished by the employment of debt.

LIEN: A claim or encumbrance against property used to secure a debt, a charge or the performance of some act.

LIEN WAIVER: Waiver of a mechanic's lien rights that is often required before the general contractor can receive a draw under the payment provisions of a construction contract. It may also be required before the owner can receive a draw on a construction loan.

LIFECYCLE: The various developmental stages of a property: pre-development, development, leasing, operating and redevelopment (or rehab).

LIKE-KIND PROPERTY: A term used in an exchange of property held for productive use in a trade or business or for investment. Unless cash is received, the tax consequences of the exchange are postponed pursuant to Section 1031 of the Internal Revenue Code.

LIMITED PARTNERSHIP: A type of partnership comprised of one or more general partners who manage the business and are personally liable for partnership debts, and one or more limited partners who contribute capital and share in profits but who take no part in running the business and incur no liability above the amount contributed.

LIQUIDITY: The ease with which assets can be bought or sold without affecting the price.

LISTING AGREEMENT: An agreement between the owner of a property and a real estate broker giving the broker authorization to attempt to sell or lease the property at a certain price and terms in return for a commission, set fee or other form of compensation.

LOAN-TO-VALUE RATIO (LTV): The ratio of the value of the loan principal divided by the property's appraised value.

LOCK-BOX STRUCTURE: A structure whereby the rental or debt-service payments are sent directly from the tenant or mortgagor to the trustee.

LOCKOUT: The period during which a loan may not be prepaid.

LONG-TERM LEASE: In most markets, this refers to a lease whose term is at least three years from initial signing to the date of expiration or renewal.

LOSS SEVERITY: The percentage of principal lost when a loan is foreclosed.

LOT: Generally one of several contiguous parcels of land making up a fractional part or subdivision of a block, the boundaries of which are shown on recorded maps and plats.

LOW-RISE: A building with fewer than four stories above ground level.

LUMP-SUM CONTRACT: A type of construction contract requiring the general contractor to complete a building or project for a fixed cost normally established by competitive bidding. The contractor absorbs any loss or retains any profit.

MARK TO MARKET: The process of increasing or decreasing the original investment cost or value of a property asset or portfolio to a level estimated to be the current market value.

MARKET CAPITALIZATION: One measure of the value of a company; it is calculated by multiplying the current share price by the current number of shares outstanding.

MARKET RENTAL RATES: The rental income that a property most likely would command in the open market, indicated by the current rents asked and paid for comparable space.

MARKET STUDY: A forecast of future demand for a certain type of real estate project that includes an estimate of the square footage that can be absorbed and the rents that can be charged.

MARKET VALUE: The highest price a property would command in a competitive and open market under all conditions requisite to a fair sale.

MARKETABLE TITLE: A title free from encumbrances that could be readily marketed to a willing purchaser.

MASTER LEASE: A primary lease that controls subsequent leases and may cover more property than subsequent leases.

MASTER SERVICER: An institution that acts on behalf of a trustee for the benefit of security holders in collecting funds from a borrower, advancing funds in the event of delinquencies and, in the event of default, taking a property through foreclosure.

MATURITY DATE: The date when the total principal balance comes due.

MECHANIC'S LIEN: A claim created for the purpose of securing priority of payment of the price and value of work performed and materials furnished in constructing, repairing or improving a building or other structure.

MEETING SPACE: In hotels, space made available to the public to rent for meeting, conference or banquet uses.

METES AND BOUNDS: The boundary lines of land described by listing the compass directions and distances of the boundaries. Originally, "metes" referred to distance and "bounds" referred to direction.

MEZZANINE FINANCING: Mezzanine financing is somewhere between equity and debt. It is that piece of the capital structure that has senior debt above it and equity below it. There is both equity and debt mezzanine financing, and it can be done at the asset or company level, or it could be unrated tranches of CMBS. Returns are generally in the mid to high teens.

MID-RISE: A building with four to eight stories above ground level. In a central business district this might extend to buildings up to 25 stories.

MIXED-USE: A building or project that provides more than one use, such as office/retail or retail/residential.

MORTGAGE: A legal document by which real property is pledged as security for repayment of a loan until the debt is repaid in full.

MORTGAGE BROKER: A firm or person that serves as an intermediary, helping to facilitate a mortgage transaction between a lender (source of capital) and a borrower.

NEGATIVE AMORTIZATION: The accrual feature found in numerous participating debt structures that allows an investor to pay, for an initial period of time, an interest rate below the contract rate stated in loan documents.

NET ASSET VALUE (NAV): The value of an individual asset or portfolio of real estate properties net of leveraging or joint venture interests.

NET ASSET VALUE PER SHARE: The current value of a REIT's assets divided by shares outstanding.

NET ASSETS: Total assets less total liabilities on a market-value basis.

NET CASH FLOW: Generally determined by net income plus depreciation less principal payments on long-term mortgages.

NET INVESTMENT IN REAL ESTATE: Gross investment in real estate less the outstanding debt balance.

NET INVESTMENT INCOME: The income or loss of a portfolio or entity resulting after deducting all expenses, including portfolio and asset management fees, but before realized and unrealized gains and losses on investments.

NET OPERATING INCOME (NOI): A before-tax computation of gross revenue less operating expenses and an allowance for anticipated vacancy. It is a key indicator of financial strength.

NET PRESENT VALUE (NPV): Net present value usually is employed to evaluate the relative merits of two or more investment alternatives. It is calculated as the sum of the total present value of incremental future cash flows plus the present value of estimated proceeds from sale. Whenever the net present value is greater than zero, an investment opportunity generally is considered to have merit.

NET PURCHASE PRICE: Gross purchase price less associated debt financing.

NET REAL ESTATE INVESTMENT VALUE: The market value of all real estate less property-level debt.

NET RETURNS: Returns to investors net of fees to advisers or managers.

NET SALES PROCEEDS: Proceeds from the sale of an asset or part of an asset less brokerage commissions, closing costs and market expenses.

NET SQUARE FOOTAGE: The space required for a function or staff position.

NOMINAL YIELD: The yield to investors before adjustments for fees, inflation or risk.

NON-COMPETE CLAUSE: A clause that can be inserted into a lease specifying that the business of the tenant is exclusive in the property and that no other tenant operating the same or similar type of business can occupy space in the building. This clause benefits service-oriented businesses desiring exclusive access to the building's population.

NON-DISCRETIONARY FUNDS: Funds allocated to an investment manager requiring the investor's approval on each transaction.

NON-PERFORMING LOAN: A loan that is unable to meet its contractual principal and interest payments.

NON-RECOURSE DEBT: A loan that, in the event of a default by the borrower, limits the lender's remedies to a foreclosure of the mortgage, realization on its assignment of leases and rents, and acquisition of the real estate.

OFFER: Term used to describe a stated price or spread to sell whole loans or securities.

OPEN SPACE: An area of land or water dedicated for public or private use or enjoyment.

OPEN-END FUND: A commingled fund that does not have a finite life, continually accepts new investor capital and makes new property investments.

OPERATING COST ESCALATION: Although there are many variations of escalation clauses, all are intended to adjust rents by reference to external standards such as published indexes, negotiated wage levels, or expenses related to the ownership and operation of a building.

OPERATING EXPENSE: The actual costs associated with operating a property, including maintenance, repairs, management, utilities, taxes and insurance.

OPPORTUNISTIC: A phrase generally used by advisers and managers to describe investments in underperforming and/or undermanaged assets that hold the expectation of near-term increases in cash flow and value. Total return objectives for opportunistic strategies tend to be 20 percent or higher. Opportunistic investments typically involve a high degree of leverage—typically 60 to 100 percent on an asset basis and 60 to 80 percent on a portfolio basis.

ORIGINATOR: A company that sources and underwrites commercial and/or multifamily mortgage loans.

OUT-PARCEL: Individual retail sites in a shopping center.

PARKING RATIO: Dividing the total rentable square footage of a building by the building's total number of parking spaces provides the amount of rentable square feet per each individual parking space.

PARTIAL SALES: The sale of an interest in real estate that is less than the whole property. This may include a sale of easement rights, parcel of land or retail pad, or a single building of a multi-building investment.

PARTIAL TAKING: The taking of part of an owner's property under the laws of eminent domain.

PARTICIPATING DEBT: In addition to collecting a contract interest rate, participating debt allows the lender to have participatory equity rights through a share of increases in income and/or increases in residual value over the loan balance or original value at the time of loan funding.

PERCENTAGE RENT: Rent payable under a lease that is equal to a percentage of gross sales or gross revenues received by the tenant. It is commonly used in retail center leases.

PERFORMANCE: The quarterly changes in fund or account values attributable to investment income, realized or unrealized appreciation, and the total gross return to the investors both before and after investment management fees. Formulas for calculating performance information are varied, making comparisons difficult.

PERFORMANCE BOND: A surety bond posted by a contractor guaranteeing full performance of a contract with the proceeds to be used to complete the contract or compensate for the owner's loss in the event of nonperformance.

PERFORMANCE MEASUREMENT: The process of measuring an investor's real estate performance in terms of individual assets, advisers/managers and portfolios. The scope of performance measurement reports varies among managers, consultants and plan sponsors.

PERFORMANCE-BASED FEES: Fees paid to advisers or managers based on returns to investors, often packaged with a modest acquisition and asset-management fee structure.

PERMANENT LOAN: The long-term mortgage on a property.

PLAT: Map of a specific area, such as a subdivision, that shows the boundaries of individual lots together with streets and easements.

PORTFOLIO MANAGEMENT: The portfolio management process involves formulating, modifying and implementing a real estate investment strategy in light of an investor's broader overall investment objectives. It also can be defined as the management of several properties owned by a single entity.

PORTFOLIO TURNOVER: The average time from the funding of an investment until it is repaid or sold.

POWER OF SALE: Clause inserted in a mortgage or deed of trust giving the mortgagee (or trustee) the right and power, upon default in the payment of the debt secured, to advertise and sell the property at public auction.

PRELEASED: Space in a proposed building that has been leased before the start of construction or in advance of the issuance of a certificate of occupancy.

PREPAYMENT RIGHTS: Rights given to the borrower to make partial or full payment of the total principal balance prior to the maturity date without penalty.

PRICE-TO-EARNINGS RATIO: This ratio is calculated by dividing the current share price by the sum of the primary earnings per share from continuing operations, before extraordinary items and accounting changes, over the past four quarters.

PRIME SPACE: Typically refers to first-generation space that is available for lease.

PRIME TENANT: The major tenant in a building, or the major or anchor tenant in a shopping center.

PRINCIPAL PAYMENTS: The return of invested capital to the lender.

PRIVATE PLACEMENT: A sale of a security in a manner that is exempt from the registration rules and requirements of the Securities and Exchange Commission. An example would be a REIT directly placing an issue of stock with a pension fund.

PRIVATE REIT: An infinite- or finite-life real estate investment company structured as a real estate investment trust. Shares are placed and held privately rather than sold and traded publicly.

PRO RATA: In the case of a tenant, the proportionate share of expenses for the maintenance and operation of the property.

PRODUCTION ACRES: The area of land that can be used in agriculture or timber operations to produce income, not including areas used for crop or machinery storage, or other support areas.

PUBLIC-PRIVATE PARTNERSHIP (P3): According to the National Council for Public Private Partnerships, a Public-Private Partnership (P3) is a contractual agreement between a public agency and a private sector entity. Through this agreement, the skills and assets of each sector (public and private) are shared in delivering a service or facility for the use of the general public. Each party shares in the risks and rewards potential in the delivery of the service and/or facility.

PUNCH LIST: An itemized list documenting incomplete or unsatisfactory items after the contractor has notified the owner that the tenant space is substantially complete.

QUITCLAIM DEED: A deed operating as a release that is intended to pass any title, interest or claim that the grantor may have in the property, but not guaranteeing such title is valid.

RATING: Grade, assigned by a rating agency, designating the credit quality or creditworthiness of the underlying assets.

RATING AGENCIES: Independent firms engaged to rate the creditworthiness of securities for the benefit of investors. The major rating agencies are Fitch Ratings, Standard & Poor's and Moody's Investors Service.

RAW LAND: Unimproved land that remains in its natural state.

RAW SPACE: Unimproved shell space in a building.

REAL ESTATE FUNDAMENTALS: The factors driving the value of real property (i.e., the supply, demand and pricing for land and/or developed space in a given geographic or economic region or market).

REAL PROPERTY: Land, and generally whatever is erected or affixed to the land that would be personal property if not attached.

REAL RATE OF RETURN: Yield to investors net of an inflationary factor. The formula for calculating the real rate of return is [(1 + nominal yield) / (1 + inflation rate)] – 1.

RECAPTURE: When the IRS recovers the tax benefit of a deduction or a credit previously taken by a taxpayer, which is often a factor in foreclosure because there is a forgiveness of debt. As used in leases, it is a clause giving the lessor a percentage of profits above a fixed amount of rent; or in a percentage lease, a clause granting the landlord the right to terminate the lease if the tenant fails to realize minimum sales.

RECOURSE: The right of a lender, in the event of default by the borrower, to recover against the personal assets of a party who is secondarily liable for the debt.

REGIONAL DIVERSIFICATION: Definitions for what constitute various regions, for diversification purposes, vary among managers, consultants and plan sponsors. Some boundaries are defined based purely on geography; others have attempted to define boundaries along economic lines.

REHAB: Extensive renovation intended to cure obsolescence of a building or project.

REIT (REAL ESTATE INVESTMENT TRUST): A business trust or corporation that combines the capital of many investors to acquire or provide financing for real estate. A corporation or trust that qualifies for REIT status generally does not pay corporate income tax to the IRS. Instead, it pays out at least 90 percent of its taxable income in the form of dividends.

RENEWAL OPTION: A clause giving a tenant the right to extend the term of a lease.

RENEWAL PROBABILITY: Used to estimate leasing-related costs and downtime, it is the average percentage of tenants in a building that are expected to renew at market rental rates upon the expiration of their leases.

RENT: Compensation or fee paid for the occupancy and use of any rental property, land, buildings, equipment, etc.

RENT COMMENCEMENT DATE: The date on which a tenant begins paying rent.

RENT-UP PERIOD: The period following construction of a new building when tenants are actively being sought and the project is approaching its stabilized occupancy.

RENTABLE/USABLE RATIO: A building's total rentable area divided by its usable area. It represents the tenant's pro rata share of the building's common areas and can determine the square footage upon which the tenant will pay rent. The inverse describes the proportion of space that an occupant can expect to actually use.

RENTAL CONCESSION: What landlords offer tenants to secure their tenancy. While rental abatement is one form of a concession, there are many others such as increased tenant improvement allowance, signage, below-market rental rates and moving allowances.

RENTAL GROWTH RATE: The expected trend in market rental rates over the period of analysis, expressed as an annual percentage increase.

REO (REAL ESTATE OWNED): Real estate owned by a savings institution as a result of default by borrowers and subsequent foreclosure by the institution.

REPLACEMENT COST: The estimated current cost to construct a building with utility equivalent to the building being appraised, using modern materials and current standards, design and layout.

REPLACEMENT RESERVES: An allowance that provides for the periodic replacement of building components that wear out more rapidly than the building itself and must be replaced during the building's economic life.

REQUEST FOR PROPOSAL (RFP): A formal request, issued by a plan sponsor or its consultant, inviting investment managers to submit information on their firms' investment strategy, historical investment performance, current investment opportunities, investment management fees, other pension fund client relationships, etc. Firms that meet the qualifications are requested to make a formal presentation to the board of trustees and senior staff members. Finalists are chosen at the completion of this process, and contract negotiation begins.

RESERVE ACCOUNT: An account that a borrower has to fund to protect the lender. Examples include capital expenditure accounts and deferred maintenance accounts.

RETAIL INVESTOR: When used to describe an investor, retail refers to the nature of the distribution channel and the market for the services, selling interests directly to consumers.

RETENTION RATE: The percent of trailing 12-month earnings that have been ploughed back into the company. It is calculated as 100 minus the trailing 12-month payout ratio.

RETURN ON ASSETS: The income after taxes for the trailing 12 months divided by the average total assets, expressed as a percentage.

RETURN ON EQUITY: The income available to common stockholders for the trailing 12 months divided by the average common equity, expressed as a percentage.

RETURN ON INVESTMENTS: The trailing 12-month income after taxes divided by the average total long-term debt, other long-term liabilities and shareholders equity, expressed as a percentage.

REVERSION CAPITALIZATION RATE: The capitalization rate used to determine reversion value.

REVERSION VALUE: A lump-sum benefit that an investor receives or expects to receive at the termination of an investment.

REVPAR (REVENUE PER AVAILABLE ROOM): Total room revenue for the period divided by the average number of available rooms in a hospitality facility.

ROLL-OVER RISK: The risk that a tenant's lease will not be renewed.

SALE-LEASEBACK: An arrangement by which the owner-occupant of a property agrees to sell all or part of the property to an investor, then lease it back and continue to occupy space as a tenant.

SALES COMPARISON VALUE: A value indication derived by comparing the property being appraised to similar properties that have been sold recently.

SECOND-GENERATION OR SECONDARY SPACE: Previously occupied space that becomes available for lease, either directly from the landlord or as sublease space.

SECONDARY FINANCING: A loan on real property secured by a lien junior to an existing first mortgage loan.

SECONDARY MARKET: A market where existing mortgage loans are securitized and then bought and sold to other investors.

SECURITY DEPOSIT: A deposit of money by a tenant to a landlord to secure performance of a lease. It also can take the form of a letter of credit or other financial instrument.

SENIOR CLASSES: With regard to securities, describes the classes with the highest priority to receive the payments from the underlying mortgage loans.

SETBACK: The distance from a curb, property line or other reference point, within which building is prohibited.

SITE ANALYSIS: Determines the suitability of a specific parcel of land for a specific use.

SITE DEVELOPMENT: The installation of all necessary improvements made to a site before a building or project can be constructed on the site.

SITE PLAN: A detailed plan that depicts the location of improvements on a parcel.

SLAB: The exposed wearing surface laid over the structural support beams of a building to form the floor(s) of the building.

SOFT COST: The portion of an equity investment other than the actual cost of the improvements themselves that may be tax-deductible in the first year.

SPACE PLAN: A graphic representation of a tenant's space requirements, showing wall and door locations, room sizes and sometimes furniture layouts.

SPECIAL ASSESSMENT: Special charges levied against real property for public improvements that benefit the assessed property.

SPECIAL SERVICER: A firm that is employed to work out mortgages that are either delinquent or in default.

SPECIFIED INVESTING: Investment in individually specified properties or portfolios, or investment in commingled funds whose real estate assets are fully or partially specified prior to the commitment of investor capital.

SPECULATIVE SPACE: Any tenant space that has not been leased before the start of construction on a new building.

STABILIZED NET OPERATING INCOME: Projected income less expenses that are subject to change but have been adjusted to reflect equivalent, stable property operations.

STABILIZED OCCUPANCY: The optimum range of long-term occupancy that an income-producing real estate project is expected to achieve after exposure for leasing in the open market for a reasonable period of time at terms and conditions comparable to competitive offerings.

STEP-UP LEASE (GRADED LEASE): A lease specifying set increases in rent at set intervals during the term of the lease.

STRAIGHT LEASE (FLAT LEASE): A lease specifying a fixed amount of rent that is to be paid periodically, typically monthly, during the entire term of the lease.

STRIP CENTER: Any shopping area comprised of a row of stores but smaller than a neighborhood center anchored by a grocery store.

SUBCONTRACTOR: A contractor working under and being paid by the general contractor, often a specialist in nature, such as an electrical contractor, cement contractor, etc.

SUBLESSEE: A person or identity to whom the rights of use and occupancy under a lease have been conveyed, while the original lessee retains primary responsibility for the obligations of the lease.

SURETY: One who voluntarily binds himself to be obligated for the debt or obligation of another.

SURFACE RIGHTS: A right or easement granted with mineral rights, enabling the possessor of the mineral rights to drill or mine through the surface.

SURVEY: The process by which a parcel is measured and its boundaries and contents ascertained.

TAKING: A common synonym for condemnation, or any interference with private property rights, but it is not essential that there be physical seizure or appropriation.

TAX BASE: The assessed valuation of all real property that lies within a taxing authority's jurisdiction. When multiplied by the tax rate, it determines the amount of tax due.

TAX LIEN: A statutory lien for nonpayment of property taxes that attaches only to the property upon which the taxes are unpaid.

TAX ROLL: A list or record containing the descriptions of all land parcels located within the county, the names of the owners or those receiving the tax bill, assessed values and tax amounts.

TENANT (LESSEE): One who rents real estate from another and holds an estate by virtue of a lease.

TENANT AT WILL: One who holds possession of premises by permission of the owner or landlord. The characteristics of the lease are an uncertain duration and the right of either party to terminate on proper notice.

TENANT IMPROVEMENT (TI): Improvements made to the leased premises by or for a tenant.

TENANT IMPROVEMENT (TI) ALLOWANCE: Defines the fixed amount of money contributed by the landlord toward tenant improvements. The tenant pays any of the costs that exceed this amount.

TENANT MIX: A phrase used to describe the quality of a property's income stream. In multi-tenanted properties, institutional investors typically prefer a mixture of national credit tenants, regional credit tenants and local non-credit tenants.

TERM: The lifetime of a loan.

TITLE: The means whereby the owner has the just and full possession of real property.

TITLE INSURANCE: A policy issued by a title company that insures against loss resulting from defects of title to a specifically described parcel of real property, or from the enforcement of liens existing against it at the time the title policy is issued.

TITLE SEARCH: A review of all recorded documents affecting a specific piece of property to determine the present condition of title.

TOTAL ACRES: All land area contained within a real estate investment.

TOTAL ASSETS: The sum of all gross investments, cash and equivalents, receivables, and other assets presented on the balance sheet.

TOTAL COMMITMENT: The full mortgage loan amount that is obligated to be funded if all stated conditions are met.

TOTAL INVENTORY: The total square footage of a type of property within a geographical area, whether vacant or occupied.

TOTAL PRINCIPAL BALANCE: The total amount of debt, including the original mortgage amount adjusted for subsequent fundings, principal payments and other unpaid items (e.g., interest) that are allowed to be added to the principal balance by the mortgage note or by law.

TOTAL RETAIL AREA: Total floor area of a retail center less common areas. It is the area from which sales are generated and includes any department stores or other areas (such as banks, restaurants or service stations) not owned by the center.

TOTAL RETURN: The sum of quarterly income and appreciation returns.

TRADE FIXTURES: Personal property that is attached to a structure that is used in the business. Because this property is part of the business and not deemed to be part of the real estate, it is typically removable upon lease termination.

TRIPLE NET LEASE: A lease that requires the tenant to pay all expenses of the property being leased in addition to rent. Typical expenses covered in such a lease include taxes, insurance, maintenance and utilities.

TURN-KEY PROJECT: The construction of a project in which a third party is responsible for the total completion of a building, or for the construction of tenant improvements to the customized requirements and specifications of a future owner or tenant.

UNDER CONSTRUCTION: The period of time after construction has started but before the certificate of occupancy has been issued.

UNDER CONTRACT: The period of time after a seller has accepted a buyer's offer to purchase a property and during which the buyer is able to perform its due diligence and finalize financing arrangements. During this time, the seller is precluded from entertaining offers from other buyers.

UNDERWRITER: A company, usually an investment banking firm, that guarantees or participates in a guarantee that an entire issue of stocks or bonds will be purchased.

UNENCUMBERED: Property that is free of liens and other encumbrances.

UNIMPROVED LAND: Most commonly refers to land without improvements or buildings but also can mean land in its natural state.

USABLE SQUARE FOOTAGE: The area contained within the demising walls of the tenant space that equals the net square footage multiplied by the circulation factor.

USE: The specific purpose for which a parcel or a building is intended to be used or for which it has been designed or arranged.

VACANCY FACTOR: The amount of gross revenue that pro forma income statements anticipate will be lost because of vacancies, often expressed as a percentage of the total rentable square footage available in a building or project.

VACANCY RATE: The total amount of available space compared to the total inventory of space and expressed as a percentage.

VACANT SPACE: Existing tenant space currently being marketed for lease excluding space available for sublease.

VALUE-ADD OR VALUE-ADDED: A phrase generally used by advisers and managers to describe investments in underperforming and/or undermanaged assets that possess upside potential. NOI and property value can be positively affected through a change in marketing, operating or leasing strategy; physical improvements; and/or a new capital structure. The objective is to generate 13 to 18 percent returns. Leverage could fall in the 60 to 70 percent range.

VARIABLE-RATE: A loan interest rate that varies over the term of the loan, usually tied to a predetermined index. Also called adjustable-rate.

VARIANCE: Permission that allows a property owner to depart from the literal requirements of a zoning ordinance that, because of special circumstances, cause a unique hardship.

WEIGHTED-AVERAGE RENTAL RATES: The average proportion of unequal rental rates in two or more buildings within a market.

WORKING DRAWINGS: The set of plans for a building or project that comprise the contract documents that indicate the precise manner in which a project is to be built.

WORKOUT: The process by which a borrower attempts to negotiate with a lender to restructure the borrower's debt rather than go through foreclosure proceedings.

WRITE-DOWN: The accounting procedure used when the book value of an asset is adjusted downward to better reflect current market value.

WRITE-OFF: The accounting procedure used when an asset has been determined to be uncollectible and is therefore charged as a loss.

YIELD: The effective return on an investment, as paid in dividends or interest.

YIELD MAINTENANCE PREMIUM: A penalty, paid by the borrower, designed to make investors whole in the event of early redemption of principal.

YIELD SPREAD: The difference in yield between a debt instrument or other investment and a benchmark value, typically U.S. Treasuries of the same maturity.

ZONING: The division of a city or town into zones and the application of regulations having to do with the architectural design and structural and intended uses of buildings within such zones.

ZONING ORDINANCE: The set of laws and regulations controlling the use of land and construction of improvements in a given area or zone.

ACKNOWLEDGMENTS

THIS BOOK WAS MADE possible through the success of my company, Washington Street Properties, and there's a long list of people who played a role in that achievement. Among others, it includes every employee, contractor, service provider, and tenant that I've had the privilege of working with since I first started in commercial real estate. That said, there are a few individuals whose contributions merit special acknowledgment.

First and foremost, I'd like to thank my wife, Tricia, who's been my partner in this whole endeavor. When Tricia came into my life, I only owned one property, and my motivation had waned. But my passion returned when Tricia became my best friend, my property manager, and eventually my wife. We make a great team, and together we've accomplished some pretty remarkable things. I'm eternally grateful for everything she has done and continues to do for me.

I'd also like to acknowledge our children, Alexa, Jack, Ryan, and Kyle, whose presence in my life inspires me to be my best in everything I do. I'm proud of them and blessed to have such extraordinary kids.

In addition to my wife, Tricia, I've had some stellar team members at Washington Street Properties, starting with the amazing Allison Carlos, who has basically made me dispensable. I'm pretty sure she's going to fire me one of these days, if Tricia doesn't do it first. Other key contributors past and present include Samantha Brothers, MaryLu Moriarty, Sasha Spinks, Kevin Woodcock, Jessica Renzi, Tony Gouty, Eric Lugo, Jamal Phillipus, Steve Calhoun, John Einbeck, Alison Williams, Chris Dillon, Jackie Jimenez, Sharon Duke, and our "honorary employee" Garrett McCarthy. I'm privileged to have worked with so many good people who care about making a difference in the community and in the lives of our tenants.

For her guidance and contributions to this book, I'd like to thank Maria Gagliano, who started off as my fantastic developmental editor and ended up managing the entire production process. She helped make this book the best it could be. Maria also assembled a talented team of professionals, including Jennifer Eck (copyediting), Zoe Norvell (cover design), and Pauline Neuwirth (interior design and index). I'm grateful to each of them for their respective roles in making this a publisher-quality book.

I would also like to thank David Fugate of LaunchBooks Literary Agency for his advice and help in navigating the evolving world of book publishing. Even after not hearing from me for almost nine years David was generous with his time and kind enough to represent my interests. He also put me in contact with Maria. David, you're a rock star.

For taking time out of their busy lives to do peer reviews, I would like to acknowledge Matthew Turcotte, MaryLu Moriarty, Michael Layton, Todd Murray, Alison Williams, Amanda Macikowski, Tricia Murray, and Steven Calhoun. *Crushing It in Apartments and Commercial Real Estate* reflects their thoughtful feedback.

I'd like to thank my friend Addison "Trey" Vars III for reviewing the manuscript and sharing his sound legal advice, which has helped me throughout my real estate journey. I was incredibly fortunate to connect with Trey and his capable assistant Donna Jareo on my very first deal. Since then, Trey's sage counsel has helped me navigate more complicated situations than I care to remember. In exchange, I'm pretty sure my escapades in real estate have helped to keep him suitably amused and entertained.

Finally, I would like to acknowledge you, the reader, for your interest in commercial real estate and for purchasing this book. Your desire and willingness to learn from my experience is both humbling and gratifying. If you found *Crushing It in Apartments and Commercial Real Estate* to be of value, I hope you will take a moment to share your feedback by posting a review online or recommending this book to a friend.

INDEX

NORM JOHNSTON, *NNY BUSINESS*

BRIAN MURRAY started Washington Street Properties in 2007 when he acquired his first investment property. Without raising any outside capital, Brian bootstrapped his way from newbie investor to the owner of a nationally recognized real estate investment and property management firm. In 2014, Washington Street Properties won a Gold Stevie Award for Real Estate Company of the Year.

Washington Street Properties has been ranked on the Inc. 5000 list of the nation's fastest-growing private companies for the past three years in a row. The company's success has been achieved through a value-add approach, focusing on the renovation and turnaround of underperforming, strategically located properties.

With a focus on core values of integrity, excellence, value, and innovation, Washington Street Properties owns and operates a large portfolio of assets in Upstate New York, including apartments, office buildings, retail centers, storage, parking, and mixed-use properties.

In addition to his endeavors in real estate, Brian Murray has worked as a professor, technology executive, management consultant, and engineer. His media appearances include interviews on CNN, PBS, and CBS *MarketWatch*. Brian has been quoted by the *Wall Street Journal*, the *New York Times*, and dozens of other major newspapers around the world.

Brian holds degrees from Syracuse University, Johns Hopkins University, and the Darden School of Business at the University of Virginia. In 2015, he was honored with a Gold Stevie Award for Real Estate Executive of the Year at the 13th Annual American Business Awards in Chicago.

Made in the USA
Middletown, DE
16 June 2017